VOLUM

BOB AND DEBBY GASS
WITH RUTH GASS HALLIDAY

COLLECTOR'S EDITION

Synergy Publishers
Gainesville, Florida

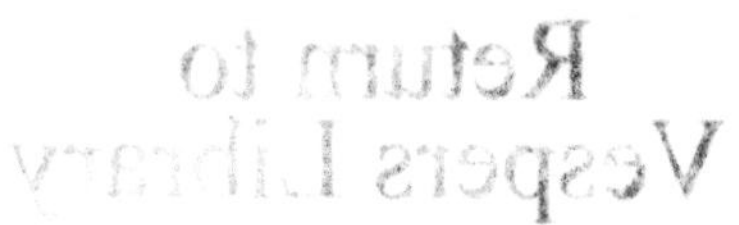

The Best of The Word for Today, Volume Two
by Bob Gass
International Standard Book Number: 1-931727-91

P.O. Box 11045
Roswell, GA 30077-1045

Synergy Publishers
Gainesville, Florida 32635

Return to Vespers Library

Dedication

To Tony and Colette, "Faithful Friends," and
to Jack and Nicki, who have enriched our lives.

Index of Abbreviations

NIV	New International Version
TM	The Message
NAS	New American Standard
NCV	New Century Version
NKJV	New King James Version
KJV	King James Version
CEV	Contemporary English Version
AMP	Amplified Bible
NLT	New Living Translation
TLB	The Living Bible

Old Testament

Listed Alphabetically

Amos	AM
1 Chronicles	1 Ch
2 Chronicles	2 Ch
Daniel	Dn
Deuteronomy	Dt
Ecclesiastes	Ec
Esther	Es
Exodus	Ex
Ezekiel	Ez
Ezra	Ezra
Genesis	Gn
Habakkuk	Hb
Haggai	Hg
Hosea	Ho
Isaiah	Is
Jeremiah	Jr
Job	Job
Joel	Jl
Jonah	Jon
Joshua	Js
Judges	Jg
1 Kings	1 K
2 Kings	2 K
Lamentations	Lm
Leviticus	Lv
Malichi	Ml
Micah	Mic
Nahum	Nh
Nehemiah	Ne
Numbers	Nu
Obadiah	Ob
Proverbs	Pr
Psalms	Ps
Ruth	Ru
1 Samuel	1 S
2 Samuel	2 S
Song of Songs	Sgs
Zechariah	Zec
Zephaniah	Zep

New Testament

Listed Alphabetically

Acts	Ac	Mark	Mk
Colossians	Col	Matthew	Mt
1 Corinthians	1 Co	1 Peter	1 P
2 Corinthians	2 Co	2 Peter	2 P
ephesians	Eph	Philemon	Phm
Galatians	Ga	Philippians	Phil
Hebrews	He	Revelation	Rev
James	Jas	Romans	Ro
John	Jn	1 Thessalonians	1 Th
1 John	1 Jn	2 Thessalonians	2 Th
2 John	2 Jn	1 Timothy	1 Ti
3 John	3 Jn	2 Timothy	2 Ti
Jude	Jd	Titus	Titus
Luke	Lk		

NEW YEAR'S RESOLUTIONS

I keep working toward that day when I will finally be all that Christ . . . wants me to be."

Philippians 3:12 TLB

If your goal this year is to become all God wants you to be, then *more* resolutions aren't the answer. Based on last year's track record you know just about how long they last, don't you?

Here's an important key: focus *only* on the end result and you won't get overwhelmed. Tackle one thing at a time. Start with a specific area, even a difficult one. Arnold Palmer says, "The most rewarding things in life are often ones that look like they cannot be done!" Here's a four-step game-plan to get you started:

(1) *No more excuses.* Stop saying, "That's just the way I am," or, "Everybody does it." You're rationalizing disobedience and killing your own motivation. Believe that with God's help you can change!

(2) *Set manageable goals.* Approach your target with a rifle, not a shotgun. Instead of reaching for everything, focus only on those things that are important to your personal growth this year.

(3) *Be reasonable.* It requires at least twenty-one days for a habit to take root. Setbacks are part of the process. If you get off track, just get back on again. Perseverance is the secret!

(4) *Be optimistic.* Paul says, "We are saved by hope" (Ro 8:24). Keep reminding yourself, "With God's help I can do it," and you'll discover you can!

Change is painful; *not* changing is even more painful! Remember, Paul didn't say he had arrived, he said, "I'm working toward that day" (Php 3:13 TLB).

FINANCIAL AMNESIA!

Be careful that you do not forget the Lord.
Deuteronomy 6:12 NIV

In Egypt God's people lived as dependents, with no ability to improve their lot in life. To wean them from reliance on others, God brought them into the wilderness to teach them reliance on *Him.* When they reached The Promised Land He warned them, "When you build fine houses and settle down . . . and all you have is multiplied . . . Be careful that you do not forget the Lord" (Dt 8:11-18; 6:12 NIV).

This is what's called "financial amnesia." We remember God in times of crisis, but forget Him as soon as they're over. We can't count our blessings because we're too busy counting our money. We feel like we don't need Him as much, because everything's going our way. We say, *"My* power and the strength of *my* hands have produced this wealth for me" (Dt 8:17 NIV).

People don't change much, do they? When we had nothing we praised God with abandon. But once we get a little something and want to look dignified, we keep the name of Jesus locked behind our lips when questioned about our success. The danger of entering The Promised Land is this: forgetting where you came from.

A little food in your stomach can make yesterday's hunger seem like a long time ago. A few clothes in your closet and a new sofa in your living room can make the old stuff you used to get by with seem like a distant memory. The word for you today is, *"Be careful that you do not forget the Lord."*

ON THE OTHER SIDE OF THE WALL

And the Lord said unto Joshua,
See, I have given into thine hand Jericho.
Joshua 6:2

Everything God promised to Joshua was on the other side of Jericho's wall. From that we learn two important things:

(1) *Your blessing is on the other side of your problem!* The land will be yours once the wall comes down. And it will, for Jesus is your enemy-exposing, strategy-giving, wall-toppling conqueror.

(2) *You've got to fight for it.* Don't let that intimidate you. You're not fighting in your own strength, and you're not fighting alone. You ask, "What can I do?" (a) Realize that victory begins on your knees. Everything changed when Joshua prayed, "What saith my lord unto his servant?" (Jos 5:14). God has a plan, and He'll reveal it to you if you seek Him. (b) The enemy has no defense against God's Word. Three different times Jesus used The Word to "face him down." After the third time we read, "The devil leaveth Him and . . . angels came and ministered unto Him" (Mt 4:11). If your stand outlasts the enemy's, he'll flee, and God will send in reinforcements!

Paul says we are to, "Withstand in the evil day" (Eph 6:13). Note, your enemy only has a day; his time will soon be over. Don't give up when you are just moments away from victory, or inches from the prize. What would have happened if Joshua had quit on the third or fourth time around the walls? Keep going! *Your blessing is waiting – on the other side of the wall!*

RESURRECTION LIFE

You have been raised with Christ.
Colossians 3:1 NIV

What is it that seems dead to you today? Your marriage? Your career? Is your creativity dead from too much rejection? Your heart from too much sorrow? Your witness from too much fear? Your peace from too much unrest?

Grasp this: God causes dead things to live again! Not only does He raise them from the dead, He gives them purpose. He doesn't just give life, He gives *meaning* to life.

When you realize that God wants to bring your marriage back to life because it has eternal meaning and significance before Him, *you'll* want to see it restored too. When you realize that He wants to see the talent that's lying dormant within you come alive, *you'll* want to dust it off and start using it again for His glory. When you realize that He wants your paralyzed, disappointed heart to live and express God's love to others so that they can be saved, blessed, and spend eternity in heaven, *you'll* want to start loving again, even if it means being vulnerable.

Listen, "I pray that you will begin to understand the incredible greatness of his power *for us* who believe him. This is the same mighty power that raised Christ from the dead and seated him in a place of honor at God's right hand" (Eph 1:19-20 NLT). Did you hear that? His power is "for us." That means it's available to *you* today!

JESUS IS THE ANSWER

And hath put all things under His feet [authority], and gave Him to be the head over all things.
Ephesians 1:22

In the Greek mathematical system when numbers are added, the total is put at the top instead of the bottom. Where we might say, "Jesus is the bottom line," the Greeks would say "Jesus is the top line." I like that better, don't you? No matter how you cut it, when everything's added up, Jesus is the answer!

Think: God has given Jesus as a gift to us. That makes us the most privileged people in the history of mankind, because we have the Lord Jesus Christ as our head.

In Him no weapon formed against you shall prosper! (Isa 54:17). *In Him* you have authority over the enemy! (Lk 10:19). *In Him* you're tapped into the limitless, universe-shaking power of God! (Eph 1:19).

Paul says *all* things are under His control! That means the problems you're having with your family today are under His control; He has a strategy for your home. That means the problems you're having in your career today are under His control; He has a strategy for your life, your talents, and your dreams.

Just as the head commands the body, so Jesus: (1) directs you by His wisdom; (2) empowers you by His Spirit; (3) moves you by His compassion; (4) completes you by His love. Everything you need today, *absolutely everything,* can be found in Him! He doesn't just *have* the answer, He *is* the answer!

ALL THROUGH THE NIGHT

All that night the Lord drove the sea back.
Exodus 14:21 NIV

The miracle of rolling back The Red Sea happened "all that night." The morning simply revealed what God had done the night before while they were sleeping. Good news: God works the night shift! Even though you feel lost and alone, He's still on the job working "all things after the counsel of his own will" (Eph 1:11). Have you heard of *"songs in the night?"* Here's one of them:

"When darkness seems to veil His face,
I rest on His unchanging grace.
When all around my soul gives way,
He then is all my hope and stay.
On Christ the solid rock I stand,
all other ground is sinking sand."

You may not be able to see Him today, but His eyes are still on you. Whether you're a student off at school, a young couple hard-pressed financially, a divorcee struggling to get back on your feet, a servant of God laboring in difficult circumstances, or just lonely and in need of companionship, here are some words to help get you through until the morning:

(1) "I have been young, and now I am old; yet have I not seen the righteous forsaken [have you?] nor his seed begging bread" (Ps 37:25). (2) "Weeping may endure for a night, but joy cometh [it's on the way!] in the morning" (Ps 30:5). (3) "In all these things [whatever you're facing] we are more than conquerors through him that loved us" (Ro 8:37). *Be encouraged – God's working in the dark!*

AMAZING GRACE

The gift that came by the grace of one man, Jesus Christ.
Romans 5:15 NIV

During a British conference on comparative religions, experts from around the world gathered to debate what belief, if any, was *unique* to the Christian faith. Was it resurrection? Other religions had accounts of people returning from the dead. Was it healing? Other religions had accounts of miraculous healing too. The debate continued until C.S. Lewis stood up and said, *"That's easy, the answer is: grace!"*

If you were raised to believe that God forgives you, albeit reluctantly and only after you've squirmed a while, then "grace" probably sounds too good to be true. The idea that God's love is unconditional is hard to grasp, because acceptance for most of us has always been based on *our performance.*

But not with God. Listen, " . . . it is the gift of God – not by works" (Eph 2:8-9 NIV). If you believe you're *saved* by God's grace but kept by your own works, every time you fail you'll have to prove all over again that you're worthy of His love. That's not salvation; that's probation! James says, "He gives us *more* grace" (Jas 4:6 NIV). Relax, God's grace won't run out before you get your act together!

Peter says we are "kept by the power of God through faith" (1Pe 1:5). The word *faith* means "trusting in Christ alone." No more is required, no less will do! When Jesus said, "It is finished," He satisfied *all* of God's claims against you. "But what about doing good deeds?" you ask. They're just a "PS" to say, *"Thanks for all You've done."*

REMINDERS

Jesus saith . . . take up thy bed, and walk.
And immediately the man was made whole.
John 5: 8-9

Picture a wretched street in Calcutta and you'll have an idea of what people witnessed at the Pool of Bethesda. What did they hear? Endless groans. What did they see? Faceless need. What did they do? Walk on by. But not Jesus; He went there to find a paralyzed man who'd spent 38 miserable years lying on a cot.

But why did Jesus tell this man to take up his bed and walk? Don't faith-healers usually break crutches over their knees, and dance on discarded eyeglasses? Two reasons:

(1) *His bed was a constant reminder of what he'd been delivered from.* Why did God tell His ancient people to put tassels on the corners of their garments (Nu 15:38-39 NIV)? To help them recall His commandments and obey them. Why did He tell them to build a monument of stones taken from the Jordan River? To remind them of *Who* had parted the waters and brought them safely through (Jos 4:5-7). Why did He tell them to keep The Passover? To reinforce the truth that their very existence depended on Him. Our problem isn't that we're slow learners – we're just quick forgetters!

(2) *To confirm the rumors about his healing.* When people asked, "Did that really happen?" there'd be evidence. Like Jacob's limp, when God delivers us, sometimes He leaves just enough to remind us of what *He* did – that *we* couldn't do.

GET TO THE SECRET PLACE

Let's take a break.
Mark 6:31 TM

People's needs are endless! With the best of intentions you try "being there" for them, and before you know it, you're drained. If that's where *you* are today, listen to Jesus: "Let's take a break" (Mk 6:31 TM). Jesus understood that solitude was necessary for intimacy with God, and intimacy with God was necessary for impartation to others. You see information may change people's *minds,* but only divine impartation can change their *lives!*

You've got to get away from the clamor and demands of others in order to discern the voice of God. Job said, "The breath of the Almighty hath given me life" (Job 33:4). Until God breathes *His* thoughts into you, you're just recycling the ideas of others.

In Genesis God said, "Be fruitful, and multiply, and *replenish"* (Ge 9:1). Have you learned yet how to "replenish" your flagging emotions and your drained energies? David said, *"He* maketh me to lie down in green pastures. *He* leadeth me beside the still waters. *He* restoreth my soul" (Ps 23:2-3). Those things only happen in *His* presence.

Ponder these 3 scriptures: (1) "Three times a day he got down on his knees and prayed, giving thanks to his God" (Dan 6:10 NIV). (2) "In the morning I lay my requests before you and wait in expectation" (Ps 5:3 NIV). (3) "Very early in the morning . . . Jesus got up, left the house and went off to a solitary place, where he prayed" (Mk 1:35 NIV). The message is clear – you need more time alone with God!

FEELING REJECTED?

On the day you were born you were despised.
Then I passed by and saw you.
Ezekiel 16:5-6

When you've been abused you not only carry the memories, but also *anger* over the fact that nobody stepped in to help you. Listen, "No one looked on you with pity . . . you were thrown into the open field" (Ez 16:5 NIV).

Private rejection is bad enough, but when it happens in public you feel vulnerable and worthless. You think to yourself, "If *they* don't think I'm worth anything, then maybe I'm not."

Wrong! Never allow somebody else's opinion of you to determine how you see yourself! That's too much power to give anybody. If others don't value you, that's their problem – unless you make it *yours!*

When people reject you, it's usually because *they don't have the ability* to see inside you, or hear the meaning behind your words, or feel the quality of your touch. They've bought into a lie; make sure you don't buy into it also!

Until you can learn to care for yourself, you won't really be able to care for anybody else. You can only give to others out of the well of your own self-esteem. Most physical abusers don't hate their victims, they hate themselves. It just overflows to those nearest them. Paul says, "He who loves his wife loves himself" (Eph 5:28 NIV). But what if he doesn't love himself?

"What's the answer?" you ask. Listen, "Then I passed by and saw you" (Ez 16:6 NIV). God sees you, He loves you, and He has a wonderful plan for your life. When you can fully accept that your healing will begin.

WHAT WILL YOU LEAVE BEHIND?

The plans of the diligent lead to profit.
Proverbs 21:5 NIV

Life is an investment. You can't pay what you like and still have what you want in the end. Solomon says, "Look at the ant . . . let it teach you a thing or two . . . all summer it stores up food . . . it stockpiles provisions. So how long are you going to laze around doing nothing? A nap here, a nap there, a day off here, a day off there, sit back, take it easy – do you know what comes next? . . . *a dirt poor life"* (Pr 6:6-11 TM). Strong language!

If you don't do the right things now, you'll end up in the winter of your life depressed and resentful, cursing your wasted youth, and spending your days in want. Ants stockpile food. Birds build nests. All creation prepares, delaying gratification in the interests of a better future. Follow its lead!

Prosperity and piety *can* abound in the same life. Indeed they *should,* for visions die without funding. Listen to these two scriptures: (1) "My chosen ones will long enjoy the works of their hands" (Isa 65:22 NIV). (2) "A good man leaves an inheritance for his children's children" (Pr 13:22 NIV).

Enjoy every moment of your present, but don't fail to invest for your future. If you're practical, try to be godly. If you're godly, try to be practical. One should compliment the other. Ask God to add days to your life, and then life to your days. Strive to leave a legacy that enhances your memory and blesses those you leave behind.

S.E.C.R.E.T.S.

Remember the Lord in all you do, and
He will give you success.
Proverbs 3:6 NCV

Cartoonist Walt Kelly once pictured his character *Pogo* fishing, when a duck asks him, "Have you seen my cousin? He's migrating north by kiddy car." Pogo exclaims, "By kiddy car?" "Yep," says the duck, "He's afraid to fly in case he falls into the water." Pogo says, "Why doesn't he swim?" The duck responds, "Cause he gets seasick." Pogo replies, "When your cousin decided to be a duck, he chose the wrong business, didn't he?"

Blessed is the duck that walks like a duck, quacks like a duck, and does what ducks are supposed to do! *Only then will he succeed!* Want to know the secret of success? Follow these guidelines, based on S.E.C.R.E.T.S.

(1) *Sense of purpose:* write down your goals and review them regularly. Jesus said, "Blessed are the meek [focused]: for they shall inherit the earth" (Mt 5:5). (2) *Excellence:* need a standard to reach for? "Work . . . as if . . . for the Lord" (Col 3:23 NCV). (3) *Contribution:* "God is fair; he will not forget the work you did [for others]" (Heb 6:10 NCV). (4) *Responsibility:* take responsibility for your actions. "You can't whitewash your sins and get by with it" (Pr 28:13 TM). (5) *Effort:* without hard work success is impossible. "Diligence brings wealth" (Pr 10:4 TM). (6) *Time management:* time is the one thing you can't get more of. Listen, "Teach us to live wisely and well" (Ps 90:12 TM). (7) *Stick with it:* "We will receive our harvest . . . if we do not give up" (Gal 6:9 NCV). There's the formula, now put it to work!

THE LIMP

The sun rose above him as he passed Peniel,
and he was limping.
Genesis 32:31 NIV

Jacob didn't know who he was until God told him. All his life he'd been labeled a "deceiver," until the Lord explained to him that he was "a prince . . . with God." (Ge 32:28). Notice those words *"with God."* God was in essence saying, "From now on Jacob, you're just my puppet. Unless I pull the strings, you'll fall over. I'm the source of every good idea you'll ever have and every blessing you'll ever receive. Don't forget that!"

Becoming a Christian is the work of a moment. Learning to depend on God is the work of a lifetime. That's why you can walk with Him, yet still limp in certain areas. Your limp is what keeps you from "believing your own press." It's what makes you say, "If God can use *me,* He can use anybody." It reminds you that you're still a work in progress; it forces you to lean more on God and less on yourself.

In a way, Paul had a limp. Listen, "To keep me from becoming conceited . . . there was given me a thorn in my flesh . . . three times I pleaded with the Lord to take it away from me. But he said to me, 'My grace is sufficient for you, for my power is made perfect in weakness' " (2Co 12:7-9 NIV).

Here's a word to *you* who've spent your entire life trying to hide your limp, or deny it. *Your limp, like Jacob's, is just a testimony to what God has brought you through; it proves that He's touched you!*

HOW'S YOUR VOLUME LEVEL?

People with good sense restrain their anger;
they earn esteem by overlooking wrongs.
Proverbs 19:11 NLT

The emotional intensity level in your home is similar to the volume on your radio; when it's set too high you live in an atmosphere of continual crisis. One disagreement with your spouse, and you're headed for divorce court. Your child misses his or her curfew by 5 minutes, and it's World War III. And let's not even *talk* about how you behave when you're behind the wheel of a car! Listen, "Do not be quickly provoked . . . for anger resides in the lap of fools" (Ecc 7:9 NIV).

So, how's *your* volume level these days? When it's set too high your emotions dictate your reactions, you talk without thinking and leave a trail of pain and resentment. Dad, every time you storm out of the house because you don't get *what* you want *when* you want, has it occurred to you that you're teaching your children to act the *same* way? Mom, when your daughter hears you say, "All men are alike; they're no good," has it dawned on you that *she* might grow up never trusting, or allowing herself to be emotionally available to any man? How will you feel living with *that?*

Reduce the volume! Lower the intensity level! Destinies are being shaped by your words, your behavior, and your attitudes. God says, "Refrain from anger and turn from wrath, do not fret – it leads only to evil" (Ps 37:8 NIV). Today, listen to what He's telling you!

FAITH TRAINING

In accordance with the measure of faith God has given you.
Romans 12:3 NIV

When it comes to building muscle, how *much* weight you lift isn't nearly as important as how many *repetitions* you do. The more "reps," the stronger you become. So it is with your faith. When you face tough times and come through them, you develop the faith needed to handle even tougher times. You learn that since God brought you through *that,* He can also bring you through *this.*

It's necessary to experience both success and failure, for built into each is the ability to be stronger and wiser tomorrow. David destroyed Goliath because he'd "faith-trained" with a lion and a bear! He also refused to wear King Saul's armor, because he knew you can't use somebody else's workout regimen to kill your Goliath. David said, "I cannot go with these; for I have not proved them" (1Sa 17:39).

What you're going through right now is just equipping you to handle what God has for you in the future. It's been sent so that you can work on your training formula.

Have you ever noticed how some people can lose *everything,* yet a few years later they're back on top again? That's because they know the formula, and that's better than riches because the formula will work anywhere. If you can cook, you can cook anywhere. If you can sing, you can sing anywhere. Learn God's formula for your life. Use the situation you're in right now as a faith-training opportunity.

IT'S ALL A LEARNING EXPERIENCE

It's what we trust in but don't yet see that keeps us going.
2 Corinthians 5:7 TM

A traveler in The Far East tells of watching a tapestry maker shouting instructions at a loom, and threads suddenly appearing in the tapestry. When asked for an explanation, his guide said, "The man you see is the master weaver. He's shouting to his apprentice behind the loom, telling him what color thread to use and where to put it. Only the master knows the design, so the apprentice has to listen carefully and do exactly as he says." "What happens if the apprentice makes a mistake?" the traveler asked. "Well," replied the guide, "The weaver being the artist that he is, just works it into the design."

Do you feel like you're standing on the *wrong* side of the tapestry today, looking at a bunch of knots and threads that seem to have no purpose? And just when you *think* you're starting to understand, the Master calls for a thread that changes everything? Don't worry, He knows exactly what He's doing!

Don't be so hard on yourself! When you put a blue thread where a red one was supposed to be, or tie a knot in the wrong place, God doesn't fall off His throne. No, He just takes your mistakes, turns them into wisdom, and works them into His overall design.

Hannah Whitehall-Smith says, "All the attacks the enemy hurls at us through others, are not only powerless to harm us, but are transformed into blessings along the way." Aren't you glad?

SINGLE, AND ENJOYING IT

Let every man abide in the same calling wherein he was called.
1 Corinthians

Learn to enjoy being single. Instead of constantly struggling with it or trying to change it, discover its advantages. Here are three advantages you might not have considered:

(1) You can set your own schedule. You can attend conferences every night, or pray out loud at 3:00 a.m. without disturbing anyone. (2) You can belong to a person who can do *some* things, or to the One who can do *everything*. (3) The greatest visitation of The Holy Ghost in history happened to a single girl named Mary. And that same life-giving Spirit can also come upon you and cause you to give birth to greatness, bringing you incredible joy in the process.

Before you ask God for *another* partner, learn to minister to the one you've got. If you can't treat the perfect partner right, what would you do with an imperfect one? There's nothing wrong with wanting to be married; just learn to minister to the Lord while you're waiting.

When God picks a partner, He *always* chooses one from among those who are faithful to Him. When you've proven you can keep your vow to Him, He'll trust you to keep it to somebody else. Therefore, commit yourself fully to God today. Bond with Him. Learn to relate to Him as the Lover of your Soul. *When you can do that, you're not single – you're whole!*

BEFORE YOU PASS JUDGMENT

God's people should be big-hearted and courteous.
Titus 3:2 TM

Have you heard about the two taxidermists who stopped to look at an owl on display in a store window? Immediately they began to criticize. Its eyes weren't natural; its wings weren't in proportion to its head; its feathers weren't properly arranged. Just as they started to walk away the owl turned its head – and winked at them!

Before you pass judgment, ask yourself these questions. Have I waited long enough to get *all* the facts? What do I *not* know yet? Am I relying strictly on what I've heard? Am I eager to believe the best, or think the worst? If mistakes have been made, do I feel as though that gives me the upper hand? If so, what am I going to do about it? What would *Jesus* do? Will my actions add to the problem or lead to a solution? If the situation was reversed and I was on the other end, what would I need? Am I magnifying something which in a month or two will make little or no difference, but could hurt any future relationship I may have with this person?

Listen carefully to this verse: "Don't pick on people, jump on their failures, criticize their faults – unless, of course, you want the same treatment. Don't condemn those who are down; that hardness can boomerang. Be easy on people; you'll find life a lot easier" (Lk 6:37 TM). Now, *those* are words to live by!

GOD WANTS YOU TO BE FREE

Go, and sin no more.
John 8:11

Can you imagine being "caught in the act" of adultery? And worse – all the local clergy wanting to stone you? That was the scene when Jesus stepped in, saved this woman, and said to her, "Go and sin no more." You say, "But if she couldn't live right before, how will she manage it now?" Listen, "To them gave he power to *become* the Sons of God" (Jn 1:12). When you meet Jesus He gives you the power to become a better person!

It's as if a light comes on; now you no longer need what you needed before. The affair is over. You're free from what drove you to it. You have the power to unhook from that person (or substance, or habit), walk away and say, "I'm done with that!" You don't need a long drawn-out discussion or a confrontation or a redefining. You can say with confidence, "I'm not vulnerable to that anymore," and leave!

But there are two things you need to know: (1) Those who've used you to their own advantage, won't take kindly to the fact that you're not available anymore. (2) When God looses you from something, it's to join you to something better, otherwise you're likely to go back and seek out your old connections.

"What's the answer?" you ask. Two things: (1) When Jesus quenches your thirst, you won't have to go back to the old dry wells any more. (2) As you develop a relationship with Him, you'll begin to attract the *right* kind of people into your life.

WALKING WITH GOD!

Look carefully then how you walk.
Ephesians 5:15 AMP

How long are you going to keep wandering in the wilderness, delaying your growth, avoiding your calling, denying who you really are, and focusing on lesser things? This is not who you are or what you're supposed to be! Your mandate is to be *light,* expelling the darkness and bringing solutions wherever you go. But to do that you've got to walk *God's* way, not your own. Here are some things about walking with God you need to think about today.

(1) *It's a responsible walk.* You're supposed to bring honor to the One who saved you, by staying on the path He designated for you; to demonstrate His character and compassion to all you meet.

(2) *It's a Spirit-empowered walk.* You must continuously rely on God's ability and not your own in order to succeed. If by nature you're self sufficient, you'll have to work on this each day.

(3) *It's a Word-directed walk.* It's not based on *your* ideas or perceptions, but on the very mind and heart of God which He's revealed to you in His Word.

(4) *It's a relational walk.* You're not walking alone. You're walking hand in hand with Jesus, and in unity with your brothers and sisters in God's family. That's what gives us the collective power to reach and transform this world.

The truth is, your walk can bring results and rewards which reach far beyond your own little sphere of influence – in this life, and in the one to come.

YOUR POSITION AND YOUR CONDITION

In Whom we have redemption through His blood.
Ephesians 1:7

Stop worrying about your *condition* and start focusing on your *position!* Your condition probably won't improve until you understand your position. Any condition is temporal and subject to change. But your position "in Him" is eternal. Paul says, "If any man be *in Christ,* he is a new creature" (2Co 5:17). That means you're forgiven, accepted, and perfected in the eyes of God – present tense!

The word redemption means "payment of ransom." It depicts God holding you in prison under a death sentence because of your sin. But then He sees the blood of Jesus, and all claims against you are thrown out of court, your prison door swings open and you're free. Awesome!

No matter how hard you try or how dedicated you become, you couldn't *in 50 lifetimes* pay off your debt. Only Jesus could do that, because only He could offer a life completely free from sin.

But it's not enough to issue a declaration of emancipation; the slaves need to know about it! And the last person on earth who wants them to know is the slave-master. You see, if you don't *know* you're free you'll remain in bondage in your mind, and live accordingly.

So today when the devil points to your *condition,* remind him of your *position.* Tell him, "Some areas may be under construction, but I'm still loved, accepted, and approved one-hundred-percent by God!"

DARE TO DISTURB!

There was a division among the people because of Him.
John 7:43

Wayne Dyer came home from school one day and asked his mom, "What's a scurvy elephant?" She told him she'd never heard of one, and asked him where he'd heard it. "From my teacher," he replied. When his mother called the teacher, he told her, "As usual, Wayne got it wrong. I didn't say he was a scurvy elephant; I said he was a *disturbing element!*"

Do people see you that way? They did Jesus! His enemies said, "He stirreth up the people" (Lk 23:5). Imagine that: The Prince of Peace was also The Great Disturber!

Daniel refused to eat the King's meat or bow to his gods because he'd been sent to bring change, not build a consensus. When you compromise what's right in order to gain acceptance with men, you forfeit acceptance with God. Make your choice!

You are where you are today for a purpose! The question is, are you willing to become a disturbing element in order to fulfill it?

Joseph Bayly writes, "Lord of reality, make me real, not plastic. I don't just want to keep a prayer list, I want to pray. I don't want to agonize to find Your will, I want to obey what I already know of it. I don't want to explain the difference between Eros, Philos, and Agape. I just want to love. I don't want to *tell* it like it is, I want to *be* like You want it." Make that *your* prayer today, too.

TELL THE TRUTH!

Truthful lips endure forever, but a lying tongue lasts only a moment.

Proverbs 12:19 NIV

Too many of us are like the little boy who, when he was asked by his Sunday School teacher, "What is a lie?" replied, "Sometimes it's an abomination unto the Lord, other times it's a very present help in trouble!" You may smile, but God says, "No one who practices deceit will dwell in my house; no one who speaks falsely will stand in my presence" (Ps 101:7 NIV).

Do you think God's serious about that? He exposed King David for living a lie, and killed Ananias and Sapphira for telling one. Whether it's to . . . save face or somebody else's feelings . . . earn an extra buck or keep from losing one . . . gain acceptance or keep somebody else from getting it . . . the bottom line is, God hates lying!

And He doesn't mince words when He talks about it. Listen: (1) "The Lord detests lying lips, but he delights in men who are truthful" (Pr 12:22 NIV). (2) "A fortune made by a lying tongue is a fleeting vapor and a deadly snare" (Pr 21:6 NIV). (3) "A false witness will not go unpunished, and he who pours out lies will not go free" (Pr 19:5 NIV). (4) "Therefore each of you must put off falsehood and speak truthfully to his neighbor" (Eph 4:25 NIV).

Today, make up your mind to tell the truth – always!

DON'T SETTLE FOR MEDIOCRITY!

Woe to you who are complacent.
Amos 6:1 NIV

When you get to the seventh church in Revelation, Jesus is standing outside knocking, trying to get in, *and nobody inside seems to have missed Him!* Does that shock you? It should! Listen to what He told them, "You are neither cold not hot. I wish you were either one or the other! So, because you are lukewarm . . . I am about to spit you out of my mouth" (Rev 3:15-16 NIV). Bottom-line – don't settle for mediocrity!

Ponder these words by Wilbur Rees: "I'd like to buy $3 worth of God please. Not enough to awaken my soul or disturb my sleep, just enough to equal a cup of warm milk or a snooze in the sunshine. I want ecstasy, not transformation; the warmth of the womb, not the new birth. I want a pound of the eternal in a paper sack. No, not the flesh and blood one, He'll keep me from my appointment with the hairdresser, or make me late for my cocktail party. I can't put up with wise men from Persia, or sweaty shepherds trampling all over my carpet with their muddy feet. My name isn't Mary you know. I don't want a living Christ – I just want one I can keep in a crib."

Want to know the answer to complacency? Jesus gives it to you: "Be earnest and repent. Here I am! I stand at the door and knock. If anyone hears my voice and opens the door, I will come in" (Rev 3:19-20 NIV). That's *you* He's speaking to today!

"TO ENCIRCLE BEFOREHAND"

In love He predestined us to be adopted as His sons.
Ephesians 1:4-5 NIV

There's just enough ego in each of us to want to claim part of the credit for our salvation, and just enough pride to say, "I decided to live for Jesus." No way! Dead men can neither respond nor initiate, and you were spiritually dead when He found you.

The truth is the guilt you felt, the crisis that brought you to your knees, the person who told you about Christ – *every* circumstance that drew you – was orchestrated by Him.

Love was His motive; predestination was His method. Don't let the word predestination scare you; it just means, "to encircle beforehand." Have you ever searched the newspaper to find a house? First you scan the listings, then you take a red pen and circle the one you want. That's a crude example, yet it illustrates the fact that God specifically chose *you* for Himself.

He didn't choose you because of your actions, your lifestyle, or your pleadings. He decided to be good to you without provocation, inducement, or cajoling. None of your weaknesses, failures, or personality flaws had *any* effect on His decision. You had neither influence over Him or access to Him, because you didn't even exist yet. Listen, "Long ago, even before he made the world, God loved us and chose us in Christ" (Eph 1:4 NLT). Aren't you glad?

"But I don't understand that kind of love," you say. No, and you never will! That's why we'll *all* spend eternity singing the debtor's anthem – "Amazing Grace!"

CHRIST IS EVERYTHING

For me to live is Christ, and to die is gain.
Philippians 1:21

"For me to live is Christ." Those words don't work any other way. For example: (a) For me, to live is *money* . . . to die is to leave it all behind. (b) For me to live is *fame* . . . to die is to be quickly forgotten. (c) For me to live is *power and influence* . . . to die is to be replaced by others. (d) For me to live is *possessions* . . . to die is to depart empty-handed. Somehow these words fall flat, don't they?

When money's your obsession you can never get enough, and you live in constant fear of losing it. When fame's your goal you become competitive and manipulative lest others upstage you; that makes you insecure. When power and influence drive you, you become self-serving and strong-willed; that makes you arrogant. When possessions become your God you become materialistic; that makes you greedy.

Whether you have or don't have, are known or unknown, live or die – *only* Christ can satisfy! And death? That only sweetens the pot. J.B. Philips writes, "Living to me simply means Christ, and if I should die, I merely gain *more* of Him."

So what's the bottom line? It's this; the secret to living is the same as the secret to joy. Both revolve around Christ. *Don't try to pursue happiness, just cultivate a Christ-centered, Christ-controlled life, and you'll have more happiness than you know what to do with!*

FROM THE LESSER TO THE GREATER

A kernel of wheat . . . if it dies . . . produces many seeds.
John 12:24 NIV

What do you say to those who believe in miracles yet don't seem to get one? Or when your life suddenly hits the wall of adversity? Or your building burns to the ground and your insurance won't cover it? Or your mate becomes involved with someone else? There lie your hopes for a marriage that would last forever. There lie the ashes of what you had to lose, in order to gain what God has in store for you next. It's both a place of death and a place of birth. And it hurts!

To reach the next dimension of *anything,* something you presently have may be the sacrificial offering required. Jesus taught that certain things in our lives must die in order to be reborn at the next level.

When trouble comes, our questions often place God's integrity on the line. Indeed He has to be extremely secure to stick to His plan in the face of our vacillating and complaining.

The truth is, it's not until we *look back* that we realize what we went through was just the bar mitzvah (coming of age) of our faith; the time in our life when weak faith evolved into a faith previously beyond our grasp.

It's on the *other side* of pain that faith gets its diploma. From then on it refuses to be intimidated by anyone or anything.

PRACTICE MAKES PERFECT

Though your beginning was insignificant,
yet your end will increase greatly.
Job 8:7 NASB

George's first job as a landscaper was removing a big tree stump for a farmer. It was also his first time to use dynamite. With the farmer watching, George calculated the size of the stump, the right amount of dynamite, then pushed the plunger. Suddenly there was an explosion. The big tree-stump rose gracefully into the air and came crashing down – on top of the cab of George's new truck! Filled with admiration, the farmer turned to him and said, "Son, with a little more practice those stumps will land in the *bed* of that truck every time!"

No matter what we're doing, few of us ever get it right the first time. Remember Edison? One thousand attempts before the lights came on. And do you recall his answer to his critics? "I didn't fail 999 times, the electric light bulb was just *a one-thousand-step process!"* It's all in how you see it.

What will you learn or accomplish if you give up? Instead of dwelling on how far short you fell, look at how *close* you came. The truth is, if your life is failure-free you're not taking enough risks or growing in obedience to God!

Refuse to allow the opinions of others to limit you. The road to success winds through multiple failures. The people who tell you today that you can't or shouldn't, will be the first to claim credit tomorrow when you succeed.

Should that make you resentful? No, it should just make you smile and keep you pressing forward.

WHERE IS YOUR FAMILY GOING?

As arrows in the hands of a mighty man; so are children.
Psalm 127:4

You may be ready for sex, but are you ready for marriage and children? No more tantrums; no more staying home from work because you don't feel like going; no more leaving your family to fend for themselves because you want to go out and party. Marriage means growing up!

Every team needs a game plan and a good coach; without one, all-stars can look like *The Bad News Bears.* Parent, the most important job you have is to create a vision for your family. What values will you live by? What will you do to help develop your children's talents? Listen, "Like arrows in the hand of a warrior, so are the children of one's youth" (Ps 127:4 NAS). Shoot those arrows as far as you can, using all the strength God's given you! Give your children purpose and direction. Aim them toward worthy goals and help them to reach them!

That means first having direction for your *own* life! What's *your* purpose? Are you living it every day?

If you want to create a better future, don't squander your money and your time. Invest them wisely! Determine where you want to go, and start taking steps to get there.

But before you try to lead anybody else, make sure you know how to follow God yourself. That means hearing from Him – which means *spending time* with Him! Are you doing that?

IT'S TIME TO RECONNECT

It is not good for . . . man to be alone.
Genesis 2:18 NIV

When we isolate ourselves, everything gets blown out of proportion. Minor setbacks become major catastrophes. We get angry with the people who don't notice us, and distrusting of those who seem to go out of their way to become our friends. What's the answer? *Connecting!* By connecting we're able to see that our giants are only knee-high, and most of our fears are made out of smoke. That's why God said, "It is not good for . . . man to be alone" (Ge 2:18 NIV).

If you wrestle with either rejection or self-sufficiency, consider this thought provoking poem by Charles H. Towne:

> *"Around the corner I have a friend, in this great city that has no end. Yet days go by and weeks rush on, and before I know it a year is gone. And I never see my old friend's face, for life is a swift and terrible race. He knows I like him just as well, as in the days when I rang his bell. And he rang mine – we were younger then; but now we are tired, busy men. Tired of playing a foolish game, tired of trying to make a name. 'Tomorrow,' I say, 'I'll call on Jim, and let him know that I'm thinking of him.' But tomorrow comes and tomorrow goes, and the distance between us grows and grows. Around the corner, yet miles away, then comes the news . . . Jim died today! And that's what we get and deserve in the end, around the corner – a vanished friend!"*

Today *reconnect* with the people in your life who really matter!

HE CAN MAKE IT UP TO YOU

My father and mother walked out and left me,
but God took me in.
Psalm 27:10 TM

Has death or divorce robbed you of a parent? Are you still grieving lost hugs and birthdays without bicycles? These losses can cause you to struggle all your life to find your identity.

When you grow up listening to endless arguments but never seeing affection, it's easy to think that's normal. Then later you find yourself asking, "How should I act as a parent? And why do I still feel like a lost child?"

David said, "My father and mother walked out and left me, but God took me in" (Ps 27:10 TM). How wonderful! God can hold you and heal your pain. When you're hurting, He can put you on His couch and be your "Wonderful Counselor" (Isa 9:6). When you feel like an orphan, He can be to you an "Everlasting Father" who doesn't abandon His kids no matter what.

With Him you're always safe and protected, because *that's* what loving fathers do. You're His child – which means if something's important to you it's important to Him too!

What's more, He can send people into your life who'll be to you the father, the mother, the brother, or the sister you never had. Listen, "God sets the lonely in families" (Ps 68:6 NIV).

Don't be so focused on your losses that you fail to see Him at work, or receive the people He sends into your life today to make it better.

BELIEVING

Great is thy faithfulness.
Lamentations 3:23

Don't be too hard on Thomas for doubting. He'd already given up his job once to follow a man he'd seen crucified and buried. So when they said, "Jesus is alive," Thomas wasn't taking any chances.

That's what we do when our faith seems to fail, isn't it? Discard it in favor of something we think is absolute. Listen, "Unless I see . . . I will never believe" (Jn 20:25 AMP). Did Thomas's lack of faith do away with the resurrection? No! And when somebody says, "Miracles are not for today," does that do away with them? No! It just means *they'll* probably never experience one, for Jesus said, "These signs shall follow them that believe" (Mk 16:17).

Thomas almost missed the greatest event of his life because he limited himself to one method of believing – seeing. Yet eyewitnesses are often the most unreliable. Do you think a magician *really* saws the lady in half, or makes the table float in mid-air? Remember the brilliant people who looked through a telescope and told us the earth was flat and that the sun revolved around it? Today's scientific fact can become tomorrow's scientific nonsense.

Every time you fly trusting a pilot you've never met, or drive your car trusting that the other drivers on the road will stay in their lanes, you're operating in faith. You can't function without it.

The question is *who* is worthy of your trust? The only sure answer is – God! Why? Because, "Great is thy faithfulness" (Lam 3:22-23).

MORE ON BELIEVING

Blessed are they who have not seen, and yet have believed.
John 20:29

There are times when faith seems to make no sense at all. How can a sea be parted, or one man defeat an army, or the world be created by a word? Intellectuals think Christians are "simple minded" for believing such things. Yet they base their entire future on the stock market, or sell their home and move their family halfway across the country based on a promise of employment – or a 90-day probationary period! What's the difference? Their faith is in *man* – ours is in *God.* Who's wiser?

Jesus said, "Have faith in God" (Mk 11:22). That takes our faith from the unreliable, and places it in a God who is faithful, dependable, and sure. We can't see tomorrow, but we can trust the God who does. We can't trust ourselves, so we depend on His wisdom to know what's best for us. Sounds smart to me!

When you get down to the fine print, even some who call themselves Christians remain doubtful. When you tell them God's blessed you in a certain way, they say, "Yeah, but what did you *do?"* Because they haven't developed *their* faith, they go around like Delilah trying to find out the secret of *yours.* The simple answer is this, when you walk with God, He blesses you. He does it because He promised to, because He can, and because it pleases Him. Selah! So put your trust in God today!

MIX AND MATCH

Bearing with one another in love.
Ephesians 4:2 NJKV

Single parent, if you're fortunate enough to meet someone you want to marry, seek God's help from the outset. Mergers are challenging enough, but add visitation rights, custodial care, court intervention, and ex-in-law meddling, and it can be like negotiating an international peace treaty!

Here are some of the questions your kids should be asked when you attempt to blend families. "Do you take these children to be your brothers and sisters? Do you promise to accept this new mom or dad, while keeping ties with your biological parent and obeying your step-parent every day? Do you promise to share the toys your father bought you with the child of the man your mother just married?"

You can't just turn your child's world upside down, then say, "Play nice." Children need *time* to digest the situation and adjust to it. Indeed, some of them may *never* adjust. But you must help them through it and love them regardless.

If you want the merger to be as painless and stress-free as possible, try to do these 4 things:

(1) Give yourself totally; half measures don't build successful families. (2) Talk less and listen more. (3) Be patient: it may take years to win a child's love and respect, not to mention healing the scars of the past and erasing the fears of the future. (4) Pray! Pray! Pray! Even if it doesn't change them, it'll change you, and *that* could be the best thing for all concerned.

MORE ON JOY

I will continue to rejoice, for I know that . . .
what has happened to me will turn out for my deliverance.
Philippians 1:18-19 NIV

Paul's greatest desire was to go to Rome and testify before Caesar. As a Roman citizen he had that right. Instead, he was illegally arrested in Jerusalem, misrepresented before the court, incorrectly identified as an Egyptian renegade, lost in the red-tape of political machinery, and then granted a trip across the Mediterranean only to encounter a storm and be shipwrecked. When he finally arrived in Rome, they imprisoned him and threw away the key for two years. In total he received 2,340 welts on his back from the Roman cat-o-nine-tails. And for *what?* He never even spat on the sidewalk! All he did was preach Christ and love people. Yet he could write, "What has happened to me will turn out for my deliverance" (Php 1:19 NIV).

How do you develop an attitude like that? Here's how: instead of asking *"Why* did this have to happen to me?" ask, *"How* can I use it to grow stronger, *see* more clearly, and *reap* the benefits God has for me?" Paul chose to count his blessings, not his disappointments.

Recently I came across a book called *14,000 Things To Be Happy About.* The trouble is not *one* of them will work unless you give yourself *permission* to be happy. The secret lies in your mind-set! Listen again, *"Think* about all you can praise God for and be glad about" (Php 4:8 LB). *That's* the secret of joy – now put it to work!

YOU'VE GOT TO PRESS THROUGH!

When she heard about Jesus, she came up behind Him in the crowd and touched [Him].

Mark 5:27 NIV

This woman faced two challenges. (1) *Self-doubt!* "Can a person like me touch a God like Him?" The answer is yes! (2) *Getting through the crowd!* The enemy will do everything he can to keep you from getting to Jesus. You'll have to press through the flesh realm to get to the spiritual realm. You'll have to say to those who doubt what you're doing, "Excuse me, I've got to get to Jesus!" To those who want you to stop and stroke their egos, "Sorry, I don't have time, I have to get to Jesus!" To those who offer you their expert but unscriptural opinions, "Please step aside, I'm on my way to Jesus!"

Just take the first step, and God will work with you. When justice says, "You can't get to Him," mercy will let you through. When the law tries to stop you, grace will open the door. When the world says, "Don't go," God will whisper, "Come. Just press through; I'm waiting for you!"

But don't expect it to be easy. This woman had to press through the naysayers and the doomsayers, the doctor's reports, the piles of unpaid bills, the laws that shut her out, and the people who preached them.

But look what happened! Immediately the life of Jesus poured into every part of her and she was healed. And He'll do the same for you if you'll only *press through* and touch Him today.

FINDING THE RIGHT ANSWER

When she heard of Jesus [she] came in the press behind.
Mark 5:27

Remember the sick woman we talked about yesterday? A lot of people are just like her. Sometimes it's hard to tell they're even suffering. In some cases they've been told by church folk, "If you were really saved you wouldn't have that problem." Interestingly, if it's a problem *we've* experienced it's okay; but when it's something we've never struggled with, we're quick to pass judgment.

All God's heroes had problems! Samson fought lust. Noah got drunk. David stole somebody's wife. What a cast! Yet the Bible says, "These all died in faith" (Heb 11:13). The truth is you can be a Christian and still struggle. It's not a lack of faith, or not being saved, it's a matter of living in a fallen world!

The Bible says this woman had "suffered many things of many doctors and . . . grew worse" (Mk 5:26 NIV). Now it's one thing to have a problem; it's another to suffer at the hands of those who're supposed to be solving the problem! Be careful who you allow to treat you; they may only be after your money, or they may be ego-tripping because you're dependent on them, or they may be gossiping about you to everybody they know. The trouble with ungodly counselors is they'll give you plenty of advice, but no lasting help.

If you want real help, go to somebody who can give it. Go to Jesus! He's the Problem-Solver, the Direction-Giver, the Burden-Bearer, and the Way-Maker. One touch from Him – and you're whole!

LONGING FOR FORGIVENESS

If we confess our sins, He is faithful and just to forgive us our sins.

1 John 1:9

An organization in Los Angeles operates an *Apology Sound-Off Line.* It gives callers an opportunity to confess their sins anonymously for just the price of a phone call. At last count, about 500 callers a day were contacting them; people who've given up on organized religion; people who believe God's given up on them; people trying to find peace by saying, "I'm sorry for the things I've done."

At some point we *all* need forgiveness. If that's where you are today, listen: "If we admit our sins . . . he won't let us down; he'll be true to himself. He'll forgive our sins" (1Jn 1:9 TM). Guilt is an anchor that keeps you chained to the past and shuts out any possibility for change. God's forgiveness is the laser that breaks that chain, ends the cycle of blame, and frees you to be all that God called you to be.

"But you don't know what I've done," you say. Listen again, "God made him [Jesus] who had no sin to *be* sin for *us*" (2Co 5:21 NIV). Whatever you are, Jesus became it. Whatever you've done, Jesus took it. When you cry, "Father, I've sinned," God doesn't even look at you; He looks at His crucified Son, charges your sin to *His* account, and says, "I forgive you." What an arrangement!

What is it that you've been carrying around for years? Give it to Him today, for His Word says, "He will have mercy . . . He will abundantly pardon" (Isa 55:7).

REJOICE

I delight greatly in the Lord; my soul rejoices in my God.
Isaiah 61:10 NIV

Here's something to help you smile: "Yes, I'm tired. For several years I've been blaming it on middle-age, iron-poor blood, lack of vitamins, air pollution, water pollution, saccharin, obesity, dieting, underarm odor, yellow wax build-up, and a dozen other things that make you wonder if life is really worth living.

"But now I find out that it isn't *any* of those. It's because I'm overworked! The population of this country is over 200 million; 84 million are retired, leaving 116 million who do the work; 75 million are in school, leaving 41 million to do the work; 22 million are employed by the government, leaving 19 million to do the work; 4 million are in the armed forces, leaving 15 million to do the work; 14.8 million work for the state or city, leaving 200,000 to do the work; 88 thousand are in hospitals, leaving 112,000 to do the work; 111,998 are in prison, leaving only 2 to do the work: you and me. And *you're* sitting reading this – *no wonder I'm tired!"*

Seriously, if you want to be happy, learn to *let go!* "Let go of what?" you ask. Let go of . . . looking at the negative . . . fixing everybody . . . competing and comparing . . . needing to rescue your adult children . . . and all the other stuff that keeps you from enjoying life.

Refuse to live that way another day! God has put joy in your well and the pump in your hand. Start pumping! Start rejoicing! Start living!

ACCEPTING OUR DIFFERENCES

Whether from false motives or true, Christ is preached, and . . . because of this I rejoice.
Philippians 1:18 NIV

With 240 different denominations all claiming to preach Christ there are *bound* to be differences. If you have trouble accepting that, listen to Paul, "The important thing is . . . Christ is preached. And because of this I rejoice" (Php 1:15 NIV). Can you rejoice in that too? Or do you need to keep *categorizing* everybody?

Get rid of your judgmentalism and become broad-shouldered enough to let things be. Leave room for differences. Applaud good results, even if they weren't arrived at by *your* preferred method. It takes grace to do that. To do otherwise is to clutter your mind with thoughts that rob you of both love and faith. Remember, "faith . . . worketh by love" (Gal 5:6). If you're not careful, you'll become a petty, cranky, grim soul, who has to pour everybody into *your* mold before you can relax. And worse, you'll do it all in the name of God!

Cut it out! If God calls somebody His child then start calling him or her your brother or sister, otherwise *your* attitude is worse than *their* shortcomings. Listen, "Who are you to judge someone else's servant? To his own master he stands or falls" (Ro 14:4 NIV). They're not *your* servant, they're *God's!* They're out of your jurisdiction! Stop judging them and get your eyes back where they belong – on Jesus!

HAVE A SET TIME

Every morning, I tell You what I need,
and I wait for Your answer.
Psalm 5:3 NCV

Dr. Mike Murdock says, "What you do daily determines what you become permanently." He's right! "But is it really necessary to spend time with God early in the morning?" you ask. *Any* moment spent with God can change you; but don't you think it's wise to plan your trip *before* you take it? Why enter the day without a sense of His direction and peace? Is any voice more important than His? Or more reliable? If you're struggling to rise early and pray, start doing these 3 things:

(1) *Set an achievable goal.* Don't focus on getting up an hour earlier, try 15 minutes! You can always add to it. When you set impossible goals you create memories of failure instead of memories of success.

(2) *Learn how to enter His presence.* Listen, "Come before His presence with singing" (Ps 100:2). God loves music. He responds to worship and singing. When King Saul was depressed, we read that "David took an harp, and played . . . and the evil spirit departed" (1Sa 16:23). Music lifts your spirits and helps dispel your fears.

(3) *Educate those around you about your new prayer time.* Few things are more impacting than watching a person with a consistent prayer life. Without saying a word, you'll challenge those who don't pray and thrill those who do. They may even decide to join you!

EVERYBODY NEEDS SOMEBODY

I thank my God every time I remember you.
Philippians 1:3 NIV

Even the great Apostle Paul needed others. When he was ill he needed Dr. Luke. For his travels he needed Silas. When he was in prison he needed Titus. For his future he needed Timothy.

Just how important are you? More important than you think. A rooster minus a hen, equals no baby chicks. Kellogg minus a farmer, equals no cornflakes. Without the nail factory, what good's the hammer factory? Or the cracker-maker without the cheese-maker? Paderewski's genius wouldn't have amounted to a thing if the piano tuner hadn't shown up. The surgeon needs the ambulance driver, Rodgers needed Hammerstein – *and you need people too!*

The other side of the coin is – somebody needs you. The young need your experience, and the elderly need your care. The foolish need your wisdom, and the hurting need your compassion. Anytime you withhold or withdraw what God's given you, others suffer and you shrivel.

Looking back over my life, I see where I've connected with specific people at every significant crossroad and milestone. Most of them the world will never know, but to *me* they were absolutely vital. Each helped me to clear a hurdle, accomplish an objective, or reach a goal. Without them I wouldn't be where I am today. How about you?

God is all-powerful, all-knowing, and all-sufficient. That's what makes it all the more significant when He uses people like *us.*

Almost without exception, His favorite plan is *a combined effort;* all of us working for Him, and each of us loving one another in the process.

WORKING OUT WHAT'S ALREADY WITHIN

Praise be to the God . . . Who has blessed us . . .
with every spiritual blessing.
Ephesians 1:3 NIV

When you stumble or face a problem, God doesn't jump off His throne and say, "John's in trouble, Mary's in a mess, I'd better act!" No, He's *already* placed within you all that's necessary to handle the situation and overcome it. Maturing in Christ is simply the process by which we learn to work *out* what God has already worked *within.*

Think about a baby in his mother's womb. He *already* has the necessary genes, chromosomes, and traits built into him from conception. Likewise, when you're born again into God's family, you don't just get one or two spiritual blessings; you get *"every* spiritual blessing."

As a baby Christian you start out not knowing who you are or what you've got, so the Holy Spirit's job is to reveal it to you.

When you go through a crisis you don't need to go out and look for faith, or grace, or strength, or any thing else. You already *have* them residing within you; learn to draw on them!

Furthermore, you don't need to go looking for a more powerful person to pray for you. God wants to bring you to the place where you can . . . lay hands on your own head . . . minister to your own needs . . . speak peace to your own spirit . . . command calm within your own home! And that will happen when you *acknowledge* and *activate* the spiritual blessings He's *already* placed within you.

SERVING

So Joshua did as Moses had said to him.
Exodus 17:10

Joshua served Moses, but he looked only to *God* for his reward. Your boss may sign your check, but he doesn't determine your future; the Lord does that! Furthermore, if you really believe that, no job God gives you will ever be beneath you!

When you pray, "God use me," He'll often ask you to *serve* someone else. If you make the mistake of looking to that person for your reward and it doesn't come, you'll feel used and resentful.

It's *God* who sets the rules for you. *He's* the one who requires you to honor Him on the job by performing with submission and excellence. *He's* the one who calls you to the highest standards of behavior. *He's* the one who says it's not okay to use the company phone to call your grandma in Chicago and pretend she's a client; or take 90 minutes for lunch and say you were gone for only 30!

Listen, "Whatsoever good thing any man doeth, the same shall he receive *of the Lord*" (Eph 6:8). God balances the scales and rewards us according to our service; not what *others* think we're worth.

Stop striving and get back to serving! Listen, "God is not unjust; he will not forget your work" (Heb 6:10 NIV). Be encouraged; God records and God rewards – that should be enough for you!

MORE ON SERVING

Serving the Lord, not men,
because you know that the Lord will reward.
Ephesians 6:7-8 NIV

When we invest in something or someone it's only human to feel we should reap where we've sown. When we don't, it's easy to get upset. Yet the Bible says, "Serve wholeheartedly, as if you were serving *the Lord, not men,* because you know that *the Lord* will reward everyone for whatever good he does" (Eph 6:7-8 NIV).

Nobody knows the sacrifices you've made better than God. He sees your secret and selfless acts on behalf of others, and His Word says, "Thy father which seeth in secret Himself shall reward thee openly" (Mt 6:4). Recognition and reward come from God, not men. *He* will determine the appropriate remuneration for you.

Now if God chooses to reward you richly, don't let anybody make you feel bad about it. Just keep giving the same faithful, humble, excellent service, regardless of what He puts into your hand, or how much praise and recognition you receive, or don't receive.

The more God proves He can trust you with His blessings, the more He'll bless you; it's that simple. In God's kingdom some receive thirty-fold returns, others sixty-fold, and others one hundred-fold (Mt 13:3-8). The rate of return is up to God. *Your* part is to be grateful for whatever He gives you and not look to others to compensate you for the sacrifices you've made on their behalf.

A WORD TO LEADERS!

Masters . . . no abuse, please.
Ephesians 6:9 TM

Never take advantage of those under you! There's no place in God's kingdom for the domineering, the egocentric, or those motivated by anger toward *any* individual or group, at *any* time, under *any* circumstance! Learn from Pharaoh: when a child of God is abused the Lord will hear their cry, intervene on their behalf, and the offender will pay a high price.

To be a good leader you've first got to learn to be a good follower, for only then will you understand the challenges of serving someone else "as unto the Lord." If you practice doing that when you're at the bottom you'll keep doing it when you reach the top. And that's critically important, for as a leader you must be able to hear, submit to, and obey the leadings of the Holy Spirit.

Joshua was a great leader because he was first a faithful servant of Moses. He remembered the difficulties of submitting to a flawed human being when *he himself* became a leader. Any time you forget what it's like to walk in the shoes of those who serve under you, you can easily become insensitive to their needs, and abuse your power.

For God to trust you with a position of authority, you must first prove to Him that you can *control your need for recognition.* God-appointed leaders are servant-leaders! They never lead by threat or force. They lead through a compelling combination of love, vision, and righteousness. *Still think you're called to lead?*

SUPERWOMAN!

Many women do noble things, but you surpass them all.
Proverbs 31:29 NIV

Proverbs Chapter 31 can be either your launching pad or your gallows; it's up to you! Do you think you should be able to do it *all* – have a successful career, be a wife and a lover, win the mother-of-the-year-award, and cook like Julia Child? You *can* be all the things God wants you to be, but *not* all at once. You need to tackle each in season.

Solomon says there is, "A season for every activity" (Ecc 3:1 NIV). The secret is to enjoy the season you're in right *now.* If you don't learn to do that everybody will suffer, especially you. You'll find yourself resenting your kids, your husband, and the 101 other things that take up your time.

Don't set yourself up for failure by demanding perfection in every area of your life. Ask God to help you set obtainable goals; ones that *stretch* you, not *stress* you!

Paul says, "I consider my life worth nothing . . . if only I may . . . complete the task the Lord Jesus has given me" (Acts 20:24 NIV). What has God given you to do *today?* If it's raising children, do it with joy, for soon they'll be grown up and gone. If it's succeeding in your career, become "salt and light" on the job; influence those around you for God.

You're not a failure because you can't do it all – you're just human! The grace required comes with the assignment given.

THE "I ONLY" SYNDROME

I, even I only, am left.
1 Kings 19:10

Depression convinced Elijah that *nobody else on earth* was as badly off as him. He felt "terminally unique." We *all* go through it. Behind your neighbor's smile or the nameplate on your boss's door, there are struggles they can't talk about.

Dr. Martin Luther King Jr. said, "We may have arrived on different ships, but we're all in the same boat now." Paul wrote, "No test or temptation . . . is beyond the course of what others have had to face. All you need to remember is that God will never let you down; He'll never let you be pushed past your limit; He'll always be there to help you come through it" (1Co 10:12-13 TM).

Before every crown, there's a cross. John Bunyan wrote *Pilgrim's Progress* in prison. Florence Nightingale, too ill to move from bed, reorganized the hospitals of England. Louis Pasteur, semi-paralyzed by apoplexy, was tireless in his attack on disease. Francis Parkman couldn't work for more than five minutes at a time. His eyesight was so bad that he could only scrawl gigantic words on a manuscript, yet he wrote twenty magnificent volumes of history.

You're not unique! And you're not alone! Listen, "Nothing living or dead, angelic or demonic, today or tomorrow, high or low, thinkable or unthinkable – absolutely nothing can get between us and God's love" (Ro 8:38 TM). What more do you need?

NOT WITHOUT A STRUGGLE

Be strong in the Lord, and in the power of His might.
Ephesians 6:10

There are things you'll never know about God until you go through certain struggles with His help. Usually we only appreciate His "keeping power" when we're under attack. It's then that something we've read weeks before comes to our aid just when we need it most.

God told His people, "Jericho is yours, but you'll have to march round it seven times and drive out the inhabitants." Unfortunately, we've been taught that anything that comes against us can be removed, confessed away, or cast out. We say, "I'm a Christian, I don't have to take that!" Don't be so sure!

Think: being a Christian means your whole foundation rests on One who endured all manner of abuse and was crucified. *He's* the One who said, "If you're going to follow me, take up your cross." How can the cross symbolize our faith if we teach that with enough faith we don't have to *have* a cross?

What will you say when you get to heaven and the saints of the ages tell you about being tortured, beheaded, and skinned alive for the cause of Christ? Can you imagine telling them, "They put me in charge of the church spaghetti dinner, and nobody brought the salad!" A lot of us will be sitting in the back row with our heads down, saying, "Thank you Lord for letting me in. I'm just glad to be hanging out with these good brothers and sisters."

Hey, if you want to celebrate with the victors you've got to be willing to fight the battles!

CUT THE CORD

On the day you were born your cord was not cut.
Ezekiel 16:4 NIV

Are you still tied to the things of your past? Are you still being fed emotionally by relationships that need to be severed? You'll only *cut the cord* when you realize that you can get what you need from a better source.

Paul speaks of "His power that is at work within us" (Eph 3:20 NIV). What is that power? It's the God-given ability to cut the cord that ties you to the old mud-holes of yesterday. If a pig and a sheep fall into the same mud, one will wallow and the other will try to get out. Why? Because their *natures* are different!

Whether you fell into the mud or were dragged back into it isn't the issue. Your new nature won't let you stay there. It'll cry, "I don't belong here! I want out! Help me Lord!"

"But I've really blown it this time!" you say. Listen to these words from a man whose failures make yours look like charitable acts: "When I kept it all inside . . . the pressure never let up . . . then I let it all out; I said, 'I'll make a clean breast of my failures to God.' Suddenly the pressure was gone – my guilt dissolved, my sin disappeared" (Ps 32:1-5 TM).

Once God forgives you, pronounce the "last rites" over your failures, forgive those who've hurt you, cut the cord that connects you to the past, and start moving forward.

IF YOU LOVE YOUR CHILD!

Children, obey your parents . . . that it may be well with thee, and thou mayest live long on the earth.

Ephesians 6:1-3

If a temper tantrum can cause you to back down, what are you teaching your child about life? That the teacher, or the police officer, or the boss, or their spouse, will do the same thing? Get real!

One day a mother brought her newborn son to General Robert E. Lee for a blessing. The old southern general cradled the child in his arms and said, *"Ma'am, please teach him that he must deny himself."* What's the opposite of self-denial? Instant gratification! And that's *not* how life works! What we must wait and work for we treat with respect. Otherwise we grow up feeling "entitled" to whatever we want. That's a recipe for life-long heartache!

If you think enforcing discipline inhibits creativity, think again! It's those who work *within* the rules who see their dreams flourish! Those who learn obedience early are sensitive to God later. Parents, if you love your child teach them these 3 things:

(1) *Every relationship has boundaries.* When someone says no to your advances, respect it and back away. (2) *Life is built on rules.* Break them, and they'll inevitably break you. (3) *Obedience can lengthen or shorten your life.* If you doubt it, check the obituary column. The whole purpose of teaching your child obedience is "That it may be well with thee, and thou mayest live long on the earth" (Eph 6:3). If you love them how can you do less?

WASHED, SALTED, SWADDLED!

Neither was thou washed . . . [nor] salted . . . nor swaddled.
Ezekiel 16:4

Why is it that only one out of ten people who make a commitment to Christ is still serving Him five years later? Ezekiel gives us some answers:

(1) *You must be washed!* Your spiritual protection against dirt, disease, and spiritual death is "the washing of water by the Word" (Eph 5:26). It's not enough to step into the shower every morning – you've also got to step into the Scriptures. Jesus said, "Now are ye clean through the word" (Jn 15:3). Sin will keep you from your Bible, and your Bible will keep you from sin.

(2) *You must be salted!* In Hebrew culture they rubbed salt on newborn babies to toughen their skins so that they could be handled without bruising. Too many of us need "special handling." We're touchy. If we're corrected we get defensive. Only when you've been "salted" by mature love and non-legalistic acceptance can you really be open and honest.

(3) *You must be swaddled!* When we're first born into God's family we're vulnerable. We need to be covered and protected. That's the value of Christian fellowship; it wraps us up in the arms of love and says, "You don't *ever* have to go back to your old life again! You can begin afresh. You can be healed of your painful past. You can have good times and good relationships instead of bad ones." *Have you been washed, salted, and swaddled?*

SECRET ANGER

Better a patient man than a warrior, a man who controls his temper than one who takes a city.

Proverbs 16:32 NIV

Secret anger is very dangerous. Not only does it eat away at us replacing kindness with animosity, but when we try to keep a lid on it, it explodes, surprising (and often devastating) those who thought they knew us so well.

It can come out in schemes, maneuvers, and outright deception. In its worst form it can turn to violence, manifesting itself in physical or sexual abuse; even murder!

The truth is, secret anger hurts *most* those who carry it! It colors your world, embittering you to everything and everyone. As it percolates, you feel less and less joy and all your experiences are filtered through the lens of resentment instead of gratitude. Anger can hide behind smiles and laughter and still be simmering – even towards the person closest to you. Secret anger can take an event that happened twenty years ago and make it a basis for divorce by labeling it "irreconcilable differences."

What's the answer? Two things: (1) *Communication.* The Prodigal Son's older brother had been angry for years, but it didn't surface until his younger brother came back home. (See Lk 15). The father's response to his older son's anger was, "If only you'd told me how you felt and what you needed, I'd have been there for you." (2) *Forgiveness.* Listen, "Forgive as the Lord forgave you" (Col 3:13 NIV). Forgiveness doesn't just let the other person off the hook – it lets *you* off too and allows you to enjoy life again!

WHEN IT'S NOT WHAT YOU EXPECTED

Every detail in our lives . . . is worked into something good.
Romans 8:28 TM

Did you hear about the little boy who complained to his grandmother that things were bad? He was in trouble at school, his dad forgot his allowance, and his best friend went fishing without him. His grandmother, who was baking a cake at the time, listened patiently, then asked him if he'd like a snack. "Sure," he replied. So she said, "Here, have some cooking oil." "No way!" he said. "Well, how about a couple of raw eggs?" "Gross!" he exclaimed. "What about some baking soda?" she asked. "Grandma, those are all yucky!" he said. "Yes," she replied. "On their own each of them seem pretty bad, but when you put them together they make a great cake!"

Sometimes you ask God for one thing and He gives you another, because while you think you know what you want, He knows what you *need.* We're like the little girl who prayed, "God, I thank you for my new baby brother, but what I really wanted was a puppy."

The truth is God knows more about what you need than you do yourself. Listen, "He knows us far better than we know ourselves . . . That's why we can be so sure that *every detail* of our lives . . . is worked into something good" (Ro 8:26-28 TM).

Did you hear that? *Everything* that comes your way today will have His fingerprints on it and is designed for your good!

ARE YOU TOO SERIOUS?

A merry heart doeth good like a medicine.
Proverbs 17:22

When you can laugh *in spite* of your circumstances, it shows: (1) the world is *not* the source of your security; (2) temporal situations *don't* control your joy. Paul said, "Even if I am being poured out like a drink offering . . . I am glad and rejoice . . . so you too should be glad and rejoice with me" (Php 2:17-18 NIV). Can you do that?

Listen to these words, "Some Christians can't enjoy a meal because the world is starving, or thank God for their clothes because the world is naked, or smile because the world is sad. They can't spend an evening with their family because they think they ought to be out saving souls, or spend an hour with an unsaved loved one without feeling guilty that they haven't preached a sermon, or manifested a "sober Christian spirit." They know nothing of balance and they're miserable because of it. They have little motivation to bring people to Christ, because that would make *others* feel as miserable as they themselves feel. They think The Gospel is "good news" until you obey it, then it becomes an endless guilt-trip. There are leisure centers, sports centers, diet centers, entertainment centers, and guilt centers. The last group is called *churches!* The endless harping on the string of guilt is part of the reason for all this gloom and uncertainty."

Make sure those words don't describe you! Give yourself permission to laugh; it'll keep you healthy, and make the experience you talk about a lot more attractive to others.

HE'S GIVEN YOU THE ABILITY!

God . . . gives you the ability to produce wealth.
Deuteronomy 8:18 NIV

Without struggle you'll never develop your potential! Have you ever watched an ant carrying home a piece of bread bigger than he was? Success belongs to those who are too small to carry what they believe in but too stubborn to leave it behind!

If God the Creator lives within you, then you are "creative." That means when you can't find a job, you can go out and create one. In other words, if success doesn't come after you, get up and go after it.

There are no risk-free plans. A young man once asked an old man, "What's the secret of your success?" "Good decisions," he responded. "How'd you learn to make good decisions?" the young man asked. "By making bad ones," he replied.

Once you discover your gift and identify your dream – get on your mark, get set, go! Stop waiting for opportunity. Opportunity is the breath in your body and the strength of your mind. If you use your God-given gifts wisely there's no telling how far you'll go. *But you must be a "doer!"*

God does not give us wealth – He gives us the power to get wealth. There's a big difference! Too many of us sit on our differential waiting for everything to drop into our lap. A dream without corresponding action only aggravates the soul and amounts to nothing. God will give you the power to succeed, but you have to *take* it, develop a plan, and work it.

MAKE TIME FOR HIM TODAY!

I am with you always.
Matthew 28:20 NIV

"Hello there; when you wakened this morning, I thought perhaps you'd talk to Me and involve Me in your day, but you were preoccupied finding something to wear to work. When you'd time to spare, I thought we'd have a few moments together, but you got on the phone and started talking to somebody else. I noticed that before you ate lunch at work, you looked around and seemed embarrassed to talk to Me. Maybe that's why you didn't bow your head and give thanks, even though some of your friends did. Later at home I waited while you watched television, ate dinner, and then did paperwork. At bedtime I guess you were too tired, because you just dropped into bed and fell fast asleep. Do you know I'm always here for you? I love you so much that I wait every day for a prayer, a thought, or just a chance to speak with you. The problem as I see it is, it's hard to have a one-sided conversation. Signed, Your Friend, Jesus."

When did you last talk with the Lord? Or take time to listen to Him? There's never a time when He's not speaking; no room so dark, no lounge so crowded, and no office so busy that He's not there. Never mistake your insensitivity for His absence. Among life's fleeting promises of pleasure is this timeless assurance, "I am with you always" (Mt 28:20 NIV). *Make time for Him today!*

DON'T BE UNDERMINED

Bad company corrupts good character.
1 Corinthians 15:33 NIV

God told His people, "But they shall be as thorns in your sides and their gods shall be a snare to you" (Jdg 2:3 AMP). Was God being uncharitable? No, He just understood that if His people hung out with the Canaanites, they'd pick up their habits, seek their approval, live by their values, and end up worshipping their gods! *That's* why He laid down His law so clearly!

John Maxwell says, "You'll acquire the vices and virtues of your closest associates. The fragrance of their lives will pervade yours." You may tell yourself that bad relationships won't hurt you, or that your good will rub off on them, but who are you kidding! If you put on white gloves, go into your back yard and pick up dirt, the dirt won't get *glovey,* but the gloves will get *dirty,* right?

Wake up! A toxic relationship is like a malignant cell; left unchecked it'll eventually rob you of your health and maybe even your life. Cervantes, who wrote *Don Quixote,* said, "Tell me your company, and I'll tell you who you are."

Take another look at the influences in your life today, for they're doing two things: (1) *molding you;* (2) *motivating you.* If a constant drip can wear away a rock, then the wrong influences can undermine you little by little. But you're not a rock, you can move!

MANAGING YOUR ANGER

Be ye angry, and sin not:
let not the sun go down upon your wrath.
Ephesians 4:26

Anger is not a sin; mismanaging it is! The first thing to remember when you get mad at someone is that it means you *care!* You wouldn't let someone know how you *feel* if you didn't. You just need to learn how to express your feelings in ways that bring better results. For example, instead of yelling at your children for not doing their homework, explain to them how an education can fulfill their dreams, then help them where they're struggling. And don't constantly "preach" at your unsaved loved ones. You'll win them by attraction, not pressure!

Listen, "Neither give place to the devil" (Eph 4:27). The first territory the enemy wants to take is your home, because that's the seat of your power. Don't let him! "But I've reason to be angry," you say. So did Joseph, *yet he fed those who imprisoned him, and blessed those who betrayed him. In so doing he prospered and was set free from his anger!*

Later when he had two sons, he called the first Manasseh, meaning "God has made me forget all my trouble" (Ge 41:51 NIV). Would Joseph have become great if he'd gone back to seek revenge? No! He fulfilled his destiny and enjoyed God's favor because he controlled his emotions. He called his second son Ephraim, meaning "God has made me fruitful in the land of my suffering" (Ge 41:52 NIV). Your anger will subside when you start to dwell on the fact that *in spite* of all you've been through, God has continued to bless you.

"FAITH DEVELOPERS"

These [things] have come so that your faith
. . . may be proved genuine.
1 Peter 1:7 NIV

Let's think about the subject of photography for a moment. First, you expose your film to the light by opening the shutter. Then it goes into the dark room where it passes through a series of chemicals ("faith developers"). Then hopefully you end up with a perfect picture.

"What are these *faith developers?"* you ask. Peter answers, "These trials . . . show that [your faith] is . . . pure" (1Pe 1:7 NLT). Faith is what enabled David to survive the javelins of Saul and collect the foreskins of his enemies. It made him sensitive enough to write poetry but tough enough to cut off the head of Goliath! It's what enables you to stand up to the diagnosis, defy the odds and boldly announce, "I believe God!" (Acts 27:25).

Faith is what enabled Joan of Arc to pray while she burned at the stake for her convictions. Colonel Sanders, a committed Christian, said *faith* is what took him from living off a $105-a-month Social Security check to running a $285 billion dollar company, working with only a piece of chicken and twenty-nine spices.

Would all these people have *preferred* an easier road? Probably. But they understood that you have to go through the "faith developers" to reach your destiny.

YOUR SPIRITUAL COMPASS – PART ONE

Abraham saw the place afar off.
Genesis 22:4

Can you Imagine God sending Abraham to a place "which I will tell thee of" (Ge 22:2)? Women tend to understand this better than men. Sometimes when I ask my wife what she's shopping for, she'll say, "I'm not sure, but I'll know it when I see it!" There are things you *know,* that you can't explain. Listen, "We have an unction [insight] from God and we *know* things" (1Jn 2:20 Para).

Look what happened: "On the third day Abraham . . . saw the place" (Ge 22:4). Eureka! There's nothing like the moment you *see* what you've been looking for, the bell rings, and your spiritual compass reads, "This is it!"

When you're at sea all waters look alike. That's when you need a compass. Either you have one or you don't. When you see somebody who gets excited about things that aren't there, watch them! Either they didn't take their medication that morning, or *they* see what *you* don't!

Because they can get excited about the invisible, they usually end up doing the impossible. Why? Because they've learned to follow their spiritual compass!

David defeated Goliath because he was the *only* man who had the faith to do it. He knew this was a life-changing moment. If he missed it he'd go back to tending sheep!

When *your* moment comes rise up and say, "This giant is mine," no matter how many others are running away from him. God has given you a spiritual compass – learn to use it!

YOUR SPIRITUAL COMPASS – PART TWO

He persevered because he saw Him who is invisible.
Hebrews 11:27 NIV

Start using the spiritual compass God has placed within you. Yes, it's risky, but it'll open doors that nothing else will. Remember the widow in 1 Kings, Chapter 17, of whom the prophet Elisha requested her last meal? When fear whispered, "You only have enough for yourself," *her* spiritual compass said, "Give what you've got, and God will give you back what you need!"

When Saul saw Goliath he told David, "You're not able to go against this Philistine" (1Sa 17:33 NIV). But when David saw Goliath, his spiritual compass immediately pointed toward God and he announced, "The Lord . . . will deliver me!" (1Sa 17:37 NIV). Look at Noah; building a floating zoo in the desert because he *heard* a voice that nobody else did! As a result his family was saved, his children became leaders in the new-world order, and his name was immortalized.

History is full of them; people who defied the odds, followed their spiritual compasses, and achieved greatness. People like Benjamin Franklin who dared to fly his kite in a rain storm and discover electricity; or Annie Sullivan who saw a greatness in Helen Keller that would inspire the world for years to come. No they weren't gods – and they weren't perfect. They were just "compass-carriers," who saw what others didn't, and had the faith to *act* on it!

What has God shown you that others don't see? Whatever it is, *that's* what He'll give you power to perform!

WHEN IT'S TIME TO MOVE ON

Now faith is the substance of things hoped for, the evidence of things not seen.
Hebrews 11:1

When your passion for something fades, the grace to accomplish usually goes with it. Does that mean it's time to leave something even though you've invested a lot in it? Here are a few thoughts:

(1) *Get away and rest.* Stress-filled minds are not noted for coming up with good answers. Spend time with God. He's already determined your future (Isa 46:10). Ask Him about it!

(2) *You're not the only one involved.* If you don't know how (or you're unwilling) to pass the baton to someone who can take things to the next level, you lose, they lose, and the dream loses. When you've killed your giant, get out of the way and let the next person kill theirs.

(3) *Don't just focus on what you're leaving behind.* Think also about what you're taking with you when you go: self-worth, wisdom, faith for the next challenge, and the joy of knowing you've done the will of God. Listen, "I have brought you glory on earth by completing the work you gave me to do" (Jn 17:4 NIV).

Faith is a "substance." You can take it with you wherever you go. It'll grow in any climate, thrive in any economy, and move any mountain. It's the voice within you that says, "I can't wait to see what God has for me next." It's the greatest evidence that what you can conceive, by God's help you can achieve!

WHO ARE YOU FOLLOWING?

Remember those who rule over you, who have spoken the Word of God to you, whose faith follow, considering the outcome of their conduct.
Hebrews 13:7 NKJV

Some people can take less and do more with it because they've got faith. Speaking of these people, God says, "Follow them." He didn't say, "Criticize them," or "Cut them down to size." He said, "Follow them." Let's break this verse down:

(1) "Remember those who have the rule over you." Are you willing to submit to authority? If not, your future's not very bright. (2) "Who have spoken The Word of God to you." Who feeds you spiritually? Your hunger, not your talent, determines your future. (3) "Whose faith follow, considering the outcome of their conduct." Who should your mentor be? Someone whose faith produces the outcome you want.

How did Elisha earn the right to wear Elijah's mantle? (1) By *recognizing* and *pursuing* him, regardless of where the journey took him. (2) By *honoring* him when others didn't. (3) By drawing water from *his* well until he'd some in his own. (4) By *serving* him, knowing that if you can't *serve* you'll never qualify to *be* served.

"Isn't that glorifying an individual?" you ask. No! Paul told Timothy to follow him – *as he followed Christ.* You don't follow the man, you follow the *God* in the man. You catch his mantle by receiving his instructions, standing on his shoulders, and making his hindsight your foresight. Today, ask God to bring such a person into your life.

THE DIFFERENCE

The one who blesses others is abundantly blessed.
Proverbs 11:25 TM

It was their 25th high school reunion. Ted and Joe hadn't seen each other since graduation. Ted, the school basketball star, had gone on to become the CEO of a huge corporation. Joe, who'd captained their undefeated team, had gone into the ministry.

"Joe, I want to thank you for making me the success I am today," Ted said. "I didn't think I had anything to do with it," Joe replied in amazement. "Well, you probably never knew this," said Ted, "But it drove me crazy that I was never elected captain of the team. So just before graduation I asked the coach why the team voted for you instead of me. He said something that changed my life and it was this: 'Ted, you were the best player *on* the team, but Joe was the best player *for* the team. You wanted to be the best *player* in the State, Joe wanted to make us the best *team* in the State. That's why he became captain and you never did.'

"It's a lesson I've never forgotten," Ted said. "As I became more like you, I was voted captain of my college team and went on to climb the corporate ladder. The 'old me' would have wanted my company to be the best company *in* the world. Now I strive to make it the best company *for* the world. That's why I want to thank you."

"And I want to thank you too," Joe said. "For what?" asked Ted. *"For giving me next Sunday morning's sermon!"* he replied.

HERE COMES MY OLD FRIEND

Jesus said to him, Friend.
Matthew 26:50 AMP

When Jesus called Judas He understood exactly what he was. When He entrusted him with the money, He knew he was a traitor. So why call him? Because the purposes of God in your life *require* certain relationships. How do you learn perseverance? Through problems! Or forgiveness? Through betrayal!

As Mary worshipped Jesus, anointing him with costly ointment, Judas, under the guise of caring for the poor, revealed his real motive – greed. Now there's nothing new about the fact that some people you'd sacrifice your all for, will be the first to betray you. God will allow people into your life who *look* good, but as you spend time with Him He'll reveal to you their true motives, so that you don't get duped and side-tracked by appearances.

But why did Jesus call Judas, "Friend?" Because from *God's* perspective, those who shield you from life do you no favors, whereas, those who *cause* enough pain to make you turn to Him, help you toward your destiny.

Show me a successful Joseph and somewhere in his past I'll show you: (1) A "friend" who lied about him. (2) A "friend" who threw him into a pit. (3) A "friend" who forgot him when he needed them most. Yet without them Joseph wouldn't have reached the throne.

Grasp this principle and it'll change your life! Having a Judas means you've got a cross, and having a cross means you've got a resurrection! That way when you see Judas coming you'll be able to say, "Here comes my old friend!"

HELP, I'M A PERFECTIONIST!

It's in Christ that we find out who we are.
Ephesians 1:11 TM

What kind of perfectionist are you? *The performance perfectionist,* who always goes the extra mile, but never believes it's enough? *The appearance perfectionist,* who worries constantly about what others think, instead of thinking for yourself? *The interpersonal perfectionist,* who searches for the perfect mate, but always seems to wind up alone? *The moral perfectionist,* who can't forgive himself or others, no matter how minor the transgression?

The truth is your performance at any task will be *below* average half of the time, and *above* average the other half, contradicting the myth that doing anything less than your best makes you a failure.

God doesn't see you as a failure; He sees you as a learner! It's better to fail trying something, than to excel doing nothing. A flawed diamond is better than a perfect brick. The key to being free from the stranglehold of perfectionism and low self-esteem is – learn the lesson and forget the details!

If you're a perfectionist, you need to find out what God says about you in His Word, then refuse to believe anything different.

The negative messages you received and the flawed perceptions you formed about yourself in childhood were wrong *then*, and they're wrong *now*. They're wrong because: (1) God says so. (2) Now you have more experience, knowledge, choice, and personal power. (3) "It's in Christ that we find out who we are" (Eph 1:11 TM). Throw out the old mental tapes! They don't apply anymore! Learn to forgive yourself, accept yourself, love yourself, and believe in yourself, because God does!

VICTIMS OR VOLUNTEERS?

He asked him, "Do you want to get well?"
John 5:6 NIV

Jesus asked this man who'd been ill for 38 years, "Do you want to get well?" Why? Because not everybody does! Some folks would rather have sympathy than solutions, because solutions often mean taking responsibility, being willing to change, and committing yourself to "work on it". The worst thing you could have done for the Prodigal Son was bring him a meal and make him more comfortable in his hog pen. He knew the way home. He just needed a push in that direction. He needed – tough love!

Take another look at the people in your life today. How do they make you feel? Do you respect them? Share their values? By deciding *not* to have a relationship with them you're not judging them or putting them down, you're just deciding to use your life, the only life you've got, for higher purposes.

Face it, some people are victims, others are volunteers! This second group is like a car battery with a bad cell; no matter how much you pour into them you can't fix them, use them, or even jump-start them.

If somebody was draining your bank account you'd stop them in a heartbeat, wouldn't you? Sympathy wouldn't even be a consideration. Well, unhealthy relationships rob you of something even *more* valuable than your money – your time. Listen, "Live purposefully . . . making the very most of the time [buying up every opportunity]" (Eph 5:15-16 AMP). Ask God to show you who *really* belongs in your life, then start making some changes!

"I HEARD IT THROUGH THE GRAPEVINE!"

Someone of integrity won't violate a confidence.
Proverbs 11:13 TM

Information is power! We use it to get what we want, and in the process: (1) people who trust us get hurt, and have difficulty trusting anyone again. That's sad, because we may have robbed them of the one thing they need most – a safe place to open up and be made whole. (2) The world looks on as we betray each other's confidence under the guise of, "I'm just sharing this with you so you can pray about it." They lose respect for us, because in *their* fraternal orders and 12-step programs, they actually *live* by the principle, "What's said in this room, stays in this room."

If someone betrays another's confidence to you, do you really think they'll treat *you* any better? Wise up! We're allowing potentially good relationships to degenerate into grapevines.

Did you hear about the three friends who were sharing their weaknesses? The first one said, "My problem's drinking." The second said, "My problem's lust." After a long silence the third said, "My problem's *gossip,* and I can't wait to get out of here and talk about you guys!"

Ask yourself today, "Am I trustworthy, or is my need to impress others so great that I'm willing to violate a confidence to do it?" Before you answer, take a moment and reread these words: "Someone of integrity won't violate a confidence" (Pr 11:13 TM). They simply won't!

THE DANGER OF LITTLE THINGS

Catch . . . the little foxes that ruin the vineyards.
Song of Solomon 2:15 NIV

On Colorado's *Long Peak* lie the remains of a giant 400-year-old tree. Age, storms, and avalanches, couldn't bring it down. What did? A tiny beetle you could crush under your foot. It ate right through the bark and devoured the heart.

Be careful, it's the little foxes that ruin the vineyards. *Little* attitudes; but if you practice them often enough they become fixed. *Little* indulgences; but if you give place to them long enough they desensitize you to sin. Remember when certain things bothered you? Now you don't give them a second thought. You're being desensitized!

Every alcoholic started by telling himself, "I can handle it." Every victim of Internet pornography (and they're getting younger every day), started with a look, got hooked on a fantasy, and ended up uncaging a tiger that: (a) can devour them; (b) will never willingly go back into the cage.

Before a moral problem got out of hand in the Corinthian church, Paul hit it head on. Listen, "I also received a report . . . One of your men is sleeping with his step-mother. And you're so above it all that it doesn't even faze you . . . You pass it off as a small thing, but it's anything but that. Yeast, too, is a 'small thing,' but it works its way through a whole batch . . . get rid of this 'yeast' " (1Co 5:1-7 TM). Strong language!

Why does God make such a big deal out of this anyway? *Because sin hurts us, and anything that hurts one of His children makes Him angry.*

REFUSE TO QUIT!

Be strong and let us fight bravely . . .
The Lord will do what is good.
2 Samuel 10:12 NIV

In 1902 a 28-year-old aspiring poet received a rejection slip from the editor of the prestigious *Atlantic Monthly*. Returned with a batch of poems he'd submitted, was this curt note: "Not one worthy of publishing." That poet's name was Robert Frost! In 1905 the University of Bern turned down a dissertation by a young Ph.D., calling it "fanciful and irrelevant." The name of that physics student was Albert Einstein! In 1894 a 16-year-old boy in Harrow, England, found this note from his speech teacher attached to his report card: "Hopeless . . . seems incapable of progress." That boy's name was Winston Churchill!

There's a message there for you! Even when others offer you no hope or encouragement, refuse to quit! Listen to the words of Joab, who led King David's army: "Be strong and let us fight bravely . . . the Lord will do what is good" (2Sa 10:12 NIV). Joab knew that as long as you stay on the battlefield God can give you victory. *But if you quit, what more can He do for you?*

Never give up when you know you're right! Believe that all things work together for good if you just persevere. Don't let the odds discourage you, God's bigger than all of them! Refuse to let anybody intimidate you, or deter you from your goals! Fight and overcome every limitation! Remember, every winner – without exception – faced defeat and adversity, and you're no different!

YOU ARE IMPORTANT TO GOD!

For we are God's Masterpiece. He created us.
Ephesians 2:10 NLT

Ruth Lee writes, "It was the last day of a writers' conference and we gathered in one of the dormitories. In our pajamas we all looked alike. One by one we shared. After the introduction of two authors with published books and others with claim to fame, it was my turn. 'My name is Ruth,' I said, 'And I feel so inferior I think I'll just go back to my room.' Everybody laughed, so I ploughed ahead. 'I guess you could call me a producer. In 30 years I've produced a well-adjusted respiratory therapist, a machinist, and another happy homemaker. I'm also involved in the co-production of seven grandchildren.' I told them how full my life is. Full of checking on cows, helping fix fences, and then praying it will stop raining. I told them of busy hours spent baby sitting and contending with my household. Then I told them how hungry I was. Hungry for the type of spiritual and emotional food I'd received at this conference.

"From the far corner of the room a quiet girl spoke up. 'Would you please turn so that I can look at you?' I did as she asked, and she continued, 'I want to remember your face when I write,' she said, 'I want to write for people just like you.'

"Suddenly I had no need for title or degree. I served a purpose. With her words, she had helped me realize what I should have known all along: God doesn't make nobodies – everybody is somebody important to Him!"

GROUND RULES!

Pursue righteousness.

1 Timothy 6:11 NIV

If you want to run the race and finish strong, here are some ground rules from 1 Timothy, Chapter 6.

V.6 *"Godliness with contentment is great gain."* Be content with what you've got, not green with envy over what others have. There'll always be something bigger and better! Contentment comes from understanding that God knows the "when's," the "where's," and the "how's" of blessing you.

V.7 *"We brought nothing into the world, and we can take nothing out of it."* Enjoy what you've got but always remember, nothing tangible is eternal. No matter what you've acquired you can't take it with you.

V.8 *"But if we have food and clothing we will be content with that."* Start thanking God for what you have right *now.* Ingratitude clogs the pipeline of future blessings.

V.9-10 *"People who want to get rich fall into temptation . . . Some people, eager for money, have wandered from the faith."* God's not against your having money, He's against money having you. Money's neither good nor evil, it simply takes on your personality and makes you more of what you already are. If you're a giver, you'll be more generous. If not, you'll spend your life clinging to what you've got.

V.11 *"Man of God, flee from all this, and pursue righteousness."* The bottom line is – pursue God!

KEEP PRAISING

Then He touched her, and instantly she could stand straight. How she praised and thanked God!

Luke 13:13 NLT

So long as she remained dependent on them, the people around this woman had no problem with her. But when Jesus set her free and she started praising Him, they couldn't handle it. They actually wanted to throw her out of church!

How would *you* have acted if you'd been chronically ill for eighteen years and suddenly Jesus made you whole? People fall over themselves about getting a prize on a TV show. They scream and hug total strangers when their team wins, and the world says it's okay. But show a little emotion because of what God's done for you, and they'll call you a nut case. No problem; it's easier to cool down a fanatic than heat up a corpse!

So what are you going to do? Do what she did! She kept her rhythm, and let Jesus deal with her critics. While she was glorifying Him, He was dealing with them. That's how it works. While you're praising God, He's fighting for you. While you're exalting His name, His angels are coming into your hospital room or surrounding your loved one who's in danger, or going before you to open doors.

If people are upset about your new lifestyle, that's *their* problem! There'll always be a critic. There may even be one in your house, criticizing you for praising God in the shower. Or at work, mocking you for just giving thanks before you eat lunch. Pay them no attention. *Just keep praising God regardless of the background noise!*

GET OUT OF THAT STALL!

Stand fast in the faith . . . Be strong.
1 Corinthians 16:13

Yesterday we talked about a woman Jesus healed after eighteen years of chronic illness. Because He did it on the Sabbath some people made a big deal out of it! Listen to Jesus: "You hypocrites! Doesn't each of you on the Sabbath untie his ox or donkey from the stall and . . . give it water? Then should not this woman . . . whom Satan has kept bound for eighteen long years, be set free?" (Lk 13:15-16 NIV). Notice two things:

(1) *Whether it's a valuable ox or a lowly donkey, both need water.* We get excited when somebody famous comes to Christ, but we act under-whelmed when others come. Yet God makes no difference! This woman is never mentioned again in scripture, yet Jesus thought she was worth saving.

(2) *The same people who kept their expensive ox in one stall and their cheap donkey in another, wanted to "keep her in her place."* But she refused to stay in a religious stall designed to keep her from moving into areas where she could find for herself what *they* were incapable of giving her. Sound familiar?

Here's the score: when God delivers you, say, "No" to those who want to contain or control you. Tell them, "I've decided to live close to the living water. I won't be put into a position where I have to rely solely on *you* to lead me to what you think I need or don't need." Once Jesus has loosed you, refuse to return to captivity – even the religious kind!

GOD'S IDEAS

It is He that giveth thee power [ideas and ability] to get wealth, that He may establish His covenant.

Deuteronomy 8:18

Never laugh at somebody with an idea, for creative ideas come from God the creator. Some of the world's most successful people got to where they are because they'd a better idea for cooking chicken, or writing a computer program. Got any ideas?

When God gives you the ability to succeed, it usually begins as a *thought.* But that thought only becomes a reality when you make a plan and carry it out. Otherwise your seed rots in the ground of excuses.

The *gift* God gave you is your key to success. He didn't give it to you to be put on display, or wasted on worthless things, or denied out of a false sense of humility. No, He gave it to you to be *invested.*

Jesus told of three people who were each given money to invest. The first two doubled theirs. The third hid his out of fear, and was called "a wicked, lazy servant" (Mt 25:26 NIV). Look out! Fear is one of your greatest enemies. It numbs your spirit and incarcerates your creativity!

Use what God's given you! Stop praying for oak trees while acorns are lying all around you! Your ideas are the tiny acorns from which great oaks grow.

Money is called *currency* because it's supposed to flow through you. You are meant to be the conduit through which God's blessing is passed on to others, and by which His kingdom is established in their hearts. Think about it!

THE HUDDLE

I appeal to you . . . in the name of our Lord Jesus Christ, that all of you agree with one another.
1 Corinthians 1:10 NIV

To lead your family effectively, you need to learn how to huddle regularly. The "huddle" is where a team: (1) Sets its goals. (2) Discusses the division of responsibilities. (3) Tackles the issues that determine whether it wins or loses.

Parent, even though *you* call the plays from overhead, your family must be taught *how* to accomplish them on the field. That means . . . working through issues . . . talking through disagreements . . . motivating and appreciating each member.

Try to listen with an open heart. Don't just hear what your family members *say,* try to understand how they *feel.* Yes you're the boss, and yes you can act like the Gestapo and enforce your will if you want to. But sooner or later you'll have trouble, for resentment grows when people feel left out. *Every* member of your team has got to be a part of the decision-making process. Involve them! Ask God to help you look beyond what *you* want, to what's best for all of you.

And don't let "outsiders" into your huddle. Tell them to stay in their own. Too often their opinions are based on hearsay, self-interest, or jealousy. Respect the privacy of your team.

Begin today to build loyalty. Huddle regularly in prayer. When you do that everybody wins!

HOW LONG SHOULD I STAY? (PART 1)

They sought God eagerly, and He was found by them.
2 Chronicles 15:15 NIV

You'll always return to a place of *pleasure,* so *stay* in God's presence until you create memories strong enough to keep bringing you back. If you don't you'll be lured away by lesser things. "How long should I stay in His presence?" you ask.

(1) *Until you've truly repented.* Listen, "Godly sorrow brings repentance that leads to salvation and leaves no regret" (2Co 7:10 NIV). (2) *Until your mistakes have been dealt with.* Listen, "People who cover over their sins will not prosper. But if they confess and forsake them, they will receive mercy" (Pr 28:13 NLT). (3) *Until your anger subsides.* Listen, "My [own] peace I now give . . . to you . . . [stop allowing yourselves to be agitated and disturbed]" (Jn 14:27 AMP). (4) *Until your fear leaves.* Listen, "Do not fear, for I am with you; do not be dismayed, for I am your God. I will strengthen you and help you" (Is 41:10 NIV). (5) *Until your pain is healed.* Listen, "I will restore you to health and heal your wounds, declares the Lord" (Jer 30:17 NIV). (6) *Until your strength is renewed.* Listen, "They that wait upon the Lord shall renew their strength; they shall mount up with wings as eagles; they shall run, and not be weary; and they shall walk, and not faint" (Is 40:31).

All these things can be found in God's presence. So *stay* there until you receive from Him what you need!

HOW LONG SHOULD I STAY? (PART 2)

You will fill me with joy in Your presence.
Psalm 16:11 NIV

Memories of the good times he'd spent with his father was what eventually brought the Prodigal Son back home (Lk 15:17). The *right memories* will draw you back into God's presence, time and time again. "How long should I stay?" you ask.

(1) *Until change begins.* Listen, "But we all . . . beholding . . . the Lord, are changed . . . from glory to glory . . . by the Spirit" (2Co 3:18). (2) *Until you understand His plan for your life.* Listen, "For I know the plans I have for you," says the Lord. "They are plans for good and not for disaster, to give you a future and a hope" (Jer 29:11 NLT). (3) *Until you recapture your motivation.* Listen, "I am still confident of this: I will see the goodness of the Lord in the land of the living . . . be strong and take heart and wait for the Lord" (Ps 27:13-14 NIV). (4) *Until you receive His wisdom.* Listen, "I will instruct you and teach you in the way you should go; I will counsel you and watch over you" (Ps 32:8 NIV). (5) *Until new ideas are born.* Listen, "See, the former things have taken place, and new things I declare; before they spring into being, I announce them to you" (Is 42:9 NIV). (6) *Until Christ becomes the center of your life.* Listen, "Delight yourself in the Lord and he will give you the desires of your heart" (Ps 37:4 NIV).

Have you been spending enough time in God's presence lately?

REFUSE TO STAY ANGRY

Anger resides in the lap of fools.
Ecclesiastes 7:9 NIV

One day an eagle swooped down and caught up a weasel. As the big bird flew away its wings suddenly went limp and it dropped to the ground like a brick. With just one blow, the tiny weasel struck the eagle's heart and killed it. Bitterness will do the same thing to you!

We all get angry at times, but Solomon says only a *fool* allows it to move in and take up residence.

Max Lucado writes: "Hatred begins like the crack in my windshield. Thanks to a speeding truck on a gravel road my window was chipped. With time, the nick became a crack, and that crack a winding tributary. Now I can't drive my car without thinking about the jerk who drove too fast. Though I've never seen him, I could describe him. He's a dead-beat who probably cheats on his wife, drives with a 6-pack on his seat and keeps his television up so loud that the neighbors can't sleep."

Blind rage will sour your outlook. It'll break your back, not to mention your spirit. You'll buckle under the weight of it. The mountain before you is steep enough without carrying that load. Drop it! *You'll never be called upon to give more grace than God's already given you.*

Want to set yourself free today? Pray, "Father, forgive them for they know not what they do" (Lk 23:34). Want to please God? Listen, "If you suffer for doing good, and you are patient, then God is pleased" (1Pe 2:20 NCV).

HANDLE ME AND SEE!

Handle me, and see; for a spirit hath not flesh and bones, as ye see me have.
Luke 24:39

Jesus could say to doubting Thomas, "Handle me and see." Can *you* say that? Do you dare let people get close enough to see your strengths, *and* your weaknesses?

If we're the church we must let people in! That means taking off the mask, getting rid of the religious facade that hides our struggles, and saying to the world, "Handle me and see. I'm real. I struggle with my kids. I battle with my temper. I worry about my bills. I don't always read and pray as I should. But God's made a difference in my life, and what He's done for me He can do for you!"

Gandhi once said, "If more Christians were like Christ, I'd be one too!" Unfortunately, the ones he met preached love but practiced discrimination. They taught the new birth but perpetuated the same old system of poverty and despair that benefited the few and enslaved the multitudes.

Jesus said, "I am the good shepherd" (Jn 10:11). The word *good* in the original Greek means *"winsome or attrative."* Does that describe you? Do you make Christ attractive to others? It should be a crime to do otherwise!

When you've had all the "spiritual experiences" you can have in church, how's your influence at home? Or on the job? Can you say to those around you today, "Handle me and see?" *Ultimately, that's the only test that matters!*

REJOICE IN WHO YOU ARE

Thank you for making me so wonderfully complex!
Psalm 139:14 TLB

Stop despising the things that make you unique. You were born at just the right time, in just the right place, with just the right gifts, to fulfill a plan that *nobody* but you can fulfill. Open your Bible and see what God thinks of you. After all, *His* opinion is the only one that matters.

Listen to David the Psalmist, "You saw me before I was born and scheduled each day of my life before I began to breathe. Every day was recorded in your Book! How precious it is, Lord, to realize that you are thinking about me constantly" (Ps 139:16-17 TLB). If you want to work on your self-image, here's a prayer to help you today.

"Lord, it's taken me a long time to figure out that I'm different by divine design; that You've made me with abilities, traits, and a genetic combination that nobody else has. Nobody in all the ages of time has ever been me – and nobody ever will.

"Deliver me Father from feeling weird; from wishing I were someone else. Deliver me from envy and jealousy toward others.

"Help me to discover the unique person You created me to be. To enjoy the little things that make me special; so one-of-a-kind. Help me to realize that I can give the world something that no one else can give.

"Thank you Lord for the awesome creative work You've done – and continue to do – in making me who I am. Amen."

BEING IN THE RIGHT PLACE

Thus and thus said the maid that is of the land of Israel.

2 Kings 5:4

God used a cleaning maid to reach a 5-star general and introduce him to a God who could heal him of his leprosy. Her story's recorded in 2 Kings, Chapter 5. Take a moment and read it. There are 2 lessons in it for you:

(1) *There's a purpose in your being where you are!* Instead of complaining, start looking for somebody who needs what God's given you. This girl wasn't there just to make beds and clean toilets; she was there by divine appointment. Think: all of your life can be training for one moment, one crisis, one opportunity. Peter writes, "Always be prepared to give an answer" (1Pe 3:15 NIV). She was ready; are you?

(2) *What a difference a day can make!* Yesterday she was a nobody; today she's a gift from God and the most popular person in the house. The world focuses on the big names, but when they've run out of answers and out of hope, God says He'll pour out His Spirit upon His "handmaids" (Joel 2:29). When He does, people who normally wouldn't give you the time of day will suddenly begin to listen, because you're in the right place with the right answer.

Don't let your lack of education, your ethnic background, your subservient position, or your poor wages silence you. Keep renewing your mind and strengthening your faith! Allow God to use you as only He can! *And keep listening! The Master-conductor may be just about to give you your cue!*

WHEN JESUS IS IN THE HOUSE

It was noised that He was in the house.
Mark 2:1

If you're looking for a nice quiet God who won't disrupt your life, forget about Jesus! When *He* comes He'll stir up your business, your marriage, and your finances. He's a functioning, moving, teaching, touching, powerful God, who won't sit in the corner like an ornament!

In scripture people opened their homes for Jesus to come and preach. Maybe they thought, "We'll put out a few extra chairs . . . it'll be nice to hear a good sermon . . . we could use some prayer." Are you kidding? When word got out, the people came from everywhere! Talk about the power of advertising! He filled the house without a TV ministry, a promotions department, or a partner list!

It got so crazy that when four men carrying a sick friend on a stretcher couldn't get in, they cut a hole in the roof and lowered him down to Jesus. *That's* what we need in the church today – people who know how to "raise the roof" with their prayers, their praises, their preaching, and bring down the power of God.

Get ready: when you let Jesus into *any* area of your life, He'll ask you to *give* what you can't give, *do* what you can't do, and *be* what you can't be. He'll rearrange everything. That's because you've been in the same place and the same rut giving the same testimony for too long!

Today God wants to take you out of your comfort zone. He wants to stretch you by calling you to do more than you've ever done before. *Are you ready to say yes?*

CARPE DIEM!

Making the most of every opportunity.
Ephesians 5:16 NIV

There's no "magic age" at which excellence emerges and quality suddenly appears. With God you're never too young and never too old!

Thomas Jefferson was 33 when he drafted The Declaration of Independence. Charles Dickens was 24 when he began his *Pickwick Papers,* and 25 when he wrote *Oliver Twist.* Newton was 24 when he formulated *The Law of Gravity.*

But if you think movers and shakers are only found amongst the young, think again: Verdi was 80 when he produced *Falstaff.* Goethe was 80 when he completed *Faust.* Tennyson was 80 when he wrote *Crossing the Bar.* Michelangelo was doing his best work at 87. And how about Noah? He was 500 when he preached his first sermon, and 621 when he came out of the ark and helped start the world all over again.

Seize the day! Redeem the *now* moments of your life. The time or the age you're waiting for may never arrive.

James writes, "A word for you who brashly announce, 'Today – at the latest, tomorrow – we're off to such and such a city for a year. We're going to start a business and make a lot of money.' You don't know the first thing about tomorrow. You're nothing but a wisp of fog, catching a brief bit of sun before disappearing. Instead, make it a habit to say, 'If the Master wills it and we're still alive, we'll do this or that' " (Jas 4:13-15 TM). *The moment once past will never return. So do it now!*

THE HIGH COST OF REVENGE

Do not avenge yourselves.
Romans 12:19 NKJV

Chuck Swindoll tells the story of a lady whose doctor told her, "You've got rabies." Immediately she pulled out a pad and pencil and began writing. Thinking she was making out her will, the doctor said, "No, no, this doesn't mean you're going to die. There's a cure." "I know that," she said, "I'm making a list of the people I'm gonna bite!"

Revenge is like rabies; sometimes it devastates the one who gets hurt, but it *always* destroys the one who does the hurting. It's insidious because: (1) it convinces you that it's justified. (2) It forces you to get bogged down in bitterness and self-pity. (3) It makes you spit in the very well from which you may someday have to drink. (4) It sidetracks you. (5) It causes you to take the low road.

Listen, "Don't insist on getting even; that's not for you to do. 'I'll do the judging,' says God. 'I'll take care of it' " (Ro 12:19 TM).

You're not qualified to judge because: (a) you don't really know what's in somebody else's heart, causing them do the things they do. (b) You're setting the standard by which you yourself will be judged. Listen, "Whatever measure you use in judging others, it will be used to measure how you are judged" (Mt 7:2 NLT). Can you live with that?

If you've been hurt, forgive! Then for your own good, put it into God's hands. He's the only One who's qualified to handle it. *And He will if you let Him!*

WHAT'S YOUR REASON FOR LIVING?

To me living is Christ.
Philippians 1:21 NLB

Billy Graham published the following letter in *Call to Commitment.* It was written by a young Chinese communist to his girlfriend, breaking off their relationship because of his devotion to the communist cause.

"There is one thing I'm dead earnest about, and that is the communist cause. It is my life, my business, my religion, my hobby, my sweetheart, my wife, my mistress, my bread and meat. I work at it in the daytime and dream of it at night. Its hold on me grows, not lessens, as time goes on. Therefore, I cannot carry on a friendship, a love affair, or even a conversation without relating it to this force which both guides and drives my life. I evaluate people, books, ideas, and actions according to how they affect this cause and by their attitude toward it. I've already been in jail because of my ideals, and if necessary, I'm ready to go before a firing squad."

Measure yourself by *that* yard-stick! Paul writes, "I am already being poured out like a drink offering" (2Ti 4:6 NIV). Looking back he considers every act he performed as a moment in which he gave a little more of himself to God; like the slow emptying of a glass of wine on an Old Testament altar of sacrifice. He gave his wisdom, his time, his strength, his love – he gave all there was.

"How could he do that?" you ask. Because to Paul, Christ was *everything!* Do you feel that way too?

OPEN TO NEW IDEAS

The intelligent man is always open to new ideas.
In fact he looks for them.
Proverbs 18:15 TLB

One idea can change everything! Bill Gates had an idea, but when he went looking for investors some of his big-money friends called it "too risky." Can you imagine how they feel now?

Good ideas are great. *God* ideas are even better! You see, what God initiates, He backs up with the resources of heaven. Paul said, "My God shall supply all your need according to his riches" (Php 4:19). According to *what?* Imagine being empowered by God, and underwritten by The Bank of Heaven!

God's problem has never been a lack of ideas; it's finding people who'll leave their comfort zone and act on them – people like Abraham, who, "By faith . . . when called to go . . . went, even though he did not know where he was going" (Heb 11:8 NIV). And what was his reward? Listen, "All the families of the earth will be blessed through you" (Ge 28:14 NLT).

Usually God gives us His ideas when: (1) Ours have failed. (2) We've laid aside our pre-conditions, and we're willing to do *whatever* He says. (3) We're willing to risk. (4) We're committed to giving Him all the glory.

Think what one of *God's* ideas could do for your business this year! Or your ministry! Or your family! Listen, "What I have said, that I will bring about; what I have planned, that will I do" (Is 46:11 NIV). God's *already* spoken certain things over your life. Seek Him and He'll reveal them to you.

TAKE YOUR STAND

Put on the whole armor of God, that ye may be able to stand.
Ephesians 6:11

Before you can really appreciate a new outfit you've got to go into the dressing room and take off everything that doesn't go with it. Paul says, "Cast off the works of darkness, and . . . put on the armor of light" (Ro 13:12). That means take off lies and put on truth; take off strife and put on peace; take off doubt and put on faith; take off sin and put on righteousness; take off ignorance and put on knowledge. Are you getting the idea?

Your old armor can't stay, because *not one piece* is suitable for the fight ahead. It'll only weigh you down and cause you to stumble in the heat of battle.

In Ephesians 5 Paul speaks about our intimacy with Christ. In Chapter 6 we're suddenly moved to the battlefield of the soul. That's the way it is; one minute you're worshipping God in ecstasy, the next you're in the fight of your life. (And it's all God!) You can't win spiritual battles without first being intimate with Him.

Notice the words, That ye may be able to stand" (Eph 6:11). The *armor* is God's; the *stand* is yours! You don't need armor if you're running away. It's strictly for those who're willing to stand for what's truly important: like the salvation of your family, the survival of your marriage, the restoration of your health, your finances, your ministry, or anything else God's promised you. So today, suit up, stand up, and hold your ground!

GOD'S ARMOR – PART 1: TRUTHFULNESS

Stand therefore, having your loins girt about with truth.
Ephesians 6:14

For the next few days let's look at God's armor, and make sure we have it on. *First,* "Having your loins girt about with *truth*" (Eph 6:14). A Roman soldier's girdle was all-important, because his breastplate rested on it and his sword hung from it. It was the *foundation* of his entire armor.

Truthfulness! You'll accomplish nothing worthwhile if your life isn't based on it, or if you're lying to yourself, deceiving others, and trying to "block out" what God's saying to you.

Just as a girdle squeezes you, so the truth will make you uncomfortable in dishonest situations. Just as your loins represent your most private areas, so your innermost secrets must be laid bare before God in order for Him to heal them. If you don't want to reap the consequences, don't reproduce anything that's not rooted in truth!

And it's not just the lies you *tell* that hurt you; it's the ones you *believe.* The enemy will try to sidetrack you into worrying that you're not good enough to be blessed. He'll also try to make you comfortable in places of disobedience by saying, "Go head, look at that magazine; smoke that joint; have that affair; the government doesn't need those taxes; take what you want, you deserve it; God's grace will cover it."

Whenever such thoughts come, rise up and declare, "I've been called to walk in the light and I refuse to walk anywhere else!" *Today, put on the girdle of truth!*

GOD'S ARMOR – PART 2: RIGHTEOUSNESS

Having on the breastplate of righteousness.
Ephesians 6:14

The breastplate of righteousness protects your heart. Now righteousness isn't a list of "do's and don'ts." The moment you trust in Christ, you are *made* righteous before God. From that point on He sees you "in Christ" (Ro 8:1). Indeed, if He looked at you any *other* way, you'd be sunk! Listen, "By the obedience of one [Jesus] shall many be *made* righteous" (Ro 5:19). That word "made" means *"a permanent condition of being."*

Now that doesn't mean you can say, "I'm righteous because I fasted for fourteen days, therefore, this promise is mine." Nor can you say, "My parents were good Christians, therefore, great blessings are coming to me." No, the blood of Jesus alone transforms you from the inside out, *and wraps you up* in His identity. Your defense against the enemy is not what *you* have made of yourself, but what *Christ* has made you to be.

Listen to these two scriptures. (1) "And be found in him, not having mine own righteousness . . . but . . . the righteousness which is of God" (Php 3:9). That's *positional* righteousness. (2) "Being filled with the fruits of righteousness" (Php1:11). That's *practical* righteousness. Positional righteousness is how God sees you. Practical righteousness is how *others* see you – and *that's* what you must work on every day!

Because of your position of righteousness you are empowered to *choose* the right things, *do* the right things, *say* the right things, and *stand* blameless before the enemy. When you do, he's got to flee!

GOD'S ARMOR – PART 3: PEACE

And your feet shod with . . . the Gospel of Peace.
Ephesians 6:15

Roman soldiers wore shoes called *caligas,* which were wrapped tightly around their ankles and studded on the bottom with nails. This provided them with three things needed to win a battle: (1) Stability. (2) Balance. (3) Forward momentum. Can you imagine being in battle without *those?*

"But what does 'having my feet shod with the Gospel of Peace,' mean to me?" you ask. Two things: (a) *God's peace* will keep you standing when others around you are falling. It'll keep your priorities in place as you move toward your God-given goals. (b) You'll refuse to go anywhere, do anything, or think any thought, unless it maintains the peace of God in your life.

Listen to these scriptures: "Ye shall go out with joy, and be led forth with peace" (Is 55:12). "Let the peace of God rule [decide] in your hearts" (Col 3:15). God's peace is your compass! When the enemy tries to take you down the wrong road, it'll keep you on the right one. When you're not sure what to do, your inner *peace* will make a ruling on it! When you're walking in these shoes, you'll measure *every* decision and *every* relationship by one standard – how will it affect my peace?

Listen, "Write the vision . . . that he may run that readeth it" (Hab 2:2). Whatever God has told you to do – write it, read it, and run with it! *Don't* get into situations where God's not honored, or get tangled up in things that are not His will. Go *only* where He is glorified, and stay *only* where your heart is "at peace."

GOD'S ARMOR – PART 4: FAITH

Taking the shield of faith, wherewith ye shall be able to quench all the fiery darts of the wicked.
Ephesians 6:16

A Roman soldier's shield covered him from head to toe. It was the first piece of armor to come in contact with the enemy. When the attack comes, your *faith* is what should meet it and defeat it!

In Paul's day, soldiers would light their arrows so that they ignited whatever they hit. When a soldier saw one coming he put up his shield which was made of iron, covered in layers of leather, and soaked in water. When the arrow hit the shield it fizzled out in a puff of smoke.

What are *we* to soak our shields in? The water of God's Word! (Eph 5:26). That'll quench *every* fiery dart that comes at you. For example, when the fiery dart of, "Your children will never be saved" comes, quench it with, "All [my] children shall be taught of the Lord, and great shall be the peace of [my family]" (Is 54:13). When the fiery dart of, "Your problems are too big, you'll never make it" comes, quench it with, "I can do all things through Christ which strengtheneth me" (Php 4:13). When the fiery dart of, "It's flu season, get ready to be sick" comes, quench it with, "The Lord will keep me free from every disease" (Dt 7:15 NIV). Getting the idea?

Knowing God's Word won't keep the enemy from shooting at you, but it'll keep his fiery darts from breaking your heart and penetrating your soul. *When your shield of faith meets his attack, you'll be a winner every time!*

GOD'S ARMOR – PART 5: ASSURANCE

And take the helmet of salvation.
Ephesians 6:17

Some parts of a Roman soldier's armor were so elaborate because they were designed to make a statement of strength and authority.

Apart from a soldier's shield, his helmet made the biggest impression. It was bronze, with feathers on the top, and made him look ten feet tall!

By calling this "the helmet of salvation," Paul could not have made a more powerful statement about your redemption. When you truly understand that you are *eternally* and *absolutely* saved – you'll stand ten feet tall. And people will notice the difference! When everyone around you is "losing their cool," they'll notice you keeping yours, because of the joy of your salvation.

Because the helmet of salvation covers your head, Paul said that your *mind* must be focused at all times on the most basic of all spiritual truths – you are saved! Keep that in the forefront of your thinking!

When the disciples returned, rejoicing in the miracles they'd done, Jesus said, "Rather rejoice because your names are written in heaven" (Lk 10:20). *None of the blessings of this life compare to eternal life in Christ!*

When the enemy brings up your past, remind him that he has no authority over you. He can't touch what belongs to God. He can't set foot in the life of anyone who's been redeemed by the precious blood of Jesus. *When you take that position, you stand ten feet tall in the Spirit!*

GOD'S ARMOR – PART 6: THE WORD

And the sword of the Spirit, which is the Word of God.
Ephesians 6:17

So far, all of your armor has been "defensive." Now you must put on the one piece which is "offensive." The sword referred to here was a large dagger used for fighting at close range.

Understand this clearly: you'll have to stand toe-to-toe with your enemy! To defeat him, you'll need to know how to use the Word of God, because it is "Living . . . Sharper than any double-edged sword, it penetrates . . . it judges . . . the thoughts and attitudes of the heart" (Heb 4:12 NIV). God's Word can determine with pinpoint accuracy exactly *what's* going on in your life. When you come face to face with the devil, it's the *only* weapon capable of rendering him powerless.

But to use it, you must first *know* it! It must become your automatic response to every challenge. If a situation calls for *thanksgiving,* then a word of praise should come alive in your mind and flow from your lips. If a situation demands *confrontation,* then a word of rebuke, deliverance, and counsel, should come alive in your mind and flow from your lips. If a situation is rooted in *lies,* then a word of truth should come alive in your mind and flow from your lips.

If you really want to *hurt* the enemy where it counts, start declaring The Word of God to him and he'll flee. He must! He can't handle being repeatedly stabbed and slashed by the sword of God's Word, *which is the very life of God.*

THE REAL BATTLEGROUND

Praying always . . . for all saints.
Ephesians 6:18

After telling us to put on the whole armor of God, Paul writes, "Praying always." Why? Because prayer is the real battleground. *That's* where you take back what the enemy has stolen from you. *That's* where you bring to pass on earth what God's already decided in heaven.

It was when Joshua *prayed* that he received both the strength and the strategy to conquer Jericho (Jos 5:13-14). *Think: Until you pray, what do you have to obey? Until you hear from God, whose authority are you acting on?*

The large shields used by Roman soldiers in battle could be locked together in such a way that an entire row could move forward as one single unit, each soldier being fully protected. They looked like a moving wall! Their protection was multiplied because of their *unity!* Their power was increased because of their ability to work *together!*

The call of God to us today is a call to unity. As we join together in prayer, the power of God to save, heal, and deliver, is released and multiplied – millions of times over! The Bible says, "One [can] chase a thousand, and two [can] put ten thousand to flight" (Dt 32:30).

There are times when we are *alone* in the lions' den, and God delivers us. There are other times when we are *together* in the fiery furnace, and our collective faith brings us through. In most cases, it's "the prayer of agreement" that releases the greatest degree of power and wins the biggest victories (Mt 18:19). Start looking for some prayer partners today!

WANT WHAT SUCCESSFUL PEOPLE HAVE?

Be diligent in these matters; give yourself wholly to them, so that everyone may see your progress.

1 Timothy 4:15 NIV

When it comes to golf, Ben Hogan is at the top of the totem pole. His accomplishments include 242 "Top 10" finishes on the PGA tour. When he returned from the army in 1946, he won thirty major tournaments in just twenty-four months.

But Hogan is best remembered for the fact that on February 2, 1949, his car crashed head-on with a Greyhound Bus and he was almost killed. Initially the doctors doubted that he'd survive. Next, they predicted he'd never walk or play golf again. But Ben thought differently!

Within sixteen months he was walking down the 18th fairway of the Marion Golf Club in Ardmore, Pennsylvania, putting the finishing touches on a storybook victory in the 1950 *U.S. Open.*

Today people still comment on: (1) His absolute unwillingness to settle for anything less than his best. (2) His radical commitment to practice from dawn till dusk. (3) His total concentration on the issue at hand. He liked to say, "The only shot that really matters, is the *next* one." Wow! Those qualities will take you to the top in *any* profession!

Do you want what successful people have? Start doing what successful people do! Here's God's formula: "Be diligent in these matters; give yourself wholly to them, so that everyone may see your progress" (1Ti 4:15 NIV).

THE POWER OF INFLUENCE

Demetrius is well spoken of by everyone –
and even by the truth itself.
3 John 12 NIV

Compare these two stories. The first is about a major cross-country race in Malaysia that covered a seven-mile course. Two hours after the race began there wasn't a runner in sight, so officials became concerned. When they sent out a car to find them, they discovered that all of them were six miles away, running in the wrong direction. What happened? The runner leading the pack took a wrong turn at the fifth check point – and *all the others followed him.*

The second story is about a sociology class that conducted a study of two hundred young people from the inner city of Baltimore. It concluded, "Not one of them has a chance." Twenty-five years later a sociology professor did a follow up study, and located one hundred and eighty of the original two hundred. Of that number, one hundred and seventy six had become doctors, lawyers, ministers, and successful business people. When he asked each of them how they were able to escape their predicted future, they all pointed to one teacher. The professor found that teacher and asked her what she'd done to make such an impact on them. She just smiled and said, *"I loved them, and they knew it!"* Paul writes, "Love *never* fails" (1Co 13:8 NIV).

John Maxwell says, "During your lifetime you will directly or indirectly influence the lives of at least ten thousand other people." *The question you need to ask yourself is, "How* will I influence them?"

WHAT'S THE BIG DEAL ABOUT EASTER?

I am he that liveth and was dead;
and, behold, I am alive for evermore.
Revelation 1:18

Simply this: His resurrection guarantees ours! With more time behind me than ahead of me, that really does interest me. How about you?

If I'm going to trust anybody, I'll trust the One who's been through it – and lived to tell the tale. *Jesus is the only man who ever made an appointment beyond the grave – and showed up to keep it!* That makes Him "the ranking expert" on the subject.

What gives courage to the bereaved as they stand beside a fresh grave? Or ultimate hope to the handicapped and the abused? What do you say to the parents of a brain-damaged child, that'll keep them from living their entire lives exhausted and demoralized? What's the final answer to pain, mourning, senility, insanity, terminal disease, sudden calamity, and fatal accidents? The promise of the resurrection! (1Co 15:4). That's the mental glue that holds our shattered thoughts together.

More than once I've looked into the swollen eyes of despairing people and assured them, "There's a land that is fairer than day." John saw it, and he said, "There shall be no more death . . . sorrow or pain" (Rev 21:4). Just imagine – the physically disabled will leap for joy. Those who've spent their entire lives in darkness will suddenly see their first face – the face of Jesus! No wonder we get excited about Easter! Listen, "He died for us so that we can live with him forever" (1Th 5:10 NLT).

WHAT YA GONNA DO WHEN THE ROOSTER CROWS?

Peter remembered . . . and he went out, and wept bitterly.
Matthew 26:72

Listen: "The rooster crowed . . . then Peter remembered his words . . . 'Even if I have to die with you, I'll never disown you'" (Mk 14:72&31 NIV). And before you criticize him, listen: "All the others said the same" (Mk 14:31 NIV). Wow!

The moment of truth came for Peter, and it'll come for *you* too. When it does, you'll see in yourself: (1) Things you've denied. (2) Things you've excused. (3) Things you never thought were there. Sometimes the very point at which you thought you were strongest is actually your point of hidden weakness, and God's showing it to you.

Maybe you were raised to look like you "always have it together," and now He's shaking some things up and permitting others to be stripped away.

Hebrews Chapter 12 says God's going to do, "A thorough house cleaning, getting rid of all the . . . junk, so that the unshakable essentials stand clear and uncluttered" (Heb 12:27 TM). *Only* when you reach that point, can you start laying a true foundation for your future, for only *then* have you come to terms with the fact that you can do *nothing* of real value in your own strength. It's a painful lesson!

Peter was never the same after that night. He'd been humbled; now God could use him. The lesson had been burned into his conscience; now he could write, "Be clothed with humility: for God resisteth the proud, and giveth grace to the humble" (1Pe 5:5). Has God been shaking *you* up lately?

WHY YOU NEED A SHEPHERD

He gathers the lambs in his arms and
carries them close to his heart.
Isaiah 40:11 NIV

If you grew up in the city you've probably no idea of the dangers a sheep faces every day. It has no defensive skills and no sense of direction. It doesn't know the difference between a dangerous river and a gentle stream. It's just driven by its thirst. That's why it needs a shepherd – and it's why you need one too! Your shepherd will:

(1) *Protect you!* Jesus warned us, "The man who does not enter . . . by the gate, but climbs in by some other way, is a thief" (Jn 10:1 NIV). Notice the words "some other way." Certain people with their own agenda will try to get to you through "the back door." Some, like the pedophile and the pornographer, will come through the Internet (it's been well named "The Web!"). What's the answer? Keep your eyes on the Shepherd.

(2) *Feed you!* What you eat determines your health, your strength, and whether you live long enough to fulfill your destiny. Sheep don't know the difference between poisonous weeds and healthy pasture, because they look alike. Listen, "Beware of false prophets . . . they are devouring wolves" (Mt 7:15 AMP). Some will sell you dates for The Rapture, others, formulas for getting rich quick. Watch what you eat!

A hundred years ago Australia had millions of wolves and thousands of sheep. Today they have millions of sheep and thousands of wolves. Why? *Because the sheep have learned to stay close to the shepherd. And you must too!*

DON'T LOOK BACK

Remember Lot's wife.
Luke 17:32

When the Sunday school teacher told her class, "Lot's wife looked back and turned into a pillar of salt," one child responded, "That's nothin'! My mom was driving home yesterday, and she looked back and turned into a telephone pole!"

Lot's wife only appears briefly in one scripture, so why did Jesus tell us to remember her? Two reasons:

(1) *She invested her life in something that had no future.* John writes, "This world is fading away, along with everything it craves. But if you do the will of God, you will live forever" (1Jn 2:17 NLT). God tried to get Lot's wife out of Sodom, but he couldn't get Sodom out of her. When she thought of what she was leaving, she looked back and turned into a lifeless monument. When God says it's time to move, don't hesitate! Don't become like those who once walked with Him, witnessed on the job, stood out as shining lights in their communities, but now have turned cold and unresponsive.

(2) *Your decisions have consequences.* If Lot's wife had kept moving forward she'd have been there to protect her daughters when they got to the cave. Instead they became victims of abuse and incest. Before you lose your children, poison your marriage, and tear up your life by refusing to break with your past, "Remember Lot's wife." She didn't make it to safety, but she did make it into scripture long enough to warn us about three things: (1) Complacency. (2) Involvement with the wrong things. (3) A divided heart!

LIFE – AT ITS BEST!

I have come that they may have life . . . to the full.
John 10:10 NIV

Want the most rewarding life possible? Jesus gives us the formula: "Unless a grain of wheat is buried in the ground, dead to the world, it is never anymore than a grain of wheat. But if it is buried, it sprouts and reproduces itself many times over. In the same way, anyone who holds on to life just as it is destroys that life. But if you let it go, reckless in your love, you'll have it forever, real and eternal" (Jn 12:24-25 TM).

Paul knew that "death to the flesh" was so crucial to a victorious Christian life that it became the cry of his heart: Listen, "I gave up all that inferior stuff so I could know Christ personally, experience His resurrection power, be a partner in His suffering, and go all the way with Him" (Php 3:10 TM).

Want to be *in-dwelt* and *energized* by the force of the resurrection? Be willing to lay down: (1) Your will. (2) Your desires. (3) Your pride. (4) Your independence. We're talking here about reaching the place where the *only* thing that matters is what *God* wants! It's the exact *opposite* of all your natural instincts!

"How will I know when I've died to self?" you ask. Because you can criticize a dead man, walk on him, neglect and abuse him, and he's not affected by it. *That's because he has moved to a higher dimension!*

PASS IT ON

They are the sons God has given me . . .
bring them to me so that I may bless them.
Genesis 48:9 NIV

Every family, including yours, has a history rich in achievement. You may not know it, but in *your* family genes there are things that are unique and distinctive; strengths that are responsible for the life that you enjoy today.

To honor your family's past, you don't have to erect a monument. The greatest tribute you can pay them is to lovingly remember their contributions and continue in their ways so that their gifts live on.

A wonderful way to build your children's self-esteem is to tell them about the great things in their heritage. Challenge them to live up to the standards set by those before them. Help them to see that *your* past is something that they can build *their* future on.

We hear a lot these days about "generational curses." Don't you think it's time we started passing on some "generational blessings" to our children? They're transferable! Jacob passed them on to his children, and you can pass them on to *yours*.

You don't need a million dollars or a Nobel Prize to bestow an inheritance on your children. Just pass on to them the values, the wisdom, and the love that got you to where you are today. Tell them how you made it over *your* Jordan River and into the Promised Land. Pass on to them the recipe for life that has served your family so well. Then challenge them to pass it on to the next generation. *When you can do that, you've lived well!*

LEARNING TO SUBMIT

Submit yourselves to every ordinance of man for the Lord's sake.
1 Peter 2:13

You are to submit to the laws of man as though *God Himself* had written them. To rebel against them is to rebel against the God who created order and authority.

Most of us rebel for selfish reasons, not scriptural ones. For example, if we're in a hurry, we think nothing of breaking the speed limit. If our boss is a tyrant, or doesn't pay us what we think we're worth, we feel justified adding an hour or two to our overtime. If we think our taxes are too high, we don't report all of our income.

Even in church we struggle. When the message "gets to us," we take it out on the messenger. If we don't like the songs the choir director picks, we quit the choir, even though God wanted to teach us submission *through* that director.

The truth is you'll keep going from one endeavor to another until you finally learn to: (1) Submit to authority. (2) Stop complaining. (3) Serve "as unto the Lord."

When God places you under the authority of someone you don't like – *He's working on your level of submission!* He's preparing you for battle! If you can't follow orders, you'll be an easy target for the enemy.

There is no such thing as "selective submission." Only when you master your selfish whims, put aside your personal agenda, and obey God, can He honor and promote you!

YOU'RE BEING TESTED

If you will only obey Me and let Me help you,
then you will have plenty.
Isaiah 1:19 NLT

A group of businessmen went to a remote mountain retreat for a weekend of leadership training. Expecting graphs, statistics, and pep talks, they were "blown away" when their boss, Mr. Clarkson, asked them to trade their notebooks for shovels.

"I want you to dig a ditch two feet wide and ten inches deep, around the perimeter of my cabin," he said, and disappeared inside. At first nobody said anything. But soon their silence turned into questioning. Then they started *arguing* about nine inches being close enough to ten, and *complaining* about having risen to the top of the corporate ladder only to be forced into doing manual labor.

Finally Bill, a newcomer to the group, turned to the others and said, "Who cares why he told us to do it, let's just do it!" With those words, the cabin door opened and the boss reappeared. "Gentlemen," he said, as he grabbed Bill's hand, "I'd like you to meet your new vice-president." There are three things you can learn from this story today:

(1) When God doesn't explain something, it's because you don't need the details. (2) When He doesn't speak, it's because He's working things out. (3) When He tests you on one level, it's because He's getting ready to take you to the next. So don't question Him, just obey Him!

BY GOD'S HELP – YOU CAN!

I can do all things through Christ which strengtheneth me.
Philippians 4:13

The Great Houdini claimed he could be locked in any jail cell in the country and set himself free within minutes. And he made good on his claim in just about every city he visited – except one.

That day something went wrong. He entered the jail cell in his street clothes. As the heavy metal doors clanged shut behind him, he took from his belt a concealed piece of strong but flexible metal, and went to work on the lock.

Soon he realized he wasn't getting anywhere. For thirty minutes he worked without success; then an hour passed. This was much longer than it usually took and he began to "stress out." But still he couldn't pick the lock.

Finally after laboring for two hours and feeling like a total failure, he leaned against the door, and to his amazement it swung open. *It had never been locked in the first place!*

How many times does something look impossible, simply because you *think it is?* Then you focus your faith and energy on it, strike the word "can't" from your vocabulary, and suddenly, with God's help, the impossible becomes "do-able!"

When God called Gideon, he replied, "I don't have the right connections." When He called Moses, he replied, "I'm not a gifted speaker." When He called Jeremiah, he replied, "I'm too young." To each God said, "I will strengthen you and help you; I will uphold you with my righteous right hand" (Is 41:10 NIV). *Today He's saying the same thing to you!*

REVISIT THE PROMISES YOU'VE MADE!

Thou shalt pay thy vows.
Job 22:27

The former president of Baylor University, Rufus C. Burleson, once told an audience, "I've often heard my father talk about the *honesty* of his old friend, Colonel Ben Shirred. Threatened with bankruptcy in his old age, and staggering under a debt of $850,000, a lawyer told him, 'For just $5,000 Colonel, I can find a technical flaw in the whole thing and get you off.'

"The old Colonel replied, 'Sir, your proposition is insulting! People trusted me. I signed their notes in good faith, and the last dollar will be paid even if charity digs my grave.' My dad once took me to see him, and his face and words are imprinted on my heart and mind to this day."

Integrity is not doing what's easy or what's popular, it's doing what's *right!* Furthermore, if you have a right to hold God to *His* Word, doesn't He have a right to hold you to *yours?* Listen, "Thou shalt make thy prayer unto him, and he shall hear thee . . . thou shalt pay thy vows. Thou shalt also decree a thing, and it shall be established unto thee: and the light shall shine upon thy ways" (Job 22:27-28).

Go back and revisit the promises you've made! Why? Because *nothing* is more important than your confidence before God! Listen, "If our heart condemn us not, then have we confidence before God. And whatsoever we ask, we receive of Him" (1Jn 3:21-22).

Could this be your doorway out of trouble, or the key to the breakthrough you've been looking for?

CORE VALUES

If you possess these qualities . . . they will keep you from being ineffective and unproductive.
2 Peter 1:8 NIV

Before you set your goals, discover your God-ordained purpose. Otherwise you could finish up somewhere you shouldn't be, or succeed at something God never called you to. Or worse, your talent could carry you to heights at which your character can't sustain you. Until you know and can clearly state the *core values* of your life, your decisions will be based on what's convenient, cheap, and self-serving. Refuse to live that way!

Marshall Field once offered the following twelve principles for determining life's core values. If you're having difficulty determining yours, read these principles, focusing carefully on each one. He writes, "We need to understand: (1) The brevity of time. (2) The power of perseverance. (3) The rewards of hard work. (4) The importance of simplicity. (5) The worth of character. (6) The fruits of kindness. (7) The power of example. (8) The call of duty. (9) The value of economy. (10) The virtue of patience. (11) The development of talent. (12) The joy of creativity."

Can *you* state your core values? If not, take a moment and consider these words from Peter: "Make every effort to add to your faith goodness; and to goodness, knowledge; and to knowledge, self-control; and to self-control, perseverance; and to perseverance, godliness; and to godliness, brotherly kindness; and to brotherly kindness, love. *For if you possess these qualities in increasing measure, they will keep you from being ineffective and unproductive" (2 Pe 1:5-8 NIV).*

NEED GUIDANCE? GOD'S GOT IT!

His sheep follow Him because they know His voice.
John 10:4 NIV

E. Stanley Jones tells of a missionary who got lost in the jungle. Looking around he saw nothing but brush. Finally he came across a village, and asked one of the natives if he could lead him back to the mission station. The man agreed. "Thank you," said the missionary, "Which way do I go?" The native replied, "Just walk." And so they did, hacking their way through the jungle for the next several hours. Stopping to rest, the missionary looked around again and had that same overwhelming sense of being lost. "Are you sure this is the way?" he asked the guide, "I don't see a path." The native replied, *"In this jungle there is no path. I am the path!"*

Feeling lost today? Pray this prayer: "Lord, You said, 'I am the way,' so I'm turning to You for guidance. I'm afraid to trust my own instincts, for too often they've gotten me into trouble. You said Your sheep follow You because they know Your voice. Teach me to recognize it now. Keep me from making a wrong move, for I seek only to do Your will. You promised, 'Along unfamiliar paths I will guide them; I will turn the darkness into light before them and make the rough places smooth' (Is 42:16 NIV). Turn on the light. Smooth out the rough spots. Point me in the right direction. Today I submit my way to You, trusting You to direct my steps. In Christ's name, Amen."

GOD IS CALLING YOU

The harvest truly is great, but the laborers are few.
Luke 10:2

One of the great disasters of history took place in 1271. That year Marco Polo's father visited The Kublai Khan, supreme ruler of China, India, and the East. He was so attracted to Christianity that he told Marco Polo's father, "Tell your high priest to send 100 men skilled in your religion and I'll be baptized. All my barons and great men and their subjects will be baptized too, and soon there will be more Christians here than in all the rest of the world."

But nothing was done. After thirty years only a handful of missionaries had been sent – too little too late! Can you imagine how different the world would be today if China (1.2 billion), India (800 million), and the rest of the Orient, had been converted to Christ?

At the end of World War II General MacArthur pleaded with the church in America, "Send one thousand missionaries to Japan immediately," promising that in one generation it could be won to Christ.

Again the call was not heard, and today *less than one percent* of Japan's population is Christian. Jesus said, "The harvest truly is great, but the laborers are few: pray ye therefore the Lord of the harvest, that he would send forth laborers into his harvest" (Lk 10:2).

The words you're reading right now could be the *beginning*, or the *confirmation* of your call to the mission field – *at home or abroad.* If not, they are definitely your *call to pray* that God will send laborers to bring in the harvest.

A WORD TO CAREGIVERS

Tabitha, arise.
Acts 9:40

Do you sometimes encourage others then walk away discouraged yourself, wondering, "Who's there for *me?*" Or find yourself helping people, even when helping them is hurting you? If so, please read the story of Tabitha (Dorcas) in Acts 9:36, and notice:

(1) *God never forgets a labor of love (Heb 6:10).* Others may forget, but not Him. Just when you need Him most, He'll show up. When Dorcas died God sent Peter to raise her from the dead and show us that He cares for caregivers, and loves lovers.

(2) *No matter how strong you are, there comes a time when everybody has to leave you alone with God.* When Peter came in he sent everybody else out. Dorcas was left alone with the *only One* who could raise her up again. You can't keep giving out without taking in. A tree can't continue to bear fruit without rest. The ground can't keep yielding a harvest without replenishing the soil. Get to your prayer closet! Read your Bible! Allow God to renew you and restore you! (Is 40:31).

To you who feel burned out, stressed out, and laid out like Dorcas, God's saying, "I'm not through with you yet. I've got a plan and a purpose for your life. You may be discouraged, but it's not over until I say it's over. Put death on hold. Drive depression out. You've given so much to so many, now I'm saying to you: *today is your day. Child of Mine, arise!*"

THE ONLY THINGS THAT MATTER!

Now is the time of God's favor, now is the day of salvation.
2 Corinthians 6:2 NIV

John F. Kennedy Jr. 1960-1999. Still hard to believe isn't it? Nobody but God knew the appointment he had that hazy summer night off the coast of Massachusetts when his plane crashed into the sea. John-John, the little boy we all knew and loved, the solemn saluter at his father's final farewell, plucked from this life like a ripe apple from a tree.

The other day I saw a bumper sticker that read "Whoever dies with the most toys wins." You've got to be kidding! When you're taking your last breath it won't matter *how* many toys you've acquired.

Tummy-tucks, hair replacement, wrinkle removal notwithstanding, you can't un-age the aged, and you can't stop time. In the end you're no more than: (1) The things you've accomplished. (2) The relationships you've built. (3) And whether or not you said "Yes" to God! Just a scrapbook of moments collected. The question isn't how *long* you live, but how *well.*

So what about all the stuff you've been putting off? Afraid of failing again? Failure isn't a sin! Low-aim is. Burying your talent is. Living without purpose is. Rejecting God is.

The only time you have is right now! *Now* is the time to take responsibility for each moment. *Now* is the time to stop settling for less than you were called to be. *Now* is the time to either jump on board the train, or stay at the station. The time of your life is *right now!*

HEARING GOD

Speak, Lord; for thy servant heareth.
1 Samuel 3:9

One day an American Indian who was visiting New York City, turned to his friend in Times Square, tilted his head and said; "I hear a cricket." "You're crazy!" replied his friend. "No, I hear it," the Cherokee answered. His friend replied, "It's rush hour, the city's full of noise, and you think you can hear a *cricket?* No way!"

"Yes," said the visitor, and walked over to a big cement planter outside a building, dug into the leaves underneath it and pulled out a cricket. Turning to his friend he said, "It all depends on what your ears are tuned to hear. Let me show you." Reaching down into his pocket he pulled out a handful of change, dropped it on the pavement, and immediately every head within half-a-block turned. "See what I mean?" he said. "It all depends on what you're listening for."

The first three times God spoke to Samuel he thought it was Eli the high priest calling to him. But the fourth time he said, "Speak Lord; for thy servant heareth," and his life was changed forever. (See 1Sa 3:9).

If you're *serious* about hearing God, get rid of the distractions and set aside time to be alone with Him. Learn to be more sensitive; God will speak to you through: (a) your Bible; (b) your thoughts; (c) your desires; (d) your circumstances; (e) those He sends into your life. *But it only begins when you pray, "Speak Lord, for thy servant heareth."*

BREAKING OUT

He has sent me to . . . proclaim freedom for the captives.
Isaiah 61:1 NIV

In British Columbia a new penitentiary was built to replace the old Fort Alcan Prison. As the inmates worked to salvage building materials, they made an amazing discovery – the *walls of the old prison had actually been made from paper and clay, painted to resemble iron!* One big push and they could've escaped, yet they thought freedom was impossible. What's *your* prison?

(1) *Past failure?* You'll stay there until you decide to accept God's forgiveness. Listen, "I, even I, am He that blotteth out thy transgressions for mine own sake, and will not remember thy sins" (Is 43:25). Forget your sins (and everybody else's) for *God's sake,* for when you keep bringing them up you really bother Him.

(2) *Sickness?* Bartimaeus spent his life in a prison of blindness. But when Jesus came to town he refused to allow the crowd to either silence him or get in his way. (And they'll try both). He cried out, "Jesus . . . have mercy on me" (Mk 10:47), and Jesus responded immediately. Imagine, the *first* face Bar-timaeus ever saw was the face of Jesus!

(3) *The fear of death?* Listen, "Only by dying could he break . . . the power of death [and] . . . deliver those who have lived all their lives [in] the fear of dying" (Heb 2:14-15 NLT). Good news! Jesus is a prototype. His resurrection guarantees yours! Robert Lowry wrote, *"Death cannot keep its prey – Jesus my Savior! He tore the bars away – Jesus my Lord! Up from the grave He arose, with a mighty triumph o'er His foes . . ."*

Whatever you fear today, Jesus wants to set you free.

NOTICING THE DIFFERENCE

When they saw the boldness of Peter and John . . . they took knowledge of them, that they had been with Jesus.
Acts 4:13

Suddenly it's popular to be "spiritual." And that's good. But we must *never* let what's secular define what's spiritual – like what a church should be, or what a Christian should be, etc. When that happens, we become more concerned about *public relations* than preaching the claims of Christ.

Listen; "When they saw the *boldness* of Peter and John" (Acts 4:13). You can walk with God and be gentle, but you can't be timid! You can be compassionate, but you can't be coerced by the opinions of those around you.

Paul wrote, "Be strong in the Lord, and in the power of his might" (Eph 6:10). That kind of strength isn't arrogance, it's *resilience!* It means refusing to budge when God tells you to stand firm, and refusing to stay when He says it's time to move.

Jesus never defined His purpose by the opinions of people. Nor did He try to impress them, or fit in with their ideas. He challenged them, changed them, and then called them to a life of discipleship. And that's still the way it is!

Listen, "They took knowledge of them, that they had been with Jesus" (Acts 4:13). The world's looking for people who look and act like they've been with *Him.* They'll only be convinced by the God you *know;* the One who's met all *your* needs. So today make your prayer, "Lord, others are watching; help them to see You in me!"

THE PLACE

Then the Lord said, there is a place near me.
Exodus 33:21 NIV

His marriage was in trouble, his congregation was worshipping a cow, and Joshua, his closest friend, was having difficulty understanding God's ways. In a very real sense Moses was totally alone.

So where *do* you go when the things you love and the people closest to you, aren't enough? Here's your answer: *"There is a place near me."*

But understand this, the enemy will do *everything* he can to keep you from reaching that place. And once you're there he'll do everything in his power to keep you from staying there too long.

And there's a reason. He knows that in that place you'll find answers – real solutions to the problems you're facing. You'll also find empowerment. After Moses had been there his appearance changed, his words were more effective, and he was able to offer God's people real direction. Yet before he found that place he was no different from anyone else. It was also where he found rest. Listen, "My presence will go with you and I will give you rest" (Ex 33:14).

When you're overloaded your vision gets blurred and you become resistant to the very ideas you need, because you just can't handle any more.

What's the answer? Listen again, "There is a place near me." *Make it the passion of your life to find that place – then live in it!*

RECEIVING FROM GOD

For she said within herself, if I may but touch His garment, I shall be whole.

Matthew 9:21

Bible scholars refer to her as, "The woman with the issue of blood." Humanly speaking she was out of friends, out of money, and almost out of time. But she refused to die. Notice three things about her:

(1) *What she said.* "For she said within herself, if I may but touch [the hem of his garment], I shall be whole" (Mt 9:21). It's not what others say that determines your destiny; it's what you say "within yourself" after they stop talking. God has made certain promises to you. Get into agreement with Him – for your words create a ceiling above which your faith can't rise.

(2) *What she did!* Instead of waiting for somebody to come and rescue her, she took control of her situation, went around the system, climbed over the pain, touched Jesus, and was made whole. It doesn't matter *how* you touch Him, or *where* you touch Him, it only matters *that* you touch Him! She may not have been welcome in their church, but she was welcome at His feet. So are you!

(3) *What she knew.* "She *felt* in her body that she was healed" (Mk 5:29). You can know things in your "knower" that you can't explain to anybody else. You can have the assurance that your answer is on the way, before a single circumstance has changed. Listen, "This is how we know . . . by the Spirit He gave us" (1Jn 3:24 NIV).

Are you ready to receive from God today?

WHEN YOUR ELIJAH LEAVES

Elijah went . . . into heaven. And Elisha . . . saw him no more.
2 Kings 2:11-12

No relationship lasts forever. When God gives you a mentor, prepare for the day when he or she won't be around. Elijah raised the dead, called down fire from heaven, and led a nation. People thought there'd never be another like him – until Elisha showed up and did *twice* as much. David's reign was the high-water mark in Israel's history, yet Solomon his son had the joy of doing what his father had been denied – building the temple.

In his final hours Paul closed the book, handed the ministry over to Timothy, walked to Nero's chopping block, and was thereby relieved of his duties.

Moses spoke for God, stood up to Pharaoh, and worked miracles. But when he died Joshua wanted to know if God would be with him too. God said, "I will." There are some things you'll never know until the mentor you've learned from and leaned on, is no longer there. Stop thinking that God will use anybody but you, or bless others more than you!

People will enter your life and people will leave it. Circumstances will change overnight. Life will hit you like a bulldozer and you'll struggle to get back up, wondering if you can even go on. But through your tears you'll hear Him saying, "As I was with Moses, so I will be with thee" (Jos 1:5).

God is into "succession." He's *always* preparing someone to carry His work on to the next level. The question is, will *you* be ready when He needs you?

GO HEAD – JUMP!

Though a righteous man falls seven times, he rises again.
Proverbs 24:16 NIV

One day a young guy sat on a park bench watching a squirrel in a tree. It was aiming for a limb so far above that it looked like "a leap of suicide." Suddenly it jumped, missed, and landed on a branch several feet lower down. Immediately, it steadied itself, got up, and prepared to jump again.

An old man sitting on the same bench said, "Funny, I've seen hundreds of 'em jump like that, even with dogs barking at them from the ground. And a lot of them miss. But I've never seen one get hurt tryin'." Then he added. "I guess they must think it's better to take a risk than spend their whole life where they *don't* want to be."

What are you aiming for? Does it seem out of your reach? Do you have less nerve than a squirrel? Go ahead, use your faith and take the leap. God will catch you if you fall! Otherwise where you are today is as far as you're ever going to get.

Look at Moses: an interrupted childhood, a foster family, a violent temper, a stammering tongue, and a criminal record. What a resume! He could have given up before he even started! Yet God used him to lead the greatest migration of people in the history of the world. And Peter: sinks trying to walk on water, denies his Lord, yet he becomes head of the New Testament Church.

Failing doesn't make you a failure, quitting does. Get up and try again! Next time with God's help, you'll make it!

GOD'S WAYS

He made known His ways *unto Moses,*
His acts *unto the children of Israel.*
Psalm 103:7

It's one thing to know what God *does,* it's another to understand how He *works.* There's a big difference.

Ever hear something about somebody and think, "That doesn't *sound* like them; surely there's more to it?" That's because you know their character! Well, God wants you to know Him that way too – and you can only do that by spending time with Him!

Getting to know God is like a child trying to keep pace with his father. It's hard because His legs are longer than yours, and His thoughts are higher than yours. But as you keep walking with Him, you begin to know Him better.

Regardless of how hot the furnace gets, when you know God's *ways,* your comfort comes from the fact that *His* hand is on the thermostat. If He turns up the heat, it's because you need a little more refining. David said, "Teach me Your way . . . that I may walk and live in Your truth" (Ps.86:11 AMP).

Even things that seem chaotic suddenly begin to have purpose when you can pray: "Lord, even if You don't *act,* I thank You for Your *ways.* If You don't deliver me and I have to go through this, I'm glad You're in control, and that You'll do what's best. You don't have to explain; I'm going to trust that when it's all over, *everything* You've permitted will work together for my good and Your glory, because I'm called according to Your purpose. Amen." (See Romans 8:28)

HOVERING

And the spirit of God was hovering over the face of the waters.
Genesis 1:2 NKJV

Before God completed His creation, He "hovered" over it until it became something beautiful. And you've got to learn to hover too; to watch, to protect, to nourish, while you wait for good things to happen.

Your marriage needs hovering. Even though you may have both started out with baggage too heavy to carry and too painful to share, with God's help it can still mature into a great relationship.

Your children need hovering too. So does your business, and anything else worth living for. If greatness is going to be born, expect it to take time! Don't just try to *make* things happen, have faith – and hover! Your situation may look chaotic today, but with God chaos is curable. Look what He did at creation!

Not all eggs hatch at the same time. Not all marriages mature at the same speed. Not all children develop at the same pace. Maybe you're anxious to see things happen in your life as quickly as they did in somebody else's. Rest assured if you apply God's principles and keep hovering, it'll happen in God's time! It may not happen the way it did for the Smith family down the street, but it'll be "just right" for you.

Instead of saying, "If things don't improve, I'm leaving," pray, "Lord, I'm in this for the long-haul. I've invested too much. I'm going to sit on these eggs until You make them hatch." When hatching time comes, you'll be glad you did!

LOOK OUT FOR THE AMALEKITES

The Lord will be at war against the Amalekites from generation to generation.
Exodus 17:16 NIV

From the moment Israel entered The Promised Land the Amalekites kept attacking them and having to be defeated. That's why God declared war on them, "from generation to generation."

There's a lesson here for you. The devil isn't going to send you a "congratulatory telegram" because you've decided to serve the Lord. No, every chance he gets he's going to attack: (1) Your wounded areas. (2) Your weak areas. (3) Your unfocused areas. The greatest weapon he has against you – is *you!* Listen, "For we naturally love to do . . . the *opposite* from the things the Holy Spirit tells us to do . . . two forces within us are constantly fighting each other to win control over us, and our wishes are never free from their pressures" (Gal 5:17 TLB).

One day a hunter came across a bear in the woods. "I want a full stomach," said the bear. "I want a fur coat," said the hunter. *"Let's compromise,"* suggested the bear – and promptly ate the man. As a result, the bear went away with a full stomach, and the man went away wrapped in fur! The lesson's clear; when you compromise with the enemy, you lose! God says, "I have set before you life and death . . . Now choose life, so that you . . . may live" (Dt 30:19 NIV).

God has declared war on *anything* that keeps you from walking in His blessing. There can be no half-measures. Unless the Amalekites in your life are thoroughly defeated, they'll keep coming back.

10 COMMANDMENTS FOR PARENTS

Children are God's best gift.
Psalm 127:3 TM

If you're a parent read this. Better yet, keep it where you can read it regularly.

(1) My hands are small; don't expect perfection when-ever I make a bed, draw a picture, or throw a ball. My legs are short; slow down so that I can keep up with you. (2) My eyes have not seen the world as yours have; let me explore it safely; don't restrict me unnecessarily. (3) Make time for me. Housework will always be there; I'm only little once. (4) I have feelings too; don't nag me about my inquisitiveness. Treat me as you'd like to be treated. (5) I'm a gift; treasure me as God intended. Hold me accountable, give me guidelines to live by, discipline me with love. (6) I need encouragement to grow, not empty praise. Go easy; you can correct the things I do without putting me down. (7) Give me the freedom to make decisions, even if they're not always right. Permit me to fall so that I can learn to walk. (8) Don't do things over for me; that makes me feel like my efforts don't measure up to your expectations. And don't compare me with others; I'm me, not them. (9) Don't be afraid to leave for a weekend together. Kids need vacations from parents just like parents need vacations from kids. Besides, it shows us that your marriage is something special. (10) Take me to God's house and introduce me to Him, because I'm gonna need Him for the rest of my life.

DON'T BE AFRAID TO START SMALL

Do not despise . . . small beginnings.
Zechariah 4:10 NLT

Everything big starts with something small. For example, one kernel of corn can produce a stalk with two ears, each having 200 hundred kernels. From those 400 kernels come 400 more stalks, producing 160,000 kernels. From those 160,000 kernels come 160,000 more stalks, producing a total of 54 million kernels. Keep it up, and the whole world becomes a cornfield!

Too many of us are not willing to take the *small steps* God places before us. If God's called you to a particular area, leap at the opportunity, no matter how small. For example, if you're called to be a youth pastor, don't sit around waiting for an invitation from some big church – it probably won't come! Go out and find the first young person you can and begin to minister to them.

Fred Craddock writes, "We think giving our all to God is like taking a $1,000 bill, laying it on the table and saying, "Here's my life, Lord. I'm giving it to You." But that's not how it works! God sends us to the bank to cash the $1,000 bill for quarters. Then He asks us to give twenty-five cents here, and fifty cents there. To teach a Sunday school class, volunteer at an AIDS clinic or an animal shelter, or just attend another committee meeting." Small things!

But if you're faithful in small things, He'll put you in charge of bigger things. Listen, "Well done . . . thou hast been faithful over a few things, I will make thee ruler over many" (Mt 25:23).

IN THE PRESENCE OF THE LORD

In the shelter of Your presence You hide them.
Psalm 31:20 NIV

Here are six things you'll find in God's presence that you *won't* find anywhere else:

(1) *Hope.* "I was right on the cliff-edge, ready to fall, when God grabbed and held me . . . thank you for responding to me, you've truly become my salvation" (Ps 118:13,17 & 21 TM).

(2) *Love.* "God has poured out His love into our hearts by the Holy Spirit, whom He has given us" (Ro 5:5 NIV).

(3) *Protection.* "In the shelter of your presence you hide them from the intrigues of men . . . you keep them safe from the accusing tongues. Praise be to the Lord, for He showed His wonderful love to me" (Ps 31:20-21 NIV).

(4) *Forgiveness.* "The angel said, 'Take off his filthy clothes.' [Then] he said . . . 'See, I have taken away your sins, and now I am giving you these fine new clothes.'" "Come now and let us reason together saith the Lord: though your sins be as scarlet, they shall be as white as snow; though they be red like crimson, they shall be as wool" (Zec 3:4 NLT & Is 1:18 KJV).

(5) *Direction.* "[And] whether you turn to the right or to the left, your ears will hear a voice behind you, saying, 'This is the way; walk in it'" (Is 30:21 NIV).

(6) *Joy.* "In thy presence is fullness of joy; at thy right hand there are pleasures forevermore." "Ask and you will receive, and your joy will be complete" (Ps 16:11 KJV & Jn 16:24 NIV).

All of these things are waiting for you today – in the presence of the Lord!

472 EXPERIMENTS LATER!

The time approaches when the vision will be fulfilled. If it seems slow, wait patiently, for it will surely take place.

Habbakuk 2:3 NLT

In 1877 photographers had to work *outdoors* to have enough light, carry bulky equipment and use a corrosive agent called silver nitrate. But George dreamed of a time when the wonderful world of photography would be accessible to the average person.

Working in a bank by day, he spent his nights reading books on chemistry, and studying magazines about photography. He even took foreign language lessons so that he could read the latest information published in France and Germany. Then with a partner he began his own company in 1881.

Almost immediately a problem arose with the new "dry-plates" he'd invented. Refusing to give up, George refunded the money to those who'd purchased them, and returned to his lab. He spent many nights sleeping in a hammock at his factory, after long days designing equipment.

Then *472 experiments later* he came up with a durable emulsion that worked on photographs. To replace the glass used for photographic plates, he created a roll of thin, flexible material, now known as film. In place of heavy tripods he developed a pocket camera. By 1895 (18 years after he began), photography was at last available to the common man.

Even though he failed 471 times, his vision kept George Eastman motivated and enabled him to give birth to the Eastman-Kodak Company.

This story is for all of you who've drawn a line beyond which you won't go, or set a price above which you won't pay a penny in order to succeed!

WHERE'S GOD WHEN IT HURTS?

When I get really afraid I come to You in trust.
Psalm 56:3 TM

Are you feeling overwhelmed today? Can't see your way through? Feel misunderstood, confused, hurt, alone? Are the heavens like brass, and God silent? Here's a prayer that will encourage you, and remind you that God's still in control no matter how you *feel.*

"Lord, I feel *beaten* . . . yet You've made me more than a conqueror (Ro 8:37). *Bound* . . . yet You're my deliverer (Ro 11:26). *Confused* . . . yet You're my counselor (Is 9:6). *A failure* . . . yet You've made me an overcomer (1Jn 5:4). *Fearful* . . . yet You haven't given me a spirit of fear, but of power, love, and a sound mind (2Ti 1:7). *Friendless* . . . yet You're a friend who sticks closer to me than a brother (Pr 18:24). *In darkness* . . . yet You're a light unto my path and a lamp unto my feet (Ps 119:105). *Lonely* . . . yet You promised never to leave me nor forsake me (Heb 13:5). *Misjudged* . . . yet I'm accepted and approved by You (Eph 1:6). *Poor* . . . yet You supply all my need according to your riches in glory (Php 4:19). *Sick* . . . yet You're the Lord who heals all my diseases (Ps 103:3). *Troubled* . . . yet You're my peace (Jn 14:27). *Unclean* . . . yet You're the purifier and refiner of my life (Mal 3:3). *Vulnerable* . . . yet You're my strength and my strong tower (Ps 18:2). *Worthless* . . . yet You see me as a pearl of great price (Mt 13:46).

"Lord, since that's how You see me, then I *choose* to see myself that way too, and act accordingly. In Christ's name, Amen."

FREE FROM THE OPINIONS OF OTHERS

It matters very little to me what you think of me . . .
the Master makes that judgement.
1 Corinthians 4:3-4 TM

If you let it, criticism will: (1) steal your individuality; (2) rob you of your creativity; (3) stop you from fulfilling your God-given assignment.

Insecure people will always criticize you. Why? Because they're threatened by things that don't conform to *their* way of thinking. On the other hand, secure people can handle you "going out on a limb" for a worthy cause. They can allow you to be different because they themselves are secure in who they are. They don't need to blow your light out in order to let their own light shine.

Paul says Jesus "made himself of no reputation" (Php 2:7). Sometimes the *worst* thing that can happen to us is getting a great reputation, because then we have to promote it and protect it.

Jesus wasn't concerned about what others thought of Him. He had a goal – to do His Father's will; no more and no less. And He knew that to do it He had to be free from the opinions of others. So do you!

The greatest tragedy in life is growing old, knowing that somewhere along the way you *lost* yourself, and never succeeded in being who God called you to be.

That's why Paul wrote, "It matters very little to me what *you* think of me, even less where I rank in popular opinion . . . the Master makes that judgement" (1Co 4:3-4 TM). Can you say that too?

CHECK YOUR FRIENDS!

A mirror reflects a man's face, but what he is really like is shown by the kind of friends he chooses.

Proverbs 27:19 TLB

Your company will shape your conduct, your conduct will shape your character, and eventually your character will shape your destiny.

Count on it: you'll become like the company you keep! That's why the damage done by sexual sin can last so long. To you it may be just "a one night stand," but the truth is when you become "one" with another person you open yourself to *the spirit* that's at work within them. Listen, "Can a man walk on hot coals without his feet being scorched? So is he who sleeps with another man's wife" (Pr 6:28-29 NIV).

On the other hand, a single conversation with the right person can turn your life around and get you moving in the right direction.

You need people who bring out the best in you and who challenge you to reach higher. People who see things from God's perspective and can speak His Word into your life because it's at work in their own. Your decision to rethink who you allow to get close to you today could be your turning point.

You see when you surround yourself with the right kind of people, you enter into a God-ordained agreement. Listen, "Two can accomplish . . . twice as much as one . . . the results can be much better . . . one standing alone can be attacked and defeated; but two can stand back-to-back and conquer" (Ecc 4:9-12 TLB). Today, take a look at your friends. They're a picture of who you *are* and where you're *headed.*

DO WHAT YOU CAN

Each part in its own special way helps the other parts.
Ephesians 4:16 LB

Doctor Boris Kornfeld, a Jewish surgeon, was imprisoned in Siberia, where he treated both staff and prisoners. There he met a Christian whose daily recitation of The Lord's Prayer really impacted him.

One day while repairing a guard's slashed artery, Kornfield seriously considered suturing it so that the man would die slowly of internal bleeding. His thoughts so shocked him that he found himself praying, "Forgive us our trespasses, as we forgive those that trespass against us." After that he refused to obey any inhumane, immoral, prison camp rule, even though doing so could cost him his life.

One afternoon while examining a man who'd undergone surgery, Kornfeld saw in the patient's eyes such a depth of spiritual misery that he told him his entire story, including his secret faith in Christ. That night Boris Kornfeld was murdered as he slept.

But his testimony wasn't in vain; the patient who heard it became a Christian as a result. That patient's name was Alexander Solzhenitsyn, Nobel Laureate, whose writings ex-posed the horrors of Russian prison camps, and ultimately saved the lives of multitudes.

It's a mistake to do nothing because you can only do little! Greatness seldom seems great at the time; usually it's just somebody seizing the moment and doing the best he or she can with what God's given them. What has He given *you* to work with today? Put it out there and see what happens!

A FAST FROM CRITICISM – TRY IT!

Take control of what I say, O, Lord.
Psalm 141:3 NLT

In *A Closer Walk* Catherine Marshall writes, "One morning last week God gave me an assignment for one day. I was to go on a 'fast' from criticism. I was not to criticize anybody or anything.

"For the first half of the day I simply felt a void, almost as if I'd been wiped out as a person. This was especially true at lunch. I listened to the others and kept silent. In our talkative family nobody seemed to notice. Bemused, I noted that the Federal Government, the judicial system, and the institutional church could apparently get along just fine without my penetrating observations! But still I didn't see what this 'fast from criticism' was accomplishing – until mid-afternoon.

"In the afternoon God gave me a *new vision* for my life. And it had His unmistakable hallmark on it – joy! *Ideas* began to come to me in a way I hadn't experienced in years. Now it was apparent what the Lord wanted me to see. My critical nature had not solved a single one of the multitudinous things I had found fault with. *What it had done was to stifle my own creativity.*"

Listen, "Words kill, words give life . . . you choose" (Pr 18:21 TM). Negative words create an atmosphere in which positive people can't live, and creative solutions can't be found. Only in a climate of faith and acceptance can risks be taken, progress be made, and dreams be fulfilled. That's why you need to pray today: "Take control of what I say, O, Lord" (Ps 141:3 NLT).

BURYING YOUR PAST

Ye shall see them again no more for ever.
Exodus 14:13

It's not enough to escape your past; its power over you must be broken, otherwise it'll chase you for the rest of your life. When you break away from something that continually tries to recapture you, it's *crucial* that you get victory over it, otherwise you can't move forward!

Jesus said, "I give unto you power . . . over all the power of the enemy" (Lk 10:19). Rise up in the Name of Jesus and say: "I refuse to have another relapse, another nightmare, another heartache, another bout of low self-esteem, confusion, or turmoil – for 'If the Son sets you free, you will be free indeed'" (Jn 8:36 NIV).

It's terrifying to think something's over only to find it isn't. But remember, it was *God* who permitted Pharaoh to pursue Israel when they left Egypt. Why? "That I may show these signs of Mine . . . that you may tell . . . your son . . . the mighty things I have done" (Ex 10:1-2 NKJV).

God wants you to know two things: (1) *The past no longer has any power over you.* Listen: "The Egyptians whom you have seen today, ye shall see them again no more for ever" (Ex 14:13). (2) *Your children don't have to repeat your mistakes.* The curse is lifted! They can grow up under God's blessing.

God could solve the problem some other way, but He takes us through the Red Sea so that when we get to the other side we can look back and "[See] the [enemy] dead on the seashore" (Ex 14:30 NKJV). Then we'll *know* that the battle is truly over!

25TH HOUR PEOPLE

Joshua spoke to the Lord . . . so the sun stood still.
Joshua 10:12-13 NKJV

Joshua was fighting with everything he had, but there was an element he couldn't control. So he told God, "I'll do what I can, but I'm calling on You to do what I can't; *arrest* the thing that controls the whole system."

When you're running out of time and you need a 25th hour in your day, there's only one place to go – God! He can stop the sun and freeze the circumstances! He can give you "extra time" to regroup, get a new strategy, and win the battle.

The 25th hour is when God allows you to redeem the time you squandered fighting others (or feeling sorry for yourself), when you should have been out fighting the enemy. Theologically we'd call it *grace.* We don't get it because of our merits; we get it because of God's favor. Ever have God do you a favor when you didn't deserve it? That's grace!

Listen, "There has been no day like that, before it or after it" (Jos 10:14 NKJV). Twenty-fifth hour people are different: (1) They pray prayers nobody's ever prayed before because they believe "nothing is too hard for the Lord." (2) They remember their wasted years and live with gratitude for the gift of a second chance. (3) They live with a sense of urgency and mission because even though the clock has run out, God has given them extra time to win the game. It's not too late for you; Joshua's God is your God! Talk to Him. He's still in control!

I WILL BE HIS FRIEND

No one intervened to help . . . so He Himself stepped in to save.
Isaiah 59:16 NLT

During the Civil War Lincoln received many requests for pardons from soldiers sentenced to die for desertion. Most appeals were accompanied by testimonial letters from friends interceding for them.

One day, however, Lincoln received an appeal that stood out from the rest. It arrived *without* any accompanying letters vouching for the prisoner. When he asked the officer in charge whether the soldier had anyone to speak on his behalf, to his amazement the officer said the man didn't have one friend, and that his entire family had been killed in the war. The president informed the officer that he would give his ruling in the morning.

Lincoln wrestled with the issue all night. Overruling a death sentence for desertion could send the wrong message, yet he found it hard not to have sympathy for someone so alone in the world. Next morning when the officer asked the president for his decision, he was surprised to hear him say that *the testimony of a friend* had helped him arrive at one. When he reminded the president that the request had come with no letters of reference, Lincoln simply stated, "I will be his friend." Then he signed the request and pardoned the man.

Isaiah said, "No one intervened to help . . . so He Himself stepped in to save" (Isa 59:16 NLT). *When God could not find a man, He Himself became a man, that we who are the sons of men might become the sons of God. Aren't you glad?*

ARE YOU WORRIED?

It's wonderful what happens when Christ displaces worry at the center of your life.
Philippians 4:6 TM

Have you seen the poster that reads, *"Who says worry doesn't work? Most of the things I worry about never happen!"* If you want to test your memory, try remembering what you worried about last year – or even last week. Jesus said, "In this world you will have trouble. But take heart! I have overcome the world" (Jn 16:33 NIV). We're not hurt so much by what happens to us as by our *perception* of it.

When researchers at King's College in London did a long-term study of fifty-seven breast cancer patients who'd undergone mastectomies, they found that seven out of ten women "with a strong faith" were alive ten years later, while four out of five "who felt hopeless" because of the diagnosis had died.

David writes, "Cast thy burden upon the Lord and he shall sustain thee" (Ps 55:22). Those who live worry-free are those who *keep* casting their burdens upon the Lord until the enemy decides there's no point *giving* them that burden anymore.

Trust is an attitude. Attitudes are nothing more than habits of thought – and habits can be acquired. If you want to change your attitude from worry to trust, do these six things: (1) Pray the right prayers. (2) Hang out with the right people. (3) Read the right books. (4) Speak the right words. (5) Listen to the right messages. (6) Do the right things.

Is a worry-free life really possible? Yes! Listen, "It's wonderful what happens when Christ displaces worry at the center of your life" (Php 4:6 TM).

"GEHAZI PEOPLE"

Let no debt remain outstanding except the continuing debt to love.
Romans 13:8 NIV

We all have people who've blessed us in ways we can never forget, and we must honor them. But there will always be a few who want *more* than their due. They're the "Gehazi people." Gehazi, Elisha's servant, couldn't stand to see Naaman receive his healing without capitalizing on it. He wanted *more* than he was due, and in the end his greed caused him to die of the very leprosy God had lifted from Naaman (2Ki 5:26-27).

This "I-am-forever-grateful-to-you" syndrome sounds noble, but actually it robs *God* of the glory; it suggests you are where you are today because of *who* He used. Promotion comes only from God! Furthermore, if He uses somebody to sow into your life, that person should look to *Him* and not you for their harvest. We shouldn't give with strings attached, or take credit for what God has done in somebody's life.

Look out for the leeches who try to overtax you and leave you in debt for life. These hangers-on want to fly when they see you going higher, and they can be hard to shake.

That may mean some hard choices on your part, like choosing between being "a nice guy," or fulfilling your destiny. *Refuse* to put niceness above your own well-being, or to continue making payments on a debt that was paid off long ago. Burn the mortgage and move on! Paul writes, "Give everyone what you owe him . . . Let no debt remain outstanding, except the continuing debt to love" (Ro 13:7-8 NIV).

FACING THE FUTURE WITH CONFIDENCE

He will speak peace unto His people.
Psalm 85:8

For weeks following the attack on America my wife Debby struggled spiritually. She couldn't sleep at night. She was glued to the television. The last time she'd experienced anything like this was back in Belfast, Ireland, in the late 70's, when she worked for the city's largest newspaper. "I thought I'd left all this behind," she said, as the memories came flooding back on September 11th.

One night, tormented by her fears, she read, "Why are you downcast, O my soul? Why so disturbed within me? Put your hope in God" (Ps 42:11 NIV). In tears she prayed, "Lord, why am I so disturbed? Why can't I shake this?" God whispered, "Debby, you thought your security was in America – now you know it's in *Me!"*

Where's *your* security? If it's in anything but God it'll fail you!

Even though Israel was surrounded by hostile armies, they were able to "celebrate with great joy because they now *understood the words* that had been made known" (Neh 8:12 NIV). God's Word produces faith in the time of fear. Paul wrote, "Faith cometh by hearing, and hearing by the word of God" (Ro 10:17).

The enemy doesn't fear your sin; he knows God can forgive. He doesn't fear your depression; he knows God can drive it away. He doesn't fear your poverty; he knows God can provide. *He fears your discovery of God's Word, because your ignorance of it is the most effective weapon he can use against you when trouble comes.* Need a refuge? You'll find it in your Bible! Have you been reading yours?

FRIENDSHIP

It makes me really glad to know that I can depend on You.
2 Corinthians 7:16 CEV

George Burns said that the secret to a long and happy life is *friendship.* He should know, he lived to be 100. He was married for thirty-eight years to Gracie Allen, until her death in 1964. He also had a life-long friendship with Jack Benny. After Jack's death in 1976 George said, "We were wonderful friends for fifty-five years. Jack never walked out on me while I sang a song, and I never walked out on him while he played the violin. We laughed together, played together, worked together, and ate together. For most of those years we talked every single day."

A friendship that lasted more than half a century. Wow! Don't you hope that when you die you'll have been *that* kind of friend to at least one person?

Richard Exley says, "A true friend is one who hears and understands when you share your deepest feelings. He supports you when you are struggling; corrects you gently and with love when you err; forgives you when you fail; prods you to personal growth and stretches you to your full potential. And most amazing of all, he celebrates your successes as if they were his own."

What will people say at *your* funeral? Will they describe you as kind and compassionate? Will they talk about missing the best friend they ever had? You may think that your eulogy is beyond your influence, but it isn't. *You're writing it today – in the hearts of those around you.*

WINGS OF WORSHIP

Thou shalt make two cherubims . . . of beaten work . . . in the two ends of the mercy seat.
Exodus 25:18

God intends for the hammer blows of life to bend our wings upward into a position of constant praise. He wants to bring us to the place where our *fixed* attitude to each challenge is, "in everything give thanks" (1Th 5:18).

When Paul wrote, "For me to live is Christ, and to die is gain" (Php 1:21), he was under house arrest waiting to be sentenced. He was saying, "Every time you hit me, all it does is move me closer to God." His visit to *heaven* happened while he was being stoned at Lystra. Anybody want to be in that position?

If you're looking for an easy three-step formula for experiencing God's power, forget it! Wings of worship can only be created one way – by being beaten into proper position and image. The hammer blows of life will always bend us God-ward if our responses are right.

Though battered, bloodied, and locked in jail, when Paul and Silas brought together their beaten wings of praise, God suddenly came down and altered everything. Doors opened. Chains broke. Circumstances changed overnight.

Feel like you're "in jail" today? Have circumstances locked you up and thrown away the key? You can soar above anything on the wings of prayer; you can worship your way through them to a new day! Praise isn't denial, nor is it refusing responsibility. It's harnessing the power of a higher law; one that either lifts you above your situation or sustains you through it. *Either way, praise is the key!*

SWITCHING SIDES

Gibeon . . . made peace with Israel and . . . were among them.
Joshua 10:1 NKJV

In The Promised Land the Gibeonites were controlled by a group of nations that Joshua planned to destroy. Although heathenistic, they were smart enough to know that they were on the wrong side. So they disguised themselves, deceived Joshua into making a covenant with them, and swore, "We will be your servants." When their old buddies heard about it, they joined forces against them. As a result, Joshua fought for them and delivered them. Notice four things:

(1) When you're tired of being controlled, there comes a breaking point where, in order to follow God, you *have* to be willing to "make the break." One of the things that hurts us is we want to move without making waves. We've got to get beyond that!

(2) When you remember where you *were,* you'll be grateful for where you *are.* The Gibeonites came on board as woodcutters and water-carriers; they were happy to just *serve.* Forget about being a spiritual celebrity; the *only* position God offers on His employment application is for slaves.

(3) The greater your problem, the greater your potential. Nobody puts out a contract on a bag lady! The level of *attack* in your life is just an indication of the level of *blessing* waiting for you on the other side of it.

(4) The Gibeonites were humble enough to ask for help. No matter how gifted you are, there'll be days when you need to reach out and say, "Hey, I'm going through some stuff, let's get together." Never forget, there's power in "Holy Communion."

YOU ARE "HIS PERSONAL CONCERN!"

Throw the whole weight of your anxieties on Him,
for you are His personal concern.
1 Peter 5:7 (PHILLIPS)

When worry comes knocking at your door, stop it on the porch; otherwise it'll move in and take up residence. "How do I do that?" you ask. Listen, *"Throw* the whole weight of your anxieties on him, for you are his personal concern" (1Pe 5:7 Phillips) How wonderful; God cares (He really does) about the things that worry you and prey on your thoughts. He cares about them *more* than you do. Not a single nagging, aching, worrisome, gut-wrenching, blood-pressure-raising thought escapes His notice. Because you're "His personal concern," you never disappear from His screen.

What qualifies as a worry? Anything that drains your tank of joy . . . anything you can't change . . . anything you're not responsible for . . . anything you're unable to control . . . anything that frightens and torments you . . . anything that keeps you awake when you should be asleep. All of that "stuff" needs to be transported from your worry list to your prayer list! Listen, "Don't worry about anything; instead, *pray* about everything. *Tell God* what you need, and thank Him for all he has done. If you do this, you will experience God's *peace"* (Php 4:6-7 NLT).

Give your worries one by one to God! The more you practice doing this the more exciting your walk with Him will become. You'll be amazed at how *easily* He handles things that overwhelm you. Always keep these three things in mind: (1) He's *able* to handle it. (2) He's *willing* to handle it. (3) He's *waiting* for you to give it to Him.

HOW'S YOUR WORK ETHIC THESE DAYS?

Lazy people are soon poor; hard workers get rich.
Proverbs 10:4 NLT

When Dave was twelve he convinced a restaurant manager that he was sixteen and was hired as a lunch-counter waiter for twenty-five cents an hour. His bosses were Frank and George, two immigrants who started out as a dishwasher and a hot dog seller. Frank once told Dave, "As long as you *try* you can always work for me."

Trying meant everything from working hard to treating customers politely. Once when Frank saw a waitress giving a customer a rough time, he fired her on the spot and waited on the table himself. The usual tip for waiters back then was a dime, but Dave discovered that if he brought the food quickly and was especially polite, he sometimes got a quarter. He set a goal for himself to see how many customers he could wait on in one night; his record was 100! R.D. Thomas, better known today as "Dave," became the founder and senior chairman of *Wendy's International, Inc.,* a chain of 4,300 restaurants.

Andrew Carnegie began working for four dollars a month, and John D. Rockefeller for six dollars a week. The remarkable thing about Abe Lincoln *isn't* that he was born in a log cabin, but that he got out of it! Listen to these Scriptures: (1) "Lazy people are soon poor; hard workers get rich" (Pr 10:4 NLT). (2) "Lazy people want much but get little, but those who work hard will prosper" (Pr 13:4 NLT). (3) "Observe people who are good at their work . . . they don't take a backseat to anyone" (Pr 22:29 TM).

WHO'S IN CHARGE?

Diotrephes . . . loves being in charge.
3 John 9 TM

One of the wisest men I ever met once told me, "After fifty-plus years in ministry, I've concluded that all church trouble comes down to one question – *who's in charge!*"

Some historians believe that Diotrephes was a wealthy businessman who found Christ, joined the church, and gave generously. But as time went on he made the mistake of assuming that professional success entitled him to authority, regardless of his maturity; and that having money automatically made him a "majority stockholder" in God's work.

Old habits die hard, and in the case of Diotrephes – not at all! Listen, "Diotrephes, who loves being in charge – denigrates my counsel. If I come, you can be sure I'll hold him to account" (3Jn 9 TM). Buddy Robinson used to say, "Pride is the only disease known to man that makes everybody sick, except the person who has it."

Oswald Chambers writes, "Pride, in essence, aims at enthroning self at the expense of God. When we measure ourselves by the life of our Lord who humbled Himself even to death on a cross, we cannot but be overwhelmed with the tawdriness, shabbiness, and vileness that's in our hearts."

When His disciples fought over who should have the "top spot" in His Kingdom, Jesus ended the argument with these words: "For who is greater, the one who [sits] at the table or the one who serves . . . I am among you as One who serves" (Lk 22:27 NIV). Can *you* say that too?

KINGDOM KINGPINS

The woman . . . said . . . come, see a Man.
John 4:28-29 NKJV

We'd have described the woman at the well as "dysfunctional" because she'd had five husbands and a live-in boyfriend. So why did Jesus walk for days to meet her? Because some people are "Kingdom Kingpins;" by reaching them you reach their sphere of influence. Often they're people in messy situations. But where there's a mess there's a message – so don't miss it!

Jesus knew this woman was worth waiting for because she was a "Kingpin" in Samaria. That day a seed would be sown in that city that hell itself couldn't destroy. You see she wasn't afraid to speak up, and because of her past she wasn't intimidated by men. Listen, "The woman . . . went . . . into the city and said to the men, 'Come, see a Man who told me all things . . . Could this be the Christ?'" (Jn 4:28-29 NKJV).

Later Philip went down to that same city and encountered Simon the Sorcerer – Satan's instrument to destroy the seed. Anytime God does something great, the enemy steps in to try and destroy it. He knows that unless he does, "the God who started this great work in you [will] . . . bring it to a flourishing finish" (Php 1:6 TM). That's why he sends things to plague you, intimidate you, and frustrate you. For every woman at the well, the enemy will send a Simon the Sorcerer. He knows you're a *Kingpin,* marked by God for destiny. So stand firm! Your past doesn't disqualify you for the future God has in mind. You've been strategically placed and "No weapon formed against you shall prosper" (Isa 54:17 NKJV).

SIGNING OFF

The time of my departure is at hand.
2 Timothy 4:6

Paul had such a great relationship with God that he was still receiving revelation in his final hours. He calls for writing paper, records his last few teaspoons of wisdom, passes them on to Timothy, and then leaves for home. He writes his best stuff on the eve of his execution. Wow!

He teaches us that *age* isn't the issue, *purpose* is! You should be more effective in your last hours than you were in your first. Like *Maxwell House* – good to the last drop!

The fact is, we are literally spending our lives. After this there will *be* no more to spend. Paul was wise enough to invest his life in things that mattered. How about you? Are you doing that?

Few words are more important than our last ones. So with his integrity still intact, Paul shares his heart, then exits with his finger pointing a dying world back to the cross. Imagine, he touched a world he didn't know! He challenged people he'd never even meet! That's called *impact,* and it's the measure of effective living! For what will *you* be remembered?

Ultimately it's how we *finish* that counts. That's why we must protect ourselves in our final years even more than we did in our early ones. People will forget all the good we do because of *one thing done wrong* at the end. That may not be right or fair, but it's true. So today, tighten your grip, refocus, and let *nothing* keep you from crossing the finish line victoriously!

LEARN TO GLEAN FROM OTHERS

Ruth . . . said to Naomi . . . let me . . . glean . . . after him in whose sight I may find favor.
Ruth 2:2 NKJV

You'd be surprised how much you can "glean" just by following somebody more advanced than you are. If you want to elevate yourself, study those who've already graduated in the areas to which you aspire, and "catch what they drop."

Ruth stayed close to her mother-in-law Naomi because Naomi knew the ropes. That was smart. If you always stay in your league you'll lose every game. The fact that Naomi was of a different nationality and at a different level of maturity didn't put Ruth off one bit. Doubtless there were times when they didn't relate to each other at all, but when God wants to stretch you, He'll put somebody into your life with *different* experiences and insights.

Naomi was Ruth's eyes in a world she didn't know; she was her tutor and guide in avoiding the pitfalls of life. Naomi understood where Ruth had *been.*

That's important, because we're all a product of our pasts. She also knew where she needed to *go;* all Ruth needed was the courage (and a little humility) to follow her. After all, if you're gonna get to The Promised Land, ya' gotta leave home!

God's raising up new leaders for the 21st Century. If you hope to be called for active duty, *recognize* and *respond* to those He sends into your life to prepare you. Whether they come to comfort, counsel, or correct you, remember these words: "He that receiveth whomsoever I send receiveth me" (Jn 13:20).

THE NEED FOR SOLITUDE

My soul, wait in silence for God . . . for my hope is from Him.
Psalm 62:5 NAS

When gold is refined over extreme heat the first thing to come to the top is the "dross." And the *last* thing to be separated from it is silver, a less precious metal that often blends with the raw gold ore. What a picture! Most of us are unable to separate the "good" from the "best," so Malachi writes, "He will purify . . . and refine them like gold" (Mal 3:3 NIV). *He* does it because we don't know how to!

Personal failure is usually the result of a slow steady build-up rather than a single act. It happens when we focus on our *career* and neglect our *character.* So God calls us to the place of solitude – a place with no distractions – in order to probe our deepest thoughts and open our eyes to certain issues that need our attention. It's here that He makes us aware of the things that we try to *hide* from others.

There's no way to have a deeper more intimate relationship with God without the rarest of all disciplines – absolute silence. Think I sound like a mystic? Listen, "Be still, and know that I am God" (Ps 46:10 NIV).

Your Bible is filled with references to the value of waiting before God. It's here that the junk we've accumulated during the busy hours of our day gets filtered out. With the debris out of the way we're able to *see* things more clearly and *feel* God's nudgings more sensitively. So, rearrange your schedule and make time to be alone with God!

A HEART FOR OTHERS

Whatever you did for one of the least of these . . .
you did for Me.
Matthew 25:40 NIV

Mother Teresa said, "If you're kind people will accuse you of selfish motives; be kind anyway. If you're successful you'll win both false friends and true enemies; succeed anyway. What you spend years building, someone may destroy overnight; build anyway. The good you do today most people will forget; do good anyway. Give the world the best you have and it may never be enough; give your best anyway. In the final analysis it's between you and God; *it was never between you and them anyway.*"

The downside of living in a *nice* house, working at a *nice* job, and attending a *nice* church is that you become *insensitive* to the hurts of those around you. Check out these two Scriptures:

(1) "If anyone has material possessions and sees his brother in need but has no pity on him, how can the love of God be in him . . . let us not love with *words* . . . but with *actions*" (1Jn 3:17-18 NIV).

(2) "Suppose a brother or sister is without clothes and daily food. If one of you says to him, 'Go, I wish you well; keep warm and well fed,' but does nothing . . . what good is it . . . faith by itself, if it is not accompanied by action, is *dead.* But someone will say, 'You have faith; I have deeds.' Show me your faith without deeds, and *I will show you my faith by what I do*" (Jas 2:15-18 NIV). Today, ask God to give you a heart for others.

FAITH AND WISDOM

The Lord will guide you continually . . .
keeping you healthy, too.
Isaiah 58:11 NLT

WebMD recently reported that people who *don't* attend church or have a strong faith in God: (1) have average hospital stays *three times* longer than those who do. (2) Are *fourteen times* more likely to die after surgery. (3) Have a *forty-percent* higher death rate from heart disease and cancer. (4) Have *double* the number of strokes. The same report also says scientists have now discovered that the human brain is hard-wired to communicate best through *prayer!*

Whether God heals you medically or miraculously, He alone is the source of all healing. His Word says: (a) "The Lord will guide you continually . . . keeping you healthy, too" (Isa 58:11 NLT). That's divine *health.* (b) "The prayer of faith shall save the sick and the Lord shall raise him up" (Jas 5:15). That's divine *healing.*

So does that mean you can treat your body any way you like and not suffer the consequences? No. Your *daily habits* determine your future. You don't just need faith to be healed, you need *wisdom* to stay healthy.

Each Israeli family left Egypt through a door sprinkled with the blood of the lamb, and "there was not one feeble person among them" (Ps 105:37). That means when you get sick you have the blood-bought privilege of praying in the name of Jesus, believing that when you do, His power is being released to heal you, set you free from crippling habits, and bring answers to your prayers. The privilege is yours – use it!

CLOSE TO THE CROSS, BUT FAR FROM CHRIST

They whiled away the time by throwing dice for His clothes.
Matthew 27:35 TM

Max Lucado writes: "They were witnessing the greatest event in history, yet as far as they were concerned, it was just another Friday, and He was just another common criminal. Casting lots, heads ducked, eyes down, cross forgotten. It makes me think of *us* who claim heritage at the cross. The stuffy, the loose, the strict, the Spirit filled. Robes, collars, three-piece suits. Are we so different? Don't we too play games at the foot of the cross? Competition. Selfishness. Personal gain. It's all there. We don't like what somebody did so we take the sandal we won and walk away in a huff.

"So close to the timbers, yet so far from the blood. We act like common crapshooters huddling in bickering groups, fighting over silly opinions. How many hours have been wasted on the trivial? How many leaders have saddled their pet peeves, drawn swords of bitterness, and battled over issues not worth discussing? We specialize in 'I'm right rallies'; major in finding gossip and unveiling weaknesses; split into huddles, then split again. Is it *that* impossible to find a common cause? 'May they all be one,' Jesus prayed. One church. One faith. One Lord. No denominations, hierarchies, or traditions – just Christ.

"Too idealistic? I don't think so. Harder things have been done. For example, once upon a tree a Creator gave His life. All we need are a few hearts willing to follow. How about you? Are you ready to leave your differences at the cross and follow Him today?"

THANK GOD FOR THE BLOOD!

You were redeemed . . . with the precious blood of Christ.
1 Peter 1:18-19 NIV

Your Bible has a crimson core. It begins with God Himself, shedding the blood of the first sacrificial lamb to cover Adam's sin, and ends with a multi-national chorus singing, "You . . . have redeemed us to God by Your blood out of every . . . nation" (Rev 5:9 NKJV). At Calvary you see two things:

(1) *The cost of your sin.* Rolled onto His shoulders was the weight of your every misdeed from the womb to the tomb. Next time you're tempted to break God's law and do your own thing, keep that in mind. (2) *The cure for your sin.* Your salvation wasn't a joint effort. You didn't contribute a cent because you were spiritually bankrupt. The truth is you were redeemed (bought out of slavery) by the crimson cash of Jesus' blood. (See 1Pe 1:18).

The blood will *always* offend those with sins to hide, a rebellious will to protect, or a Gospel that offers salvation through good works or social evolution. The blood not only saves the repentant, it condemns the defiant, for "Without the shedding of blood there is no forgiveness [of sin]" (Heb 9:22 NIV).

Plagues and apocalyptic hail could not redeem God's people from the enemy's iron grip. What did? The blood. Nothing but the blood!

The blood of Jesus can: (a) heal your painful memories; (b) cleanse the sin you dare not speak of; (c) put a canopy of protection over you and your loved ones; (d) draw a line in the sand over which the enemy dare not step. *Today, thank God for the blood!*

THE CARPENTER'S CLOTH

The cloth was folded up by itself, separate from the linen.
John 20:7 NIV

In Jesus' day when a carpenter completed a job, he'd wash his hands and face, dry them on a linen cloth, then fold it neatly and leave it on top of his work. The cloth was his trademark; whoever inspected it knew the work was finished!

On Easter Sunday after Mary Magdalene told Peter the grave was empty, Peter saw "the burial cloth that had been around Jesus' head. The cloth was folded up by itself . . . He saw and believed" (Jn 20:6-8 NIV). Peter knew instantly that Jesus had risen! His work was finished!

Science says that "infallible proof" comes from getting the same result from repeated experiments. Here are five that prove Jesus rose from the dead: (1) Mary Magdalene encountered Him. (2) The women at the grave saw Him. (3) The disciples talked with Him. (4) The apostles met Him. (5) Five hundred people witnessed Him at one time.

Listen, "He also showed himself alive . . . by many infallible proofs, being seen of them" (Acts 1:3). Listen again, "He arose from the grave . . . was seen by Peter and later by the rest of 'the Twelve' . . . After that he was seen by more than five hundred . . . Then James saw Him and later all the apostles" (1Co 15:4-7 TLB).

At a service in Bangladesh the congregation wept in disbelief at the crucifixion scene in *The Jesus Film.* Suddenly a little guy at the back jumped up and shouted, "Don't worry – He gets up again! I saw it before!" *Rejoice! He got up again – and we will too!*

RULES FOR LIVING

A cheerful disposition is good for your health.
Proverbs 17:22TM

Here are three rules you need to put into practice today:

(1) *Learn to control the climate around you.* Negativity is contagious, look out for "carriers." Love them, lift them if you can, but never let them infect you. When God wants to bless you He'll send a person, and you'll know that person by their *spirit,* for it will be the spirit of power (the "can-do" attitude), love (which always looks for the best), and a sound mind (which is stable and consistent). (See 2 Ti 1:7.)

(2) *Smile, even when you're not on Candid Camera!* A woman who'd been given a lovely plant took it home, watered it, fertilized it, and set it in the sun. Later she discovered it was *silk* – and she still laughs about it! When you're secure you can laugh at yourself, plus it's also a hallmark of true humility. Your smile muscles are linked to the part of your brain that determines your mood; that's why Solomon says, "A merry heart doeth good like a medicine" (Pr 17:22).

(3) *Employ the 90/10 rule.* When ninety percent of the circumstances are uncontrollable, focus on the ten percent you can do something about. And remember, one of God's ideas – just one – can change everything! Paul writes, "We were troubled on every side; without were fightings, within were fears. *Nevertheless God . . .* " (2Co 7:5-6). Factor God in! He specializes in "impossibilities." He can take the situation you've made into a mountain and bore a tunnel through it in a matter of seconds. All He asks is that you *involve* Him!

THE "I-KNEW-YOU-WHEN" CREW!

Only in his hometown and in his own house is a prophet without honor.
Matthew 13:57 NIV

Realize that some of the people who knew you "way back when" don't necessarily know you now. They've *slotted you,* and they won't be happy that you've moved out of that slot. Listen, "Coming to his hometown, he began teaching . . . and they were amazed . . . 'Isn't this the carpenter's son?' . . . And they took offense at him . . . he did not do many miracles there because of their lack of faith" (Mt 13:54-58 NIV).

So what did Jesus do? He left! What else could He do? If you allow them, the "I-knew-you-when" crew will keep you stuck at a stage in your life that's passed and gone. You've *got* to move beyond the good old days! If you allow people to keep taking you down memory lane, you'll eventually set up house, stay longer than you should, and miss your destiny. Don't stay where you're tolerated, go where you're appreciated!

Before David slew Goliath he had to overcome his oldest brother Eliab, one of Saul's generals. David's boldness magnified Eliab's cowardice. Had David given in he'd *never* have slain the giant and gone on to become king.

It's a gift to have people in your life who know where you've been *and* can relate to where you're going. But if you have to choose between "then" and "now," sacrifice "then," because it can't be rewritten, only replayed over and over again. Stop rehearsing your beginnings and write the rest of your story! The future is yours – grab it while you can!

HE'S THERE!

God is . . . a very present help in trouble.
Psalm 46:1

In a dream a man saw Jesus approach three praying women. He knelt beside the first with great tenderness and love. At the second He simply placed His hand on her head and gave her a look of approval. He passed by the third without even stopping.

Sensing the man's bewilderment, Jesus explained, "Without constant assurance, the first woman would stumble and fall. The second woman's faith is stronger; I can count on her. The third, however, is being trained for the *highest* calling of all. She knows Me so intimately that she doesn't need signs of My approval. No circumstance discourages her because she knows that ultimately, she can trust Me."

Being sinful, we fail. Being prone to sickness, we hurt. Being mortal, we die. Pressure wears on us. Anxiety gives us ulcers. People intimidate us. Criticism offends us. Disease scares us. Death haunts us.

What's the answer? "God is . . . a very present help in trouble" (Ps 46:1). Never doubt in the dark what God tells you in the light, for He's with you day by day on your pilgrimage. His unsearchable mind works in concert with His unfathomable will, carrying things out under His sovereign control.

When we hit rough spots, our tendency is to feel abandoned. Yet the opposite is true, for at that moment we are *more than ever* the object of His love and concern. Yes, even when our vision gets blurred, our thinking is foggy, and we look up and can't see Him clearly – He's there!

GOD'S NOT FINISHED WITH YOU YET

God has appointed another seed for me.
Genesis 4:25 NKJV

Satan's goal was to infect Adam *before* his first son was born; that way he could contaminate all the rest of us. And it almost worked! Cain, Adam's firstborn, murdered his brother Abel. But God wasn't finished with Adam yet. Listen, "Adam knew his wife again, and she bore him a son and named him Seth 'For God has appointed *another seed* for me instead of Abel, whom Cain killed'" (Ge 4:25 NKJV).

How wonderful! For everything you've loved and lost, God has another seed; for everything that has died or been stolen from you, God has another seed. You see, your seed is your *future,* and God has another one for you to birth – He has another miracle for you to hold. Where you are right now is not where you're going.

The devil knew God had a plan for you, that's why he worked so hard to wipe you out. He didn't want you to live long enough to receive what God had in mind. But he failed, didn't he? The very fact that you're *still* here says that God's not through with you yet. Start looking ahead; there's something coming up on God's calendar and it's got your name on it! "God hath appointed . . ." There's something good just over the horizon – something good for your life . . . your marriage . . . your family . . . your career . . . your ministry. Unless you're on your deathbed God *still* has an appointed task for you to finish. Rejoice, He's called you with an *eternal* purpose!

BUDGETS AND BOUNDARIES

Become wise by walking with the wise; hang out with fools and watch your life fall to pieces.
Proverbs 13:20 TM

Relationships work best when you enter them "head-first," not "heart-first." Establish boundaries and a budget up front. *Where* does this person belong? *How much* am I prepared to invest in them? Life's too short to be spent straightening out misunderstandings, hurt feelings, and damaged egos.

Avoid relationships that drain you and leave you wondering, "How'd I get into this?" When keeping somebody happy means short-changing the purposes of God in your own life, you've overdrawn the budget. You've no right to complain about what you permit!

When somebody needs too many phone calls, dinners, favors, loans, or other forms of attention, it's time to draw the line. You've only so much time and energy. Good stewardship demands that you invest your life where there's the greatest return. When people who're too needy demand more than you've the *ability* or *right* to give, you must do one of two things.

(1) Renegotiate. Bankrupting yourself to make them *feel* great might sound noble, but it's not. Bankrupt people end up with everything from nervous breakdowns to extra-marital affairs, because they're overspent.

(2) If that doesn't work – walk away! Paul said, "My life is worth nothing unless I use it for doing the work assigned me by the Lord Jesus" (Acts 20:24 NLT). Let *no one* stand in the way of your doing what God has called you to do!

"GET A LIFE!"

Well done, thou good and faithful servant.
Matthew 25:21

Check out this advice given by novelist Anna Quindlen at a Villanova University graduation:

"Don't confuse your life with your work. What you *are* will always be more important than what you *do.* There'll be many others with your same degree doing what you want to do, maybe doing it better. But you have sole custody, not only of your life, but of your mind and of your heart.

"It's easier to write a resume than it is to craft a spirit or build a character. A resume is cold comfort when you're sad, broke, lonely, or you've gotten back the test results and they're not so good. I no longer consider myself the center of the universe. I show up. I listen. I try to laugh. I make my marriage vows mean something. I pray. I'm good to my friends, because without them I'd be a cardboard cutout.

"Get a life, not a manic pursuit of the next promotion, or bigger paycheck, or larger house. Do you think you'd *care* about those things if you blew an aneurysm or found a lump in your breast?

"Get a life in which you are generous. All of you want to do well, but if you don't do *good,* doing well will never be enough."

Do it right the first time, because life's not a dress rehearsal. Discover God's will for you and give yourself unreservedly to it. Live with the end in view – the final graduation when you'll hear the words, "Well done, thou good and faithful servant" (MT 25:21).

HE'S WORKING ON YOUR PATIENCE

We glory in tribulations also: knowing that tribulation worketh patience.
Romans 5:3

The toughest times are those when all we know about God still doesn't help us to get results! That's when we learn about His *silence.*

Whenever God doesn't say a word: (1) He's teaching even in the stillness; (2) He's allowing us to grow by *forcing* us to think, study, and arrive at conclusions, while He stands by with a hushed smile and a watchful eye. He's fathering us!

Faith comes by hearing. Patience comes by silence! Patience is what God gives you when bad things remain unchanged. It's God's sedative for your troubled heart. It's the balm He rubs into your aching muscles when you feel like you're being stretched to breaking point. These are the times when the pain lasts so long that *only God* can release the patience required, the sheer grace to sustain you. The truth is, patience is just strength harnessed, power focused, and faith taking its time.

Listen, "*Keep* your eyes on Jesus, who both began and finished this race we're in. *Study* how He did it. Because *He never lost sight* of where He was headed – that exhilarating finish in and with God – He could put up with anything along the way: cross, shame, whatever. And now He's there, in the place of honor, right alongside God. *When you find yourselves flagging* in your faith, go over that story again, item by item, that long litany of hostility He ploughed through. *That* will shoot adrenaline into your souls!" (Heb 12:1-3 TM).

THE RIGHT TO LEAD

Have not I commanded you? Be strong and courageous.
Joshua 1:9 NIV

On May 28, 1970, when a landmine injured one of his soldiers, General Norman Schwarzkopf flew to where the man lay. While the helicopter was evacuating him, another soldier stepped on a mine, severely injuring his leg. That's when everyone realized *they were standing in a minefield.* Schwarzkopf knew the injured man could survive and even keep his leg, but only if he stopped flailing around. There was only one thing Schwarzkopf could do – go to him and immobilize him.

In his autobiography he wrote, "I started through the minefield one slow step at a time, staring at the ground, looking for telltale bumps or little prongs sticking up from the dirt. My knees were shaking so hard that each time I took a step I had to grab my leg and steady it with both hands before I could take another. It seemed like a thousand years before I reached the kid."

The 240-pound Schwarzkopf pinned the wounded man and calmed him down. Eventually he got him and the others out of the minefield. Later that night when the General was at the hospital, three black soldiers stopped him and said, "Sir, we saw what you did for the brother out there. We'll never forget it." Until that moment it hadn't occurred to Schwarzkopf that the soldier he'd saved was black.

The army gave General Schwarzkopf the *power* to lead. His skills gave him the *ability* to lead. But only *character* and *courage* can give you the *right* to lead!

CHRIST IS EVERYTHING!

It is no longer I who live, but Christ lives in me.
Galatians 2:20 NKJV

One night Toscanini, the famous Italian conductor, led the Philadelphia Symphony Orchestra in Beethoven's Ninth Symphony, a very difficult piece to direct. So majestic was the music that after the finale the audience stood for ten minutes applauding. Toscanini took his bows again and again then turned to the orchestra who also bowed. The audience continued to clap and cheer. Finally Toscanini turned his back to the audience, and speaking only to the orchestra said, "Ladies, gentlemen, I am nothing. You are nothing. Beethoven is everything!"

What a lesson! Regardless of how eloquent or gifted you may be, throw yourself at the feet of Jesus today and say, "I am nothing. You are everything!"

When men first learned to navigate the seas by using the stars, a whole new world opened up to them. It was said, "He who is a slave to the compass enjoys the freedom of the open sea."

Commitment to Christ is your compass! It opens the door to God's kingdom for you. When you *commit* your future to Him and let Him set your course, He'll direct you to places of freedom, fulfillment, and blessing that you never knew existed. But first you must be willing to say, "It is no longer I who live, but Christ lives in me" (Gal 2:20). You must bow before Him and declare, "I am nothing. You are everything. Here are my gifts, my abilities, and my dreams. I lay them at Your feet. I give them all to You, holding nothing back."

BEING UNDER SATAN'S YOKE

Don't become so well-adjusted to your culture that you fit into it without even thinking.

Romans 12:2 TM

Addressing a worldwide convention of demons, Satan said: "As long as Christians stay close to God we've no power over them, so here's what I want you to do:

"(1) Keep them busy with non-essentials. (2) Tempt them to overspend and go into debt. (3) Make them work long hours to maintain empty lifestyles. (4) Discourage them from spending family time, for when homes disintegrate there's no refuge from work. (5) Over-stimulate their minds with television and computers so that they can't hear God speaking to them. (6) Fill their coffee tables and nightstands with magazines and newspapers, so they've no time for Bible reading. (7) Flood their mailboxes with sweepstakes, promotions, and get-rich-quick schemes; keep them chasing material things. (8) Put glamorous models on TV and on magazine covers to keep them focused on outward appearances; that way they'll be dissatisfied with themselves and their mates. (9) Make sure couples are too exhausted for physical intimacy; that way they'll be tempted to look elsewhere. (10) Emphasize Santa and the Easter Bunny, that way you'll divert them from the real meaning of the holidays. (11) Involve them in "good causes" so they won't have any time for "eternal ones." (12) Make them self-sufficient. Keep them so busy working in their own strength that they'll never experience God's power working through them. *I promise – it'll work!"*

Have you figured out yet the difference yet between being *busy* and being *successful?* Sometimes "B-U-S-Y" just means Being Under Satan's Yoke!

"RELATIONSHIP IDOLS"

The Lord . . . is a jealous God.
Exodus 34:14 NKJV

God is jealous of anything that takes His place, especially "relationship idols." "What're they?" you ask. They're the lies that convince you that your happiness depends on *another person.*

When you look to somebody other than God for security, worth, joy, and contentment – all the things He willingly provides – He's jealous. So to tear down that idol in your life He allows you to be alone.

It's hard to have nobody to share your successes . . . or to pray with . . . or to come home to. But when God wants you to hear *His* voice He silences all the rest. You're not alone because nobody likes you, you're alone because God's jealous of your affections, and He's drawing you to a place of intimacy with Him. He does this when He's going to do something *new* in your life.

How do we know? Because Joshua was alone when God gave him the strategy to overcome Jericho. Gideon was alone when he was commissioned to save Israel. "Jacob was left alone, and a man wrestled with him till daybreak" (Ge 32:24 NIV). That's when God changed his name from Jacob, *a con artist,* to Israel, *a prince with God.*

When you don't know who you *are,* in order to find fulfillment you'll allow yourself be swallowed up in somebody else's life. You'll think you need that person in order to enjoy being you! No, let God tell you who you are. After all, who knows you better than Him? And the only way you'll discover who you really are is by being alone with Him!

HOW TO IMPROVE YOUR PRAYER LIFE

You will seek Me and find Me
when you seek Me with all your heart.
Jeremiah 29:13 NIV

Want to improve your prayer life? Francois Fenelon, a 17th century French clergyman, tells us how. Listen: "Tell God all that is in your heart, as one unloads one's heart, its pleasures and its pains, to a dear friend. Tell Him your *troubles* that He may comfort you; tell Him your *longings* that He may purify them; tell Him your *dislikes* that He may help you conquer them; talk to Him of your *temptations* that He may shield you from them; show Him the *wounds* of your soul that He may heal them; lay bare your *indifference* to good, your depraved taste for evil, your instability. Tell Him how *self-love* makes you unjust to others, how *vanity* tempts you to be insincere, how *pride* hides you from yourself and from others. If you thus pour out all your weaknesses, needs, and troubles, there will be no lack of what to say. You will never exhaust the subject, for it is continually being renewed.

"People who have no secrets from each other never want for subjects of conversation. They do not weigh their words for there is nothing to be held back. Neither do they seek for something to say. They talk out of the abundance of their heart. Without consideration they simply say *just what they think.* When they ask, they ask in faith, confident that they will be heard. *Blessed* are those who attain to such familiar, unreserved communication with God."

HINTS FOR A HAPPY HOME

Love is always supportive, loyal, hopeful, and trusting.
1 Corinthians 13:7 CEV

Here are ten reasons why relationships fail. Read them slowly, then grade yourself: (1) Communication breaks down. (2) Truth is violated. (3) Integrity is forsaken. (4) Time isn't invested. (5) Risks aren't taken. (6) Control is the goal. (7) Trust is broken. (8) Self-interest is the rule. (9) Manipulation is allowed. (10) God is ignored. Well, how'd you do? Before you answer, here are three hints to help you do better.

(1) *Become a good listener.* James writes, "Be quick to listen and slow to speak" (Jas 1:19 CEV). Sometimes the greatest gift you can give somebody is to listen, and listen with your heart. You don't need to say a word, just "being there" is enough.

(2) *Speak the truth in love* (Eph 4:15). Nobody likes to be corrected, but when you're heading down the wrong road or settling for less than your potential, love will "get in your face." If you truly care about someone, you'll "speak the truth in love" to them.

(3) *Always believe the best.* Love sees you at your worst, but never forgets your best; thinks you're a little bit more wonderful than you really are; will talk with you endlessly or just sit with you in silence; is happier about your success than you are; cares about you enough to say what it really means; doesn't try to know more, act smarter, or be your constant teacher; and listens, when what you have to say isn't particularly interesting. Why? *Because love believes you're important!*

NEVER COMPROMISE YOUR INTEGRITY

The integrity of the honest keeps them on track;
the deviousness of crooks brings them to ruin.
Proverbs11:3 TM

In what he calls *A Compromise of Integrity,* psychiatrist Leo Randall analyzes the relationship between former President Nixon and some of his closest confidants. He records a conversation between Senator Howard Baker and presidential aide Herbert Porter: *Baker:* "Did you ever have qualms about what you were doing?" *Porter:* "Yes." *Baker:* "What did you do about it?" *Porter:* "Nothing!" *Baker:* "Why?" *Porter:* "Group pressure. I was afraid of not being considered a team-player."

Joseph said no to the advances of Potiphar's wife, not because he couldn't get away with it, but because he couldn't live with himself afterwards.

Ted Engstrom writes, "The world needs people who cannot be bought; whose word is their bond; who put character above wealth; who possess opinions and a will; who are larger than their vocations; who don't hesitate to take chances; who won't lose their individuality in a crowd; who'll be as honest in small things as they are in great things; who'll make no compromise with wrong; whose ambitions are not confined to their own selfish desires; who'll not do it 'because everybody else does it'; who are true to their friends through good report and evil report, in adversity as well as in prosperity; who do not believe that shrewdness, cunning, and hard-headedness are the best qualities for winning success; who are not afraid to stand for the truth even when it's unpopular; who say 'No' with emphasis, even though the rest of the world says, 'Yes.'" Try weighing yourself on *those* scales!

KEEP GIVING WHAT YOU'VE GOT

Whoever sows generously will also reap generously.
2 Corinthians 9:6 NIV

Dr. William DeVries, the surgeon who pioneered the artificial heart, is the kind of doctor who shows up at the hospital on *Sunday* just to cheer up discouraged patients. He even changes dressings, and if a patient wants him to stick around and talk, he always does. His friends say he's "an old shoe" who fits in wherever he goes. He wears cowboy boots with his surgical scrubs and repairs hearts to the music of Vivaldi. "He's always got a smile lurking," says friend Dr. Robert Goodin, "And he's always looking for a way to let it out." DeVries believes that "arriving" isn't a place where others serve you, but where you get to serve them.

Chuck Swindoll writes, "We occupy common space but we no longer have common interests. It's like we're on an elevator with rules like 'No talking or smiling or eye-contact allowed without written consent of the management.' We're losing touch with one another. The motivation to help, to encourage, yes to serve our fellow man, is waning. Yet it's *these* things that form the essentials of a happy fulfilled life."

That's what Jesus meant when He said, "But he that is greatest among you shall be your servant" (Mt 23:11). Everything God gives you is first a *gift* to enjoy, then a *seed* to sow. Got a good education? Leadership ability? More money than you need? You've got seeds – sow them! Read God's promises regarding generosity, then start giving to others what He's given to you. *That's* the way to find happiness!

LEARN TO CONFRONT

As iron sharpens iron, so one man sharpens another.
Proverbs 27:17 NIV

If you grew up in a family where confrontation left only wounds, you may have become "a tap-dancer." That's a pity because "iron sharpens iron," and there are definite times when you need to confront, such as:

(1) *When others stand to be hurt.* Paul writes, "When Peter came to Antioch, I opposed him to his face, because he was . . . wrong" (Gal 2:11 NIV). Listen again, "Before certain men came . . . [Peter] used to eat with the Gentiles. But when they arrived, he began to . . . separate himself [and] . . . The other Jews joined him in his hypocrisy . . . even Barnabas was led astray" (Gal 2:12-13 NIV).

(2) *When somebody is settling for less.* A woman bought a pair of dingy candlesticks at a yard sale for a dollar. Assuming they were made of pewter, she took them home, dusted them, and set them on her table. One day a friend who worked in antiques dropped by, "When are you going to clean those candlesticks?" she asked. "What do you mean?" the woman asked, "I just dusted them yesterday." "Dusted?" laughed her friend. "They need to be buffed and polished. They're silver!" So they got silver polish and clean cloths and went to work, until the dull charcoal veneer yielded a pair of gleaming silver candlesticks. *Confrontation* – the right kind – removes the tarnish that keeps us from shining as God intends us to.

Ask God to make you willing to confront, and when necessary, to be confronted. Your growth depends on it!

UNCONDITIONAL LOVE

When he was still a great way off,
his father saw him and had compassion.
Luke 15:20 NKJV

When Pastor Hamon Cross' unmarried daughter told him she was pregnant, he was stunned. He'd just written a book called *Sanctified Sex,* and traveled the nation preaching, "Just Say No!" Now he was spending his nights listening to his wife sobbing, and his days refereeing family feuds. He writes:

"I asked God, 'How do I model sensitivity and strength when my family's falling apart?' God replied, 'Will you quit loving your daughter . . . investing in her . . . forgiving her, as you've been forgiven?' My answer continues to be; 'No Lord, with your help we'll make it.'"

Dr. James Dobson says, "Raising children is like baking a cake – you don't realize you have a disaster on your hands until it's too late!" In Luke 15 there's a parable about a rebellious kid who left home, and a caring dad who left the light on for his return. What can you learn from him?

(1) He was a great role model for his kids. (2) He supported them financially and emotionally. (3) He gave them a heritage. (4) He guided them without forcing them to conform. (5) He gave them room to fail – and a place to return. (6) He met them more than halfway. (7) He forgave them.

It's not an indictment on you when your kids struggle, make bad choices, or challenge authority. What does reflect on you, however, is your *attitude* towards them. They may be "still a great way off," but they need to know that you care, and that you're waiting to welcome them back home.

TOTAL SURRENDER

You're not in the driver's seat; I am.
Matthew 16:24 TM

Total surrender comes at a price most of us don't want to pay, for it means (1) forsaking our own agenda; (2) relinquishing our desire to control either the method or the outcome; (3) giving up our need for approval. Jesus said, "If anyone would come after me, he must deny himself and take up his cross" (Mt 16:24 NIV). Crosses were made to *die* on, and the thing we must crucify daily is our ego. E.G.O. – Edging God Out!

A great preacher once had a conversation with God that went like this: God said, "I've seen *your* ministry, how would you like to see *Mine?*" "What do I have to do?" said the preacher. "Give me back My church," said God. "But Lord, it *is* Your church," he said. "No," replied God, "You decide when the service starts and when it ends. Worst of all, you control everything in between. You even call it 'my church.'" Immediately the preacher fell to his knees and prayed, "Lord, from this day on, it's not my church, but Yours. Not my ministry, but Yours. Show me what You can do, because my best falls miserably short of the mark."

The foolishness of independence – the desire to be significant on our own terms – is as old as Adam. We must all come to the place where we realize that we can't take one breath, think one thought, or accomplish one thing worth doing – without God! Listen, "Anyone who intends to come with me has to let me lead. You're not in the driver's seat; I am" (Mt 16:24 TM).

THE ANTIDOTE TO LONELINESS

It is not good that man should be alone.
Genesis 2:18 NKJV

Researchers who recently studied what makes us *"truly happy"* concluded that it isn't success, looks, money, or status. The clear winner is *relationships.* Imagine that? They agreed with God, "It is not good that man should be alone" (Ge 2:18 NKJV).

Yet in our world of advanced communications, it's *easier* than ever to be lonely. One man told his buddy, "What do you mean we don't communicate? Yesterday I faxed a reply to the recorded message you left on my answering machine!"

It seems like we'll do *anything* not to be alone, including hanging out with people we don't care for. Even knowing that somebody doesn't love us fails to stop us from sleeping with them. No wonder the death rate from sexually transmitted diseases is skyrocketing. Maybe it's not popular to talk about, but it's time to stop the hearse, arrest the devil, and say, "No! You're stealing our kids!"

What's the answer to loneliness? Get involved! Volunteer at a soup kitchen; if nothing else it'll make you thankful for what's on your own table. Work at a homeless shelter; you'll be amazed how good your *own* bed feels at night. People don't care how much you know until they know how much you care! Stop thinking of reasons why you *can't* do it and find one reason why you *can!*

Somebody once said, "I can't do everything but I can do something; so I'll *do* the something I can." Amazingly, by helping others up the mountain you get to the top too – and you're a lot less lonely!

USE YOUR GIFT

A man's gift maketh room for him.
Proverbs 18:16

What you're struggling with right now is part of your *preparation.* Get ready – what the enemy meant for evil, God's about to turn to good. (Ge 50:20). When God brought David to the palace, he was a wild, uncouth shepherd boy with sheep dung on his boots. But God said, "You're about to be promoted. I saw you kill that bear and that lion; I was watching when you didn't even realize it." Solomon said, "A man's gift maketh room for him." David's gift may only have been a rag and a rock, but it opened palace doors for him.

He also used his gift to kill Goliath. Any time you fight the enemy, use only what you're gifted in! Don't try wearing somebody else's armor; it won't fit. Even if what you've got to work with doesn't seem like much, if God's behind it, it'll be *more* than enough to do the job.

When God spoke to Moses, He asked him, "What is that in your hand?" (Ex 4:2 NKJV). He answered, "A rod." Imagine, a regular old walking stick! But God used it to part the Red Sea. Know what? God's already equipped *you* to do the job too. Just *recognize* what He's given you and start *using* it.

"But I'm not trained," you say. All God needs is a teachable spirit, a yielded heart, and somebody who'll pray, "Lord, if You'll make me able, I'm more than willing." Remember, when you give God what *you've* got, He'll give you what *He's* got, and that makes your odds unbeatable!

DON'T MISS YOUR CHANCE!

Now by chance a certain priest came down that road. And when he saw him, he passed by on the other side.
Luke 10:31 NKJV

In the story of the Good Samaritan three people were given a *chance* to help a dying man lying by the side of the road. Only one took it; the other two were too busy and missed it.

We tend to think that if God's going to use us, it'll only be after we've been to seminary, fasted, prayed, analyzed every angle, weighed the pros and cons, and gotten all our ducks in a row. No: opportunities are coming at you every day. The question is will you act on them or let them pass you by?

Listen, "And by *chance* a priest was going down on that road, and . . . he passed by . . . Likewise a Levite also . . . passed by on the other side" (Lk 10:31-32 NAS). Amazing! Both men were in a helping profession, yet neither stopped to help. Often we pray, "Lord give me a *chance* to minister," yet when He does, we miss it because either we're too preoccupied to hear His voice or we're looking for something "big" that'll impress others. The danger in "passing by" is that after a while you don't even *see* the need anymore!

When was the last time you stopped to visit a sick neighbor? (Do you even *know* of any?) Or listened to a hurting co-worker? Or just gave a hug to somebody who was lonely? Keep your heart open, you might get a *chance* today to "pour in oil and wine" and make a difference in somebody's life.

IT CAN BE DONE!

So we may boldly say: the Lord is my helper; I will not fear. What can man do to me?

Hebrews 13:6 NKJV

Cripple a man and you have a Sir Walter Scott. Lock him in prison and you have a John Bunyan, author of *Pilgrim's Progress.* Bury him in the snows of Valley Forge and you have a George Washington. Raise him in abject poverty and you have an Abraham Lincoln. Subject him to bitter religious prejudice and you have a Disraeli. Strike him down with infantile paralysis and you have a Franklin D. Roosevelt. Deafen him and you still have a genius composer called Beethoven. Color him black in a society filled with racial prejudice and you have a George Washing Carver or a Martin Luther King, Jr.

And if that doesn't challenge you, consider Benjamin Franklin; at twenty-five he founded America's first library. At thirty-one he started the country's first fire department. At thirty-six he designed a heating stove that's still in use today. At forty he became one of the first people to harness electricity. At forty-five, he founded the nation's first university. And at seventy-nine years of age he invented bifocals. Economist, philosopher, diplomat, inventor, educator, publisher, linguist (he spoke and wrote five languages), and he had exactly *two years* of formal schooling!

It's a safe bet that you've *already* got more sheer knowledge than he ever had when he was your age. To that fact add these promises: "The Lord is my helper" (Heb 13:6); "I can do all things through Christ who strengthens me" (Php 4:13 NKJV), *and you have absolutely no excuse for not trying!*

PARENT, DON'T STOP PRAYING!

I prayed for this child . . . Now I give him back . . .
He will belong to the Lord all his life.
1 Samuel 1:27-28 NCV

Every terrorist was once a child; so was every missionary. What made the difference? The influence of a parent!

Samuel the prophet led the nation of Israel for forty years; he guided King David in some of his most crucial decisions. But who was the dominant influence in his life? His mother! Listen to her prayer at his birth: "I prayed for this child, and the Lord answered my prayer . . . Now I give him back . . . He will belong to the Lord all his life" (1Sa 1:27-28 NCV).

Never underestimate the power that's released when a parent pleads with God on behalf of a child. Who knows how many prayers are being answered *right now* because of faithful parents who prayed ten or twenty years ago.

If this fast-paced society is taking you away from prayer time for your children – you're doing too much! Mom and dad, there's *nothing* more precious or more important than the time you spend interceding with God on their behalf.

It's not too late for the child who's brought you tears and grief. Jesus' mother had to watch her son being crucified; but she also had the joy of seeing Him raised again from the dead. You may go to your grave wondering if your prayers will ever be answered, but don't stop praying. Why? Two reasons: (1) God works according to His schedule – not ours! (2) When godly parents pray – things change!

WINNING THE LOST

[He] will have all men to be saved, and to come unto the knowledge of the truth.

1 Timothy 2:4

The problem isn't that the world's not spiritually hungry, it's that the church has a tremendous lack of "sold-out," unselfish Christians committed to the *salvation* and *discipleship* of the lost.

Too many of us have become preoccupied with our own financial and material well-being. Instead of asking God for the salvation of our loved ones, we ask Him for houses, cars, and vacations. We quote, "Faith is the substance of *things* hoped for" (Heb 11:1), but the *things* we have in mind are material and temporal possessions rather than the *eternal things* of that "better country" which the patriarchs of the Old Testament desired. (Heb 11:16).

We're supposed to seek the Kingdom of God first and foremost, and all these other things will be added to us. In fact, we don't even *have* to ask God for them, because they're automatically given to us as we put His Kingdom ahead of ours (Mt 6:33).

We must be willing to go into the greed-ridden highways of corporate society and the sin-ravaged byways of our inner cities, and *compel* people to come to the Lord. Jesus said, "The harvest truly is great, but the laborers are few: pray ye therefore the Lord of the harvest, that he would send forth laborers into his harvest" (Lk 10:2). Today tell somebody about Jesus. If you don't, they may die without ever knowing Him!

ARE YOU GIVING IT YOUR ALL?

The ultimate master you're serving is Christ.
Colossians 3:24 TM

After spending years in Rome working on life-sized sculptures, Michelangelo went to Florence, where a huge block of white Carrara marble had been obtained for a colossal statue. Within weeks he'd signed an agreement to complete a rendition of *David,* one of his most famous masterpieces.

Contract in hand, he started working with such passion that often he slept in his clothes, resenting the time it took to change them. He faultlessly examined and precisely measured the marble to see the best pose it could accommodate. He made hundreds of sketches of possible attitudes, and detailed drawings from models. He tested his ideas in wax on a small scale, and only when he was satisfied did he pick up his chisel and mallet.

He approached painting the ceiling of the Sistine Chapel in Rome with the same intensity. Lying at uncomfortable angles on hard boards breathing the suffocating air just under the vault, he suffered from inflamed eyes and skin irritation from the plaster dust. For the next four years he literally sweated in physical distress as he worked – *but look at what he produced!*

If you're not passionate about what you do, find something you *can* be passionate about! Don't just make money, make an impact! *Significance* should be your goal, not *survival.* Listen, "Don't just do the minimum that will get you by. Do your best . . . Keep in mind always that the ultimate master you're serving is Christ" (Col 3:24 TM).

WHAT WOULD JESUS DO?

Christ . . . is your example. Follow in His steps.
1 Peter 2:21 NLT

Do you complain when your friends let you down? Do you keep score of gift giving, initiating phone calls, or picking up the tab at the restaurant? Are there times when you feel that you *give* more than you *get?*

Jesus experienced these things – and more! His closest friends let Him down; they were unreliable and immature. They learned slowly, and always the hard way. One even betrayed Him. Yet He forgave them and loved them anyway. Listen, "Having loved his own . . . He loved them unto the end" (Jn 13:1). Jesus loved His friends, but not because they were worthy of love. His love *made* them worthy!

In *Knowing God,* J.I. Packer writes, "There is tremendous relief in knowing myself. There is great cause for humility in the thought that He sees all the twisted things about me that others don't see. Indeed He sees *more* corruption in me than that which I see in myself. Yet He *wants* me as His friend, and *desires* to be my friend, and has *given* His Son to die for me in order for me to realize this purpose."

So the next time a friend disappoints you, remember God's grace. Use His Son as your role model and ask yourself, *"What would Jesus do?"*

"JERICHO SYNDROME"

Jericho was tightly shut up . . .
no one went out and no one came in.
Joshua 6:1 NIV

The Bible says, "Jacob was *left* alone" (Ge 32:24). It doesn't say he wanted to be alone or that he enjoyed it; it says he was *left* that way. When it happens to you it can be devastating. And it can lead to *The Jericho Syndrome!* "What's that?" Listen, "Jericho was tightly shut up . . . no one went out and no one came in" (Jos 6:1 NIV). You're on emotional lock-down. You're afraid to reach out, or to let anybody in. You've built a wall so you can't be hurt again.

Look out; that wall can imprison you – and everybody else in your life. You can get married in Jericho, say the vows, wear the dress, exchange the rings, go on the honeymoon, and *still* have the walls up by thinking, "If he leaves I'm ready. I've got a bank account I didn't tell him about, and a game plan just in case this doesn't work out."

Jesus said that, "A man . . . is joined to his wife" (Mt 19:5 NLT). But how can you be *joined* if you can't be *reached* because of a wall of bitterness, fear and distrust? Paul writes, "Love always looks for the best" (See 1Co 13:4-8 AMP).

It's time for an exorcism! You've got to drive out the ghosts of yesterday if you're to have any hope of a real future together.

Stop rehearsing the past and give it to the Lord. He's the wall-toppling, communication-restoring, esteem-building, healer of broken hearts and relationships. He can help you to live and love again!

WHEN THE INNOCENT PERISH

We know in part.
1 Corinthians 13:9

God *doesn't* punish the innocent for the sins of the guilty. Listen, "The son will *not* share the guilt of the father, nor will the father share the guilt of the son" (Ez 18:20 NIV).

Leonard Pitts says, "In times of crisis, God has more spokespersons than *Amway.* Some claim to know His mind as surely as if they had read His diary. What you discover is that these people have created God in their *own* image. They interpret Him according to their biases and predispositions, attributing to Him their political party, motivations, hatreds, and even their timetable."

God's character never changes! On Mount Sinai He introduced Himself as "merciful and gracious, long-suffering, and abundant in goodness." If you're used to thinking about Him any other way, change the way you think! Jeremiah writes, "This I recall to mind and therefore I have hope: because of the Lord's great love we are not consumed, for his compassions never fail. They are new every morning; great is your faithfulness" (Lam 3:21-23 NIV).

When Billy Graham was asked by some family members of the Oklahoma City bombing victims, "Why'd God let this happen?" He humbly replied, "I don't know." Paul says, "We know in part" (1Co 13:9). Let's not act as though we know more than we do! God stamps some things "will explain later." One thing you *can* be sure of, God's too wise to make a mistake, and too good to do anything bad. So trust Him because He's worthy of it!

WHAT "ISSUES" ARE DRAINING YOU?

A certain woman . . . had an issue.
Mark 5:25

Are there *issues* you've struggled with so long that they've drained you? Do they whip out their resumes and remind you that you've *already* tried every solution and nothing has worked? Do they whisper, "I'm here to stay, get used to me?" Have you said, "By this particular date my marriage will be healed, my health will be restored, I'll be out of debt, the door will have opened," but it hasn't happened and you're discouraged.

What was this woman's answer? Listen, "Behold, a woman . . . with an issue . . . twelve years . . . said within herself . . . If I may but touch [him] . . . I shall be made whole" (Mt 9:20-21). She had three options, so do you. She could have said to herself: (1) "Nothing is going to change." (2) "Look at that crowd; I'll never get through to Him." (3) "I'll never be this close again!"

She chose the third option: "If I can only touch Jesus, I'll be set free." Tune out the naysayers, silence your doubts, speak words of faith to yourself, and move in His direction!

Listen, "He relieved the inwardly tormented. He cured the bodily ill. He fulfilled Isaiah's well known sermon, 'He *took* our infirmities and *carried* our diseases'" (Mt 8:17 NIV). Refuse to carry your issues one step further; bring them to the Lord. Your past doesn't matter to Him, nor do your present circumstances. The only thing that matters is *touching* Him by faith. What He said to her *then* He says to us *now,* "Your faith has made you well. Go in peace" (Mk 5:34 NAS).

LEARN TO GIVE YOURSELF CREDIT

A man has joy in an apt answer,
and how delightful is a timely word!
Proverbs 15:23 NAS

Rochelle Pennington writes, "One day I stopped at a Dairy Queen and sat down beside a family celebrating their son's basketball game. Since the aisles were narrow, I soon felt like part of the party. 'So, your team won?' I asked. The little fellow smiled, 'No, we lost 24 to 2.' 'Well, you must have made the only basket then,' I said. 'No, I missed all 8 shots, but 3 of them did hit the rim.' I was confused. They were celebrating because his team lost and he missed 8 baskets. I had absolutely no clue.

"After another mouthful of cake, and still grinning from ear to ear, he added, 'We're having a party because last week I missed 9 shots, and none of them came anywhere near the rim. Dad says that all my practicing this week really paid off. I'm making progress.'" Wow! With a dad like that he'll probably grow up to be an NBA superstar!

Where did this boy learn the self-talk of a winner? From a dad who taught him to focus on his achievements, work on his weak areas, and treat every square inch of progress as a major milestone.

If you grew up in a family where blame came quickly and credit never came at all, you'll have to change your belief system and learn a new self-talk, one that builds you up rather than tears you down. Why's this important? Because if you don't learn to encourage yourself, you'll never be able to encourage anybody else.

WORK ON YOUR RELATIONSHIP

No matter what I say . . . and what I do,
I'm bankrupt without love.
1 Corinthians 13:3 TM

By the time Ted and Bessie celebrated their 50th anniversary, Ted's hearing was almost gone. When all the guests left Bessie looked at him and said, "I'm *proud* of you Ted." Confused and upset he looked back at her and said, "Well, Bessie, I'm *tired* of you too!" If you don't want to get *tired* of each other, keep doing these four things.

(1) *Take responsibility for your own happiness.* By blaming others you never have to face yourself or change your own behavior. That's a cop-out! Relationships aren't dumping grounds. Happiness is an "inside job," that comes from healthy self-esteem and a growing relationship with God.

(2) *Be a friend.* Ever notice how easily you accept your friends just as they are, yet have trouble doing the same thing with your loved ones? Look out; familiarity breeds contempt. Don't they deserve the same respect, loyalty, tolerance, and appreciation?

(3) *Share your dreams.* Doing this will enrich your relationship and take it to a new level. You always need something to plan for and work toward together. What's your next goal?

(4) *Have courage.* Dr. Theodore Rubin says, "The problem isn't that there are problems, it's expecting otherwise. It's thinking that *having* problems *is* the problem!" There are no perfect situations. You need courage to face whatever comes. Realize that whatever you can't solve together you can probably outlive!

Outside of your relationship with God, there's no greater joy than having a good relationship with the one you love, so work on yours today!

PRAY FOR THOSE IN AUTHORITY

Pray especially for rulers and their governments.
1 Timothy 2:1

When Pastor Joe Wright opened the Kansas State Senate in prayer, instead of the typical generalities this is what they heard:

"Father . . . Your Word says, 'Woe to those who call evil good,' but that's what we've done. We've lost our spiritual equilibrium and reversed our values. We've ridiculed the absolute truth of Your Word and called it pluralism; exploited the poor and called it the lottery; rewarded laziness and called it welfare; killed our unborn and called it choice; shot abortionists and called it justifiable; neglected to discipline our children and called it building self-esteem; abused power and called it politics; coveted our neighbor's possessions and called it ambition; polluted the air with profanity and pornography and called it freedom of expression; ridiculed the time-honored values of our forefathers and called it enlightenment. Search us oh God and know our hearts. Cleanse us and set us free."

Some people walked out in angry protest, but within six weeks the church Joe Wright pastors had received 5,000 calls (only forty-seven negative!) applauding him. Solomon says, "By the blessing of *the upright* the city is exalted" (Pr 11:11). Isaiah says: "In *righteousness* shalt thou be established . . . oppression . . . fear . . . and terror . . . shall not come near thee" (Isa 54:14). Jesus said we are "the salt of the earth" (Mt 5:13). Salt irritates, cleanses, and then heals. We're supposed to use our *influence* to get *involved!* Listen, "To him that knoweth to do good, and doeth it not . . . it is sin (Jas 4:17). Today become part of the solution. Instead of complaining – *pray* for those in authority!

"DO AS YOU PROMISED!"

Do as You promised . . . that your name will be great forever.
1 Chronicles 17:23-24 NIV

When you know God well enough to pray, "Do as you promised," things begin to happen. Jesus said, "Whatever you ask for in prayer, believe that you have received it, and it will be yours" (Mk 11:24 NIV).

Faith isn't "psyching" yourself up. Actually it's only as good as the object in which you place it. Faith in a broken bridge won't get you across the river – but faith in the God who says, "I am watching to see that my word is fulfilled," will! (See Jer 1:12 NIV).

Reminding God of His promise is like presenting a check issued to you from His account and endorsed with His signature. Whose account? *God's!* Whose signature? *God's!* Paul says, "He *always* does exactly what he says. He carries out and fulfills all of *God's* promises, no matter how many of them there are" (2Co 1:19-20 TLB).

We make promises we can't keep and people get hurt. But He's never broken one of His yet! So why don't we see more of them fulfilled? *Because they're conditional!* Follow His instructions and you'll always get what He promised. That's because: (1) His *truth* won't allow Him to deceive you. (2) His *integrity* won't allow Him to go back on His word to you. (3) His *grace* won't allow Him to forget you.

Today begin praying, "Lord, do as you promised" and watch what happens! (PS: That means reading your Bible so you *know* what He's promised!)

LEARN TO LET GO!

Casting all your care upon Him; for He careth for you.
1 Peter 5:7

"Casting *all* your care upon Him" includes "casting" those you care for deeply but don't know how to help. Got somebody like that in your life? Listen:

"Letting go" doesn't mean you've stopped caring, it just means you can't do it for them. To let go is not to cut them off but to realize you can't control them. To let go is not to enable, but to allow them to learn from their consequences. To let go is to admit powerlessness, which means the outcome isn't in your hands – it never was! To let go is not to try to change or blame somebody else but to make the most of *yourself.* To let go is not just to care *for* but to care *about;* not to fix but to be supportive; not to be in the middle arranging all the outcomes, but to allow others to affect their own destinies; not to be protective but to permit them to face reality; not to deny but to accept; not to nag, scold, or argue, but to search out your *own* shortcomings and work on them; not to adjust everything to your desires but to take each day as it comes and cherish yourself in it; not to criticize or regulate others but to try and become what you dream you can be; not to regret the past but to grow and live in the present. *The truth is, to let go is to fear less, trust God, and love more.*

DEALING WITH DEPRESSION

Anxiety in the heart of man causes depression.
Proverbs 12:25 NKJV

Long-term depression drains your energy, distorts your reality, assaults your faith, and affects everybody around you. One in five of us suffers from it. It's responsible for more workplace absenteeism than diabetes and heart disease. Poor health, stress, fear, loneliness, guilt, and anger can all cause it; so can your surroundings. And it's no modern-day phenomenon; it affected Bible characters too:

(1) David experienced it because of unconfessed sin. Listen, "I am . . . severely broken . . . my strength fails . . . my loved ones . . . stand . . . afar off" (Ps 38:8-11 NKJV).

(2) Job got so depressed about his financial, personal, and family losses that he cursed the day he was born. (Job 3:3).

(3) When Jezebel threatened Elijah, he went through the "H.A.L.T." syndrome. He was **H**ungry; he stopped eating. **A**ngry; he got mad with God and the world. **L**onely; he left his servant and went off by himself. **T**ired; he collapsed. But God had a prescription. He: (a) changed his diet; (b) told him to rest; (c) let him know he wasn't alone; (d) sent an angel to minister to him. And those are *still* the steps out of depression!

David said, "The Lord . . . brought me up out of a horrible pit" (Ps 40:2 NKJV), and He can bring you out of your depression too! Don't isolate yourself, and don't be ashamed to get help from your pastor, a trusted friend, or a good counselor. And remember, addictive behavior and destructive relationships will only make things *worse.* The moment Elijah heard God's voice he began to "get it together." With *God's* help you will too!

BELIEVE IT AND DECLARE IT!

It is with your heart that you believe . . . it is with your mouth that you confess.
Romans 10:10 NIV

Here's a timeless principle you need to apply to your life each day: *conviction + confession = results!* When somebody asks, "How can you possibly justify believing such a thing?" Your answer should be, "Because I agree with the God who promised it." Conviction without confession is like faith without works – it's dead. And confession without conviction is just empty words. But put the two together and things begin to happen!

Many of us hide our convictions because we're afraid of being criticized. It's when you "put it out there" that the battle really begins. That's because the enemy *knows* that when your mouth speaks what your heart believes, mountains are moved, giants are toppled, and circumstances are changed. You don't have to have a penny in your pocket, a friend on the phone, or a contact in high places, for God to move on your behalf. Here's the formula:

(1) *Take ownership of God's promises.* Believe in your heart that they're yours. (2) *Work on your faith.* Practice "faith-training" in small areas before you attempt to conquer big ones. (3) *Resistance is good* because it requires divine assistance. (4) *Persevere through the trial;* it's building spiritual muscle and training you for greater things.

Operating daily in these principles will take you to new heights. No matter what your enemies or your senses tell you, *believe* and *declare* what God has said – and He'll do it!

DO YOU CARE?

If anyone . . . sees his brother in need, but has no pity . . .
How can the love of God be in him?
1 John 3:16-17 NIV

Gordon MacDonald writes, "Years ago I flew to Minneapolis to speak. When my taxi stopped I noticed a homeless man lurching between the cars. When he got close to us he fell. I heard the thud. His chin split open and there was blood everywhere.

"As I got out and looked these thoughts went through my head: (a) I'm wearing a brand new suit. I can't afford to get it messed up. (b) I've got to speak at a conference in fifteen minutes. (c) I'm in a strange city; I don't know what to do. But underneath was another thought – if you're dumb enough to get drunk why should I stop and help you?

"I'm ashamed of this. I can't believe a Bible-believing Christian could find those thoughts in the filing cabinets of his soul. Before I could come to better senses, other people came rushing to his help and I was able to go on to the conference – *to speak about sensitivity and caring for the needs of other human beings!"*

Before Nehemiah rebuilt the walls of Jerusalem, he first wept over the ruins. Alan Redpath writes, "You never lighten the load for others until you've first felt the pressure in your own soul."

Want to be more like Jesus? Listen, "When He saw the crowds, He had compassion on them, because they were harassed and helpless, like sheep without a shepherd" (Mt 9:36 NIV). How do *you* look at hurting people? Do you care?

STORMS

Be of good cheer: it is I; be not afraid.

Mark 6:50

Do you feel like you're in a storm today? Afraid you're not gonna make it? If so, listen to these words: "And when even was come, the ship was in the midst of the sea, and he was alone on the land. And he saw them toiling in rowing; for the wind was contrary unto them: and about the fourth watch of the night [the darkest hour] he cometh unto them, walking upon the sea . . . and saith unto them, 'Be of good cheer, it is I; be not afraid . . .' and the wind ceased" (Mk 6:47-51).

So what are the lessons here for *you?* (1) When educators teach us they do it with charts and chalkboards. When Jesus teaches us He uses storms and adversities. It's during those waiting periods when we feel so separated from Him that He's actually teaching us the most. (2) He doesn't show up early. Usually He comes in the worst part of the storm – just in the nick of time when you think you can't take any more. (3) He takes you through *different* storms, revealing Himself to you in each one. Without storms there are divine strategies and aspects of His character you'd never truly understand. (4) His presence alone should be enough for you in any storm. The moment He shows up and says, "It is I," your every fear should be calmed.

Be of good courage! The same Jesus who came to His disciples that night is with you now. Because of that you'll make it safely through – and that's a guarantee!

YOU CAN BECOME A LEADER

I have grown and increased in wisdom.
Ecclesiastes 1:16 NIV

During a sales meeting a manager was berating his staff for their dismal sales figures. "If you can't do the job there are others out there just waiting to take your place," he said. Pointing to a newly-recruited ex pro-football player, he said, "Ask him. If a team isn't winning they replace the players, right?" "No," he replied, "If the team's having trouble they replace the coach!"

But there's good news. Leadership isn't something you're born with; the raw materials can be acquired. Link them with the desire to succeed, and *nothing* can keep you from becoming an effective leader.

Think you're called to lead? Leaders are big-picture thinkers. They: (1) see beyond the immediate crisis; (2) place emphasis on vision, values, and motivation; (3) refuse to accept the status quo; (4) develop the skills to cope with conflicting requirements; (5) manage others well by first learning to manage *themselves.*

Sandhill Cranes fly great distances across continents, and they have three remarkable qualities: (a) they rotate leadership so that no bird stays out in front all the time; (b) they choose leaders who can handle turbulence; (c) when one bird leads all the rest honk their support. Learn enough about leadership so that when God calls *you* you're ready to take your place at the head of the flock.

In every age there comes a moment when new leaders must step forward to meet the needs of the hour. So be encouraged, your time will come!

THE CRUCIFIED LIFE

I am crucified with Christ.
Galatians 2:20

"I am crucified with Christ." Those words are about as appealing to your carnal nature as a root canal! Yet His kingdom can only grow within us as ours shrinks. "Crucified" – in what areas of your life are you hearing the hammering of nails? Those are the unsurrendered areas, right? And probably the ones that give you the most trouble too.

Listen to Paul: "Among those who belong to Christ, everything with getting our own way and mindlessly responding to what everyone else calls necessities, is killed off for good – crucified. Since this is the kind of life we have chosen, the life of the Spirit, let us make sure that we do not just hold it as an idea in our heads or a sentiment in our hearts, but work out its implications in *every* detail of our lives" (Gal 5:24-25 TM).

What does it mean to be "crucified with Christ?" In *Tell Me Again, Lord, I Forget,* Ruth Calkin writes: "At first, Lord, I asked you to take sides with me. With the Psalmist I prayed, 'The Lord is for me . . . maintain my rights, O Lord.' But with all my pleading I lay drenched in darkness, until in utter confusion I cried, 'Don't take sides, Lord, just take over,' and suddenly it was morning."

One day Martin Luther answered a knock at his door. "Does Martin Luther live here?" the man asked. "No," Luther answered, "He died. Christ lives here now." To be "crucified" simply means to slide out from behind the steering wheel and allow Jesus to drive.

HALLMARKS OF A GREAT DAD

The glory of children is their father.
Proverbs 17:6 NKJV

Boswell the famous biographer tells of a day when his dad took him fishing. Later when he read what his father had written in his journal that day, he found only one sentence: *"Today went fishing with my son; a day wasted!"* Boswell was devastated! Solomon says, "The glory of children is their father" (Pr 17:6 NKJV), and here are six hallmarks of a great one:

(1) *He protects:* He guards his children *physically* when they're young, and *emotionally* as they mature. He teaches his sons to respect girls, and interviews the guys who date his daughter. (2) *He listens:* Unlike the kid who told his mom, "I'm gonna be just like Dad when I grow up. My eyebrows are already growing together, and when people talk to me I don't listen!" Listening builds a lifelong bridge to your child's heart. (3) *He's affectionate:* Nothing communicates security and worth to your kids like holding them. If you grew up without it, make sure they don't. (4) *He disciplines:* He doesn't just discipline, he models self-discipline. (5) *He's fun:* He's not so preoccupied that he's a drag to be around. Remember, "A merry heart makes a cheerful countenance" (Pr 15:13), so don't be afraid to show your kids your lighter side! (6) *He "walks the walk:"* Converted atheist, Lee Strobel, says, "When I became a Christian my five-year-old daughter said, 'Mommy I want God to do for me what he's done for Daddy,' and she gave her life to Jesus." When you walk the walk before your kids it changes everything.

THE GENERATIONAL SLIDE

As for me and my household, we will serve the Lord.
Joshua 24:15 NIV

Approaching the end of his life, Joshua called the nation's leaders together and said: "You yourselves have seen everything the Lord your God has done" (Jos 23:3 NIV). Then he threw down the gauntlet; "Choose . . . whom you will serve" (Jos 24:15 NIV). What did they do? "Israel served the Lord throughout the lifetime of Joshua" (Jos 24:31 NIV). So far so good!

But take a closer look. They served Him *partly,* and only when it was to their *advantage.* The one military action remaining to be taken after Joshua's death was to clean out the last pockets of pagan worship. But Israel "did not drive out the inhabitants" (Jdg 1:27).

While Joshua had been *fully* committed to God, the elders were only *partly* committed. And the result? Their sons and daughters began to intermarry with their neighbors and to adopt foreign lifestyles. Listen, "Another generation arose after them who did not know the Lord . . . they provoked the Lord to anger . . . They did not cease from their own doings nor from their stubborn way" (Jdg 2:10-12;19 NKJV).

And what had *shaped* their spiritual values? The compromise of their parents! This is called *the generational slide.* It helps us understand how our parents impacted us, and predicts how our commitments – or lack of them – will ultimately shape our children.

Parents, you get the first crack at it! Give your children deep spiritual roots as early as possible. That way if they rebel later they'll still have memories and *values* to return to. Don't just *tell* them about God, *model* a godly lifestyle before them everyday.

STOP WORRYING SO MUCH

Trust in the Lord . . . lean not on your own understanding.
Proverbs 3:5 NIV

A friend who'd undergone surgery was confined to crutches for a few months. What a challenge! Sometimes you'd find him panting at the top of the stairs; when you looked at his hands they were often red and sore. You see leaning on crutches can be exhausting – and so can leaning on your own understanding!

If you want to have a really bad day – exclude God! Try working things out using your *own* best judgment. Chase down every possibility. When you hit a dead-end back out and turn down another one. When that gets you nowhere, try a little manipulation and then some panic. Now look back and see where you've been!

Know what? Some of us have a quiet, hidden love for worry. When one worry's gone we immediately replace it with another. There's always a line of them at the backdoor waiting to get in; we actually enjoy entertaining them. They've become our mental and emotional companions. But Jesus says they're a waste of time. Why? Because worry preoccupies your mind and keeps you from *enjoying what you have* (See Mt 6:25).

Paul writes, "(a) Do not worry about anything; (b) pray and ask God for everything you need; (c) always giving thanks . . . (d) God's peace will keep your hearts and minds" (Php 4:6-7 NCV). Worry is assuming responsibilities you can't handle. And the truth is God never *intended* you to handle them – because they're *His.* So give them to Him today!

WHO'S COVERING YOUR BACK?

Point your spear toward Ai, for I will give you the city.
Joshua 8:18 TLB

God said to Joshua, "Point your spear toward Ai, for I will give you the city." (Jos 8:18 TLB). *It's amazing how bold you become when your back's covered!* When God's behind you, "No weapon forged against you will prevail" (Isa 54:17 NIV). Remember as a child how secure you felt in a fight, knowing your big brother or sister was behind you?

But the problem is we say all sorts of things without first checking to find out if *God's* behind us. When Satan says, "Jesus I know and Paul I know, but who are you?" (Acts 19:15 AMP), you'd better be sure of two things. (1) Your relationship with God. (2) That it's *His* fight as well as yours!

Jesus said, "Whatever you bind on earth will be bound in heaven, and whatever you loose on earth will be loosed in heaven" (Mt 18:18 NIV). There must be agreement between both realms. Jesus taught His disciples to pray "Your will be done on earth as it is in heaven" (Mt 6:10 NIV), because if it's not happening where *He* is, it won't be happening where *you* are either!

As "laborers together with God," we need to fight only what He fights. You don't want to move anything He doesn't want moved or raise anybody from the dead except the Lazarus He calls forth. You want to do on *earth* only what He's already declared to be His will in *heaven.* That way you *know* your back's covered!

FIND A PRAYER PARTNER

Peter was kept in prison, but the church was earnestly praying.
Acts 12:5 NIV

Sometimes it's hard to pray for yourself. That's when you need *somebody else* to agree with you in prayer. Not somebody who'll judge your situation or pray for the world at large, but somebody who knows how to intercede with God for *your* finances, *your* children, *your* marriage.

James had just been executed and Herod was planning to kill Peter the next morning. You'd think he'd have been up all night praying like crazy, but he wasn't. "Peter was sleeping" (Acts 12:6). Wow! Where do you get *that* kind of faith? Listen, "The church was earnestly praying to God for him" (Acts 12:5 NIV).

Anytime you can sleep in the face of death, or you experience an unnatural grace in the midst of chaos, it's usually because of two things: (1) You've learned how to hand the situation over to God, or (2) somebody else is praying for you.

The church didn't pray, "Lord, if Peter was really a man of God he wouldn't be in this mess," or "Now that he's in jail who's going to preach for us next Sunday?" No, while they prayed for a breakthrough, God was at work on the other side of the city dispatching an angel to set Peter free. That's how it works!

Feel like your prayers aren't getting the job done? Find somebody who'll agree with you in prayer, for Jesus said, "If two of you . . . agree about anything . . . it will be done for you by my Father in heaven" (Mt 18:19 NIV).

PRAYING BUT NOT EXPECTING!

Because of her gladness she did not open the [door].
Acts 12:14 NKJV

After the church prayed all night for Peter's release from prison, he suddenly showed up at their door. When Rhoda told them, "It's Peter," they replied, "You're out of your mind." Listen, "Peter kept on knocking, and when they opened the door . . . they were astonished" (Acts 12:16 NIV). There are three important lessons here for you:

(1) *Don't just ask; expect!* God will astonish you by (a) His timing: "Before they call, I will answer" (Isa 65:24); and (b) His methods: "The Lord sent his angel and rescued me" (Acts 12:11 NIV). Stop limiting God!

(2) *Be alert; you might miss it.* They were all praying, but only Rhoda responded to Peter knocking at the door. And when you've got her spirit you'll respond too: (a) You'll get a divine "intuition" that something's about to happen. (b) You'll begin looking for the answers while others are locked into a posture of praying but not really expecting anything to happen. (c) You'll recognize the answer when others don't. (d) You'll be willing to leave the crowd in order to respond to God.

(3) *Open the door.* Listen, "Because of her gladness, she did not open the [door]" (Acts 12:14). How often have you come home from church, moved but not changed? You can grow old in a pew, believing but not experiencing; rejoicing yet never receiving what God's got for you. The word for you today is: (1) don't just ask, expect; (2) be spiritually alert; (3) open the door.

YOU'RE NEVER TOO OLD TO CHANGE!

Fix your attention on God.
You'll be changed from the inside out.
Romans 12:1 TM

Chuck Swindoll says, "You're over the hill when: (a) the stewardess offers you coffee, tea, or Milk of Magnesia. (b) You sink your teeth into a juicy steak – and they stay there! (c) There's more hair stuck in the drain than on your head. (d) You still have everything you once had – except now it's all four inches lower." And let's add, when you're no longer willing to change. You see when you're through changing – you're through!

Alfred Nobel was a Swedish chemist who made his fortune by inventing dynamite and other explosives used for weapons. When his brother died, a newspaper accidentally printed Alfred's obituary instead. It described him as man who had become rich by enabling people to kill each other in unprecedented numbers. Deeply shaken, he resolved to use his fortune to reward accomplishments that benefited humanity, hence the *Nobel Prize.* Nobel had a rare opportunity to reevaluate his life toward the end and still live long enough to do something about it.

Comedian Jerry Lewis joked that his best wedding gift was a film of the entire marriage ceremony. He said that when things got really bad at home, he'd go into a room, close the door, run the film backwards, and walk out a free man! Now I doubt you'll be able to do that, or read your own obituary in the newspaper, but you can make a choice to change, and when that change is successful you'll look back and call it *growth.*

REACH OUT AND TOUCH SOMEBODY

We . . . were all made to share.
1 Corinthians 12:13 NCV

When you're afraid to ask for help in case somebody questions your experience with God, it's easy to fall by the wayside and get run over without anybody ever noticing. Refuse to live that way! Not reaching out to your brothers and sisters in Christ can: (1) keep you vulnerable to attack; (2) cut you off from your supply lines. Paul says, we "were all made to share" (1Co 12:12-13 NCV).

In wartime enemies would lock their prisoners in "the hole" for long periods, and without actually *physically* abusing them, the darkness and isolation would break them down. Sometimes the church can feel like a dark, isolated place; especially when you're hurting and you don't feel like you can reach out for help. It's filled with the greatest actors and actresses of our time; in fact, if Hollywood needed extras they'd find them in the pews!

God said, "It is not good that man should be alone." Why? Because we're *communal* by nature; we need to feel "connected." This applies not only to marriage and family, but to other close relationships as well. We need people to talk, laugh, and interact with. When that doesn't happen *we're* not strengthened by receiving, and *others* aren't blessed by giving.

A note of caution, however. Never hold others in such high esteem that your fellowship becomes idolatry. Never worship at the altar of their opinions in order to stay in their good graces. Never be intimidated into being anyone other than the person God made you. Having said that, *reach out; the help you need is available today.*

BLESSED IN SPITE OF FAMINE

I went out full, and the Lord has brought me home again empty.
Ruth 1:21

For the next few days let's take a look at the *Book of Ruth.* When famine came to Bethlehem, Naomi, her husband, and two sons moved to Moab. What they hoped would be a short stay turned into ten years. Their sons married two local girls, Ruth and Orpah. Then the unthinkable happened – Naomi's husband and sons died. Now she was bitter; everything she'd ever loved was gone. When she heard that the famine in Bethlehem was ending, she decided to go back home.

But what did she mean, "I went out full, and the Lord has brought me home again empty?" Hadn't she originally left a land of famine for a land of plenty? She was saying that despite the famine at home, she'd had her husband and sons there, but in Moab, "the land of plenty," she'd lost them.

The important lesson here is that you can be blessed and not realize it. Only later as you look back do you discover that what you *had* was more important than all the things you *didn't* have. You never miss the water till the well runs dry! When Naomi lost what she loved most, even a *famine* seemed insignificant by comparison.

Happiness doesn't come from getting what you *don't* have; it comes from appreciating what you *do* have! Next time you're tempted to whine and complain about trivialities, ask yourself, "What would I take in exchange for what I *have?"* Then count your blessings and begin thanking God!

PARTNERS IN PAIN

And the woman was left . . . with her daughters-in-law.
Ruth 1:5-6

When their husbands died Naomi, Ruth, and Orpah became partners in pain. Unless you've been there you can't relate. It's a fellowship that transcends age, race, background, and status; it brings the oddest people together.

When you're hurting, don't look for validation from those who haven't walked in your shoes. People can't give you what they don't have. Often the best they have to offer is the kind of optimism that's glib and quickly becomes annoying.

Until you can start to make sense of your pain and see the greater good in it, you'll feel like a victim. But once you see God's *grace* at work and His *purpose* in it all, you can begin to move ahead . . . to marry . . . to have another baby . . . to get another job . . . to dream another dream . . . to live again.

Spurgeon wrote: "Just as old soldiers compare stories and scars, when we arrive at our heavenly home, we'll tell of the faithfulness of God who brought us through. I wouldn't like to be pointed out as the only one who never experienced sorrow, or feel like a stranger in the midst of that sacred fellowship. Therefore, be content to share in the battle, for soon we will wear the crown."

When it feels like all hell has broken loose in your life, remember Satan hasn't snatched the steering wheel from God. No, God's got it all worked out. Victory is born out of struggle. Be encouraged! God often accomplishes *more* through our pain than He does through our successes. So hold on to His unchanging hand!

WHEN THE CLOCK'S AGAINST YOU

He shall be . . . a restorer of thy life,
and a nourisher of thine old age.
Ruth 4:15

What do you do when you've got the *wisdom* but not the *time* to do it all again? Your window of opportunity seems closed. You've still got the desire, but when you look in the mirror the wrinkles and sags confirm that the clock's against you.

Listen to Naomi, "Go your way; for I am too old" (Ru 1:12). She was saying, "Don't hang around waiting for me, my life's over!" When you feel like you've run out of time, you can get bitter and start pushing people away, especially when it seems like they're asking for what you can no longer give.

Good news! Just when you think God's forgotten you and your "sell by" date has expired, He can re-commission you. He's the God of second chances. With Him you're *never* too old!

Listen: "Boaz took Ruth, and . . . she bare a son. And the women said unto Naomi [Ruth's mother-in-law], *Blessed be the Lord, which hath not left thee . . . this day without a kin's man, he shall be . . . a restorer of thy life, and a nourisher of thine old age. And Naomi took the child . . . in her bosom, and became nurse unto it"* (Ru 4:13-16).

Biologically it was impossible for Naomi to nurse a baby! *But when God wants to give you something, even if it breaks every rule in the book . . . He'll do it.* It's not over until *God* says it's over! He can do things in your life that you've never seen happen before and can't even begin to explain. So trust Him!

THE "GIFT OF GOODBYE"

Orpah kissed her mother-in-law good-bye, and returned to her childhood home.

Ruth 1:14 LB

Certain people will leave your life, and when they do – let them go! Don't try to talk them into staying. *Your destiny is seldom tied to those who walk away!* The Bible says, "They went out from us, but they did not really belong to us" (1Jn 2:19 NIV). When people don't belong in your life anymore, even a bucket of Super Glue won't make them stay!

Orpah's leaving didn't make her a bad person; it just meant her part in the story was over. Recognize when somebody's part in *your* story is over as well, otherwise you'll keep trying to raise the dead. David pleaded with God for his baby's life. He "fasted . . . spent the nights lying on the ground . . . and he would not eat" (2Sa 12:16-17 NIV). But when the child died, he had to accept that there was nothing more he could do, so he "got up . . . washed . . . changed his clothes . . . and he ate" (2Sa 12:20-21 NIV).

Know when something's over! If God means for you to have it He'll give it to you. When you've tried to make it work and it hasn't, accept His will in the matter. Get up. Go to the mall. Buy yourself a new outfit. Treat yourself to a good meal. Start living again.

Never beg anyone to stay with you against their will. Their leaving is no accident; the "gift of goodbye" is a scriptural one. It means God's got something *better* in store for you (and possibly for them too). So keep trusting Him until it comes to pass!

IT'S ALL PART OF THE PLAN

I want to go wherever you go . . .
Ruth 1:16 TLB

Ruth sensed that her destiny was tied to Naomi, so she said, "I want to go wherever you go . . . live wherever you live . . . die where you die" (Ru 1:16-17 TLB).

You can spend your life anywhere with anybody doing anything, then suddenly get involved with another person or project and sense that your destiny is tied to them. Without *them* your story will be incomplete.

It's what made Elisha leave home and run after Elijah, his spiritual father, to wash his clothes and set up his tent. It's what made Timothy hang out with an old man preparing to be executed. As he passed books and blankets through the prison window, Timothy was saying, "There's something about you that touches me. I won't reach my potential without you in my life."

Charles West said, "We turn to God for help when our foundations are shaking only to learn that it is *God* who is shaking them." Circumstances happen like they do for a reason. Remember, "The steps [and the stops] of a good man are ordered by the Lord" (Ps 37:23). Think: if you hadn't met that *person,* or taken that *phone call,* or received that *letter,* you wouldn't be where you are today. Right?

God's always been behind the scenes orchestrating things. You're not where you are today simply because you're gifted, or smart, or holy. No, you're there because God wound you up, pointed you in the right direction, and released you to fulfill your destiny! It's all part of His plan.

"STUMBLING" INTO BLESSINGS

As it happened, the field where she found herself belonged to Boaz.
Ruth 2:3 TLB

Although Ruth started out for one destination she stumbled into another. Her plan was to pick leftover grain when she happened to "light on a part of the field" (Ru 2:3) belonging to Boaz, and it changed her life. When Boaz called her name, she came from the background to a place of blessing in the foreground. That's how *quickly* it can happen!

Ruth's life had been spiraling downward; her husband and sons had died, she'd left her old home, and she hadn't quite been accepted in her new one. She was in survival mode, making the best of a bad deal by gleaning just enough to stay alive. Then God turned things around! The reapers began deliberately dropping handfuls of wheat in her path, and she started picking up undeserved blessings. Did you know that God can leave you "a bread crumb trail?" After struggling so long just to get by, He'll begin to drop blessings into your path. All you have to do is keep following.

Even though the odds might seem stacked against you today, don't let Satan push you back. You've been through too much to be intimidated by him. You're about to come into a blessing that'll change your life. "Along unfamiliar paths I will guide them; I will turn the darkness into light before them" (Isa 42:16 NIV). God can let you "stumble" into good things by being in the right place at the right time or meeting the right person with the right answer. He has a way of "tripping" us into blessing.

BLESSED FOR A REASON!

Drop them on purpose for her to glean.
Ruth 2:16 LB

When Boaz saw Ruth in his field he told his workers, "Snap off some heads of barley and drop them on purpose for her to glean" (Ru 2:16 TLB). Even though he spoke *about* her and not directly *to* her, she still received the blessing. *You don't know what God has spoken over your life, but suddenly everything changes!*

God told His people, "I'm giving you vineyards you didn't plant" (see Dt 6:11 TLB). He can take the sweat out of your success by putting you in situations where others do the work and you receive the benefits. You don't have to worry or get jealous about somebody else getting what's yours, because nobody can glean it except *you.* All you have to do is keep following God.

Why would God do that? *Because there's a direct correlation between His blessings and His purposes!* He doesn't bless you so that you can brag! Whether His blessings come in the form of increased finances, improved health, or greater influence, God's gifts are just *tools* to maneuver you to where you can fulfill His purpose.

The enemy isn't just after your provision, he's after your purpose! After all what good is success if you've wandered away from your God-ordained assignment? When God gives you something He puts you on assignment to use it for His glory. So remember, when you pick up your provision, read the instructions that go with it. Only then will you find fulfillment!

DON'T FORGET THE LORD

When you have eaten and are satisfied . . .
do not forget the Lord.
Deuteronomy 8:10-11 NIV

Can you imagine how Ruth felt coming out of famine and suddenly having grain dropped right in front of her? She didn't deserve it, earn it, or even understand it.

When you're not used to being blessed, it's heady stuff! That's why God says, "Remember the Lord thy God, for it is He who giveth thee power to [succeed]" (See Dt 8:18 KJV). *He's* the One who enables you to do what others find difficult or impossible. Others are taking classes to do what you do naturally! Why? Because God's blessed you with ability!

And people may actually resent you for it. That's because they don't understand where you came from to get where you are. They don't know that when you were discouraged and hopeless, God told you to look ahead because "The sufferings of this present time are not worthy to be compared with the glory which shall be revealed in us" (Ro 8:18). God had something in mind for you *greater* than anything you could imagine, and He's fulfilling it, isn't He?

But be careful! This is where many of us make a mistake. We praise God in the hard times, but as soon as we get on our feet we become self-sufficient and arrogant. Listen to what God told His people: "When you have eaten and are satisfied . . . be careful that you do not forget the Lord your God" (Dt 8:10-11 NIV). Remember today that God's the source of *everything* you've got – or ever will have!

NOTHING "JUST HAPPENS!"

Every purpose of the Lord shall be performed.
Jeremiah 51:29

Even in the midst of pain, separation, and disappointment, you're *still* in God's protective custody. With Him nothing "just happens." Coincidence is what takes place when He decides to remain anonymous!

Look at Jonah; God sent him to Nineveh, but instead he boarded a ship headed in the opposite direction. Now it "just happened" that a storm blew up, he was dumped overboard, a great fish swallowed him, threw him up three days later, and the first words Jonah heard when he hit the beach were, "Go to Nineveh." You can go the easy way or the hard way; the choice is yours! But one thing is certain, *every* purpose of God shall be performed.

A little girl was running to get to Sunday school on time, praying, "Lord, don't let me be late." Suddenly she tripped, fell, and got her dress dirty. Getting back up, she brushed herself off and said, "Lord, I know I don't want to be *late* – but you don't have to *shove!"*

Sometimes God gives us a *shove* to (a) get us out of our rut; or (b) get us over our fear. That's because He's the CEO. He's in charge. When He decides to "take you, break you, and make you," He carries out His will. Satan has never *once* been able to abort God's plan.

In sickness . . . poverty . . . abandonment . . . betrayal . . . mistreatment . . . nothing ever "just happens." Behind the scenes God's orchestrating everything. Romans 8:28 tells us that, *"All* things work together . . . according to his purpose," including the things you're going through right now!

DARE TO DISCIPLINE!

Discipline your son . . . if you don't you will ruin his life.
Proverbs 19:18 TLB

When allied troops captured a young American citizen fighting alongside The Taliban, a major newspaper wrote:

"The parents of John Walker Lindh, the child of privilege turned *Taliban* terrorist, didn't put their foot down when he announced he was going to drop out of school, didn't interfere when he decided to become a Muslim, were actually proud of him for pursuing an alternative course. His mother said it was 'good for a child to find a passion.' They didn't object when he asked them to pay his way to Yemen, nor when his new circle of friends included gunmen. For as long as he could remember, his oh-so-progressive parents had said yes to his every whim, fancy, and passion. The only thing they insisted on was that *nothing* be insisted on."

Newsweek called it truly perplexing that Walker was attracted to this most illiberal, intolerant sect. There's nothing perplexing about it! He craved standards and discipline. Mom and Dad didn't offer any; *the Taliban did!* If his parents had been less concerned with open-mindedness and more concerned with developing their son's moral judgment, he wouldn't have ended up where he did. His road to ruin didn't begin in Afghanistan, it began with parents who never said no!

Listen, "Discipline your son in his early years while there is hope. If you don't, you [not he], will ruin his life" (Pr 19:18 TLB). Dare to discipline – your child's life depends on it!

"THE 24-HOUR RULE!"

Bless those who curse you,
and pray for those who spitefully use you.
Luke 6:28 NKJV

When you're criticized it's human to want to retaliate. But when you take time to try and *understand,* it makes it easier to forgive. For example, critical people often (1) Lack intimate relationships – they keep others at arm's length, rarely share feelings, and are uncomfortable with those who do. (2) Lack empathy – it's easier for them to condemn than to accept. Their hard and fast views make them inflexible. (3) Fear what they don't understand. Paul persecuted Christians because he feared their increasing popularity. (4) Can't handle freedom – they need rules that limit their choices and only feel secure within their own boundaries.

Abraham Lincoln's description of how he handled criticism is a literary gem: "If I tried to answer all the attacks made on me this shop might as well be closed for any other business. I do the best I know how, and I mean to keep on doing so. If the end brings me out right, then what is said won't matter. If the end brings me out wrong, then ten angels swearing I was right would make no difference."

So what *should* you do when you're criticized? "Bless those who curse you, and pray for those who spitefully use you" (Lk 6:28 NKJV). Don Shula, the Miami Dolphins coach, held his team to "the 24-hour rule." He gave them 24 hours to either celebrate a victory or sulk over a defeat, then they had to put it behind them. That's a rule you need to live by!

GET MOVING!

I have begun . . . now [you] begin . . .

Deuteronomy 2:31 NIV

Because so many troubles result from reckless haste, the Bible talks a lot about waiting for God. And that's a good thing. But look out; you can "blow it" by *over-waiting.* God said, "I have begun . . . now [you] begin to conquer and possess" (Dt 2:31 NIV).

You say, "But I'm waiting for God to move." Maybe He's waiting for *you* to move! God promised Abraham a great future, but it didn't happen until he left his comfort zone and "went out, not knowing where he was going" (See Heb 11:8 NAS). Scary stuff!

When Pharaoh's army trapped Israel at the Red Sea, God commanded His people to "go forward" (Ex 14:15 NKJV). The time for waiting and praying was over; they had to move in faith. Later they were told to demonstrate their faith again by marching across the Jordan when it was at flood stage. Why? Because the only way *into* your next blessing is *through* your immediate fear!

The ten lepers Jesus healed were told to go and show themselves to the priest. Luke records, "*As they went,* they were cleansed" (Lk 17:14 NIV). If they'd waited to see results first, they'd never have been healed. It only happened when they started moving.

What has God told you to do? Get moving! It's when you *begin* to fight that God joins you and makes you more than a conqueror (Ro 8:37). If you wait for Him to show up *before* you enter the battle, you'll wait in vain. Move out in boldness today and see what happens!

KNOWING YOUR FATHER

How much more will your Father in Heaven give . . . to those who ask him.
Matthew 7:11 NIV

The son of a wealthy man expected to receive a sports car for his graduation. His dad called him into his study, told him he loved him, and handed him a box. When he opened it he found a leather-bound Bible with his name inscribed inside. Angrily he said, "With all *your* money you give me a Bible!" and stormed out. They never spoke again.

Years later he got a call and learned that his dad had died, leaving him everything. Going through his father's things he found the Bible, still in its box. Tearfully he noticed that his dad had underlined Matthew 7:11, "And if ye then, being evil, know how to give good gifts to your children, how much more shall your Father . . . give . . . to them that ask him?" As he read it a car key fell from inside. It had a tag with the dealer's name on it – for the sports car he'd wanted years earlier! On the tag beside his graduation date were the words, *"Paid in full – Love, Dad."*

Your Heavenly Father knows *what* you need, *when* you're ready for it (which is more than most of us know), and *how* to get it to you. Listen, "I know what I'm doing. I have it all planned out – plans to take care of you . . . plans to give you the future you hope for . . . when you get serious about finding me and want it more than anything else, I'll make sure you won't be disappointed" (Jer 29:9-12 TM). Signed – *"Your Heavenly Father."*

IT'S IN THE BOOK

There's nothing like the written Word of God.

2 Timothy 3:16 TM

Paul writes: "There's nothing like the written Word of God for . . . showing us truth . . . correcting our mistakes, training us to live God's way." (2Ti 3:16 TM). What *you* say isn't important; what *God* says is.

You say, "It's impossible." He says, "With me *all* things are possible" (Lk 18:27). You say, "I'm exhausted." He says, "Wait on me. I'll renew your strength" (Isa 40:31). You say, "Nobody loves me." He says, "I have loved you with an everlasting love" (Jer 31:3). You say, "I can't go on." He says, "My grace is sufficient for you" (2 Co 12:9). You say, "I don't know what to do." He says, "I'll direct you" (Pr 3:6). You say, "I can't do it." He says, "You can do *all* things through Me" (Php 4:13). You say, "It's not worth it." He says, "It *will* be – just keep going" (Gal 6:9).You say, "I can't forgive myself." He says, "You *can* – because *I* have" (Eph 4:32). You say, "I can't make ends meet." He says, "I'll supply all your needs" (Php 4:19). You say, "I'm afraid." He says, "I didn't give you a spirit of fear, but of . . . power" (2Ti 1:7). You say, "I can't handle this." He says, "Give it to me; I'll carry it for you" (Ps 55:22). You say, "I don't have enough faith." He says, "I'll give you faith" (Ro 12:3). You say, "I'm not smart enough." He says, "I'll give you wisdom" (1Co 1:30). You say, "I'm all alone." He says, "I will never leave you or forsake you" (Heb 13:5).

MOVING ON

When you go through . . . great trouble, I will be with you.
Isaiah 43:2 TLB

Divorce is like an amputation – you survive but there's less of you. And it's worse if you didn't initiate the divorce, or you feel abandoned by a church that doesn't want to appear to condone it and, therefore, does nothing to help. So how *do* you move on?

(1) *Confess your mistakes and accept God's forgiveness.* God hates divorce because of the pain it causes. But He loves you. Listen, "I am He who blots out your transgressions, for my own sake, and remembers your sins no more" (Isa 43:25 NIV). God forgives and forgets; you must do the same.

(2) *Forgive those who've hurt you.* Forgiveness is the one power you always have over anybody who hurts you. So forgive and keep on forgiving until *the past* controls you no more. Make it a fixed attitude.

(3) *Take your time.* Don't make any life changes now; you're on an emotional roller coaster, vacillating between wanting your mate back and wanting them to suffer. You're vulnerable, easily drawn to anybody who pays you attention. Take time to heal. Only healthy people make healthy choices.

(4) *Start giving back.* Listen, "He comforts us . . . so that when others have trouble, we can comfort them" (2Co 1:4 NCV). Once you discover that God hasn't turned His face from you (See 2Ch 30:9), you'll begin to become whole again. Then out of what you've received you'll have something to give to others. When you can do that your future's bright and your possibilities unlimited.

NIGHT CLASSES

What I tell you in the dark, speak in the daylight.
Matthew 10:27 NIV

Suffering from sleeplessness? Ever think that maybe God's calling you to *pray?* "But I'll be tired for work in the morning," you reply. Really? Try it! Listen: "They that wait upon the Lord shall renew their strength; they shall mount up with wings as eagles" (Isa 40:31). Do you know that God:

(1) *Works the nightshift?* While Israel slept secure under the blood, God sent His angel to break Pharaoh's iron grip and set them free.

(2) *Holds night classes?* In the wee hours God wrestled Jacob into submission. He changed his priorities, his outlook, and even his name. And Jesus took His disciples through a life-threatening storm. When? At night! Why? To introduce them to a dimension of His power they knew nothing about. Listen to them: "What manner of man is this, that even the wind and the sea obey him" (Mk 4:41). How else can you become a *believer?*

Why does God sometimes speak so clearly at night? Because we tend to listen better with no distractions, no competing interests. We're desperate, open, and ready for answers. During the day we run ourselves ragged talking to people with just as many questions and just as few answers as we have. At night we're ready to slow down and listen.

Jesus said, "What I tell you in the dark, speak in the daylight" (Mt 10:27 NIV). God can give you a solution in the night that will solve a problem waiting for you in the morning. So next time you can't sleep, pray – you might be amazed what happens!

LOVE? WHAT DOES IT MEAN ANYWAY?

Love never fails.
1 Corinthians 13:8 NIV

The word love comes from two Greek words: *phileo* and *agape.* One is of human origin, the other divine. (1) *Phileo* requires two people to appreciate each other; *agape* can be entirely one-sided. (2) *Phileo* is conditional, and if the conditions aren't met, it ends. *Agape* comes with no strings attached. (3) *Phileo* relationships can end due to changing circumstances. *Agape* exists, period. (4) *Phileo* requires some level of emotional reward. *Agape* flourishes regardless; any reward only enhances it.

When Jesus said, "As I have loved you, so you must love one another" (Jn 13:34 NIV), He was using the word *agape,* not *phileo.* Why? Because He knows that we can *choose* to love one another at all times, regardless of what does or doesn't happen.

In her book, *Love Is So Much More, Lord,* Ruth Calkin writes, "*Marriage means* . . . putting up with personality weaknesses, accepting criticism, and giving each other freedom to fail. It means sharing deep feelings about fear of rejection, turning self-pity into laughter, and taking a walk to regain control. *Marriage means* – gentleness and joy, toughness and fortitude, fairness and forgiveness, and a walloping amount of sacrifice. *Marriage means* – learning when to say nothing, when to keep talking, when to push a little, and when to back off. It means acknowledging 'I can't be God to you – I need Him too.' *Marriage means* – you are the other part of me and I am the other part of you. We'll work through this with never a thought of walking out. Marriage, my love, means *us!*"

"MIND MELTDOWN!"

Trust God . . . don't try to figure out everything on your own.
Proverbs 3:5 TM

Feel like you're having a "mind meltdown?" That at any moment you might go over the edge? Listen, *"Come* to me, all of you who are tired and I will give you rest . . . *learn* from me . . . the teaching that I ask you to accept is easy; the load I give you to carry is *light"* (Mt 11:28-30 NCV).

"Mind meltdown" is brought on by our need to know all the facts ahead of time and to be in control. We're afraid things won't turn out the way we want them to. We even develop a back-up plan in case God doesn't come through for us!

When you put your money in the bank do you stay up all night wondering if it's safe? Come on, have at *least* that much faith in God!

"What can I do?" you ask. The moment you begin the downward spiral by asking, "How . . . What . . . Where . . . When . . . Why," stop and give it to God. Not the *little* God of your understanding, but the One who asks, "Is anything too hard for me?" (Ge 18:14).

Know what your problem is? You don't know God well enough! In *Knowing God,* J.I. Packer writes, "What matters is not that I know God, but that He knows me. I'm engraved on the palms of His hands. I'm never out of His mind. There's not a moment when His eye is off me, or His attention is distracted from me; no moment when His care falters. What momentous knowledge! What unspeakable comfort! God is constantly watching over me!"

NEED A NAIL?

May I never boast except in the cross.
Galatians 6:14 NIV

The youth pastor was concerned that the beaches of Florida, the site of their upcoming evangelism trip, would distract his kids from their purpose, so he made a big wooden cross. Just before they climbed onto the bus he said to them, "Our purpose in going here is to lift up Christ, so we're going to take this cross with us everywhere we go."

Feeling awkward and insecure, the kids dragged the big cross on to the bus. It banged against the seats all the way there. It went with them into restaurants; it stayed with them overnight. It stood in the sand as they shared their faith with thousands of other kids who'd come for spring break. At first it embarrassed them, then gradually it became a point of identification; a constant reminder of *who* they belonged to and *why* they'd come.

The night before they went home the youth pastor handed each kid two nails and said, "If you're willing to commit your entire life to Christ, I want you to hammer one nail into the cross and keep the other with you as a reminder wherever you go."

Fifteen years later a successful stockbroker called the youth leader and said, "I still have that nail. Whenever the pressure's on and I'm tempted to go astray, I just reach into my pocket and feel it, and immediately I'm reminded that the core of my life is – commitment to Christ." Think maybe you need to carry a nail with you too?

ON DISPLAY

That in the coming ages He might show . . .
His grace expressed . . . to us.
Ephesians 2:7 NIV

Did you know that your Heavenly Father plans to show you off one day, to display to the world your character and commitment to Him? That means what you're going through right *now* is significant, because God's weighing it in the light of the *future.* He never measures us in terms of our present condition or comfort level. No, He has a far greater plan in mind. Listen, "God knew [us] before he made the world, and he decided that [we] would be like his son" (Ro 8:29 NCV). *Just like Him;* doesn't that blow your mind?

In the coming age He's going to put us on display and say, "Look at My workmanship; can you believe that I made these glorified creatures from clay? When I first scooped them off the ground they wouldn't hold water. But I molded them and raised them up until they held relationships, and ministries, and concepts, and jobs! What you heard about them *was* true! They *were* a disgrace and a disaster, but My grace was sufficient. Now they will sit with Me forever!"

When it comes to performing the impossible Houdini and P.T. Barnum were amateurs compared to God! Could *they* have parted the Red Sea? Put the sun on hold for twenty-four hours? Resurrected the dead – and done it all with such style? Guess what! That same God is at work in *your* life today, too. Why? Because He plans to show you off! Incredible as it may sound, when He gets through with you you'll be "something else!"

WHAT IT MEANS TO BE A "MEMBER!"

You are . . . members.
Ephesians 2:19 NIV

Robert Frost wrote: *Home's the place where when you go there, they have to take you in.* If your children stood outside your house pleading to get in, wouldn't you say, "Come in, you don't need to beg, you're my flesh and blood?" Well when Jesus died He left us the keys to *God's* house. You can come in any time you want. Paul says we're "no more strangers . . . but fellow citizens . . . of the household of God . . . an holy temple" (Eph 2:19, 21). Here's what that means:

(1) As "fellow citizens" we're *ambassadors* of another kingdom. "What does an ambassador do?" you ask. He (a) knows the mind of his king; (b) stays in constant communication; (c) keeps his heart set on his king's interests alone; (d) represents him well; (e) is ready for recall on a moment's notice.

(2) Because we belong to "the household of God" we can come into His presence any time, with any need, and know we'll be received with love. God's the father you always hoped for, and you're the child He always wanted. If you've any doubts, look at the cross – *that's* how much He wanted you! But remember, every member of the family needs to (a) contribute; (b) be loyal; (c) protect the family's good name.

(3) We're a "holy temple." Once God had a temple for His people; now He has a people for His temple. Christ *lives* in you; He *thinks* and *carries* out His will through you. That means you're accepted, empowered, and more than equal to any situation.

RAISED UP TOGETHER!

[God] hath . . . raised us up together.
Ephesians 2:6

There are blessings none of us will experience until *all* of us come into the same level of blessing! God's plan is to *raise us up together.* We're intimately connected in the Spirit. We're each a living stone connected to other living stones, and God keeps working on us until we fit together.

God sees only two categories – saved and unsaved. He doesn't care about differences in denominations or races; "We are all the same . . . one in Christ" (Gal 3:28 TLB). That means when you become a member of His family you pledge allegiance to every other member.

When the Israelites were about to take the Promised Land, two of their tribes wanted to settle where they were; they didn't want to fight with the rest. But Moses challenged them, "Shall your brethren go to war, and . . . ye sit here?" (Nu 32:6). So they came back into unity and said, "We will not return unto our houses, until . . . Israel have inherited *every man* his inheritance" (Nu 32:18). They couldn't enjoy their legacy until everybody shared in it.

Walking in the unity of the Spirit means you can't *fully* enjoy your health while your brother's still sick, or *fully* celebrate your successes while he still struggles. There's something about receiving a blessing that makes you want to say to others, "The God who brought me through can bring you through too!"

When we're "raised up together" divisions will be healed, the world will be convinced, and we'll all be conformed, or become similar in character to Jesus Christ. Hasten the day, Lord!

THE "BUT GOD" FACTOR!

But God . . . hath raised us up.
Ephesians 2:4-6

Ultimately there's nothing that can fill the emptiness of the human heart – *but God.* There's no solution to war, prejudice, and injustice – *but God.* There's no satisfaction for the cravings of the flesh – *but God.* There's no healing for the brokenhearted, lonely, and desperate – *but God.* There's no turning point for human depravity – *but God.* There's no deliverance from addiction and heartache – *but God.*

The *"But God"* factor breaks every generational curse that reaches you through Adam's sin. One Greek translation of the word "spirit" is *air.* When you were "dead in trespasses and sin" (Eph 2:1), God breathed divine air into you. Paul says, "And you [He made alive] when you were dead [slain] by [your] trespasses and sins" (Eph 2:1 AMP). The truth is you never really lived until you met the Lord!

The *"But God"* factor turns tragedy into triumph; it's the turning point in your story. Hell would be partying today, "but God" chose to lavish His mercy and grace on you. Listen, "Though he was rich, yet for your sakes he became poor, that ye through his poverty might be rich" (2Co 8:9). Rich in wisdom. Rich in achievements. Rich in relationships. Rich in all things.

Despite Satan's efforts to destroy, diminish, defame and discourage you, God never once took His hand off your life. He brought you to an understanding of Jesus as your Savior and Lord; now He's raising you up to fulfill His purposes. No matter how bad things may look today, rise up and declare *"But God!"*

THAT'S GRACE!

Unto me . . . is this grace given.
Ephesians 3:8

Grace is the backdrop and framework of our salvation. It's so important, in fact, that Paul mentions it three times more than any other writer! *Grace* comes from the Greek word *charis,* meaning "pure joy." Although you didn't deserve it, God considered saving you "pure joy." Amazing isn't it?

In John 8, a woman is caught in the act of adultery. She's clearly guilty, and the law is unmistakable about her punishment. The Pharisees are ready to stone her. She knows that Jesus, being meticulously fair, must agree. She has no lawyer to defend her, not even a character witness! But suddenly Jesus begins to write in the sand. (You have to wonder if He wrote down *their* sins – times, places, etc.!) When He looks up all her accusers are gone. He says, "Neither do I condemn thee: go, and sin no more" (Jn 8:11). *That's grace!*

Jesus lifted her from a position of undeniable guilt to one of unconditional pardon. She didn't deserve it and couldn't buy it; she didn't even know it was possible. *That's grace!* And that's your story too – isn't it?

One day Abraham Lincoln watched a plantation owner bidding for a slave girl. Figuring he was going to buy her and abuse her, Lincoln paid the price to set her free. "Does this mean I can now *say* whatever I want to?" she asked. Lincoln replied, "Yes." Again she asked, "And *go* wherever I like?" Lincoln responded, "Yes, you're free!" With tears streaming down her face she replied, "Then, sir, I'll go with you." *That's grace!*

STRAIGHT TALK ABOUT WORK!

The energetic have something to show for their lives.
Proverbs 13:4 TM

Bill Gates offers these ten insights to anybody starting out. They're worth considering:

"(1) Life isn't fair – get used to it! (2) The world doesn't care about your self-esteem; it expects you to accomplish something *before* feeling good about yourself. (3) You won't make sixty thousand dollars a year right out of school, or be a vice-president with a car phone. You have to earn it! (4) Think your teacher's tough? Wait till you have a boss – *he's* not tenured! (5) Flipping burgers isn't beneath you; your grandparents called it *opportunity!* (6) Your parents weren't *always* boring; it came from feeding you, cleaning your clothes, and paying your bills. So before you save the rain forest from the 'parasites' of your parents' generation, try delousing your own closet! (7) Some schools may have abolished winners and losers, but life hasn't! They may have eradicated 'failing grades' and given you as long as you want to get the right answer. This bears *no* resemblance to reality! (8) Life isn't divided into semesters; you don't get summers off. Employers aren't interested in helping you 'find yourself'; you do that on your *own* time. (9) Unlike television, *real* people actually have to leave the coffee shop and go to work! (10) Be nice to nerds – chances are you'll end up working for one!"

Solomon says, "Sloth makes you poor; diligence brings wealth." And again, "[Laziness] wants it all and gets nothing. The energetic have something to show for their lives" (Pr 13:4 TM). Today, give it all you've got!

PICKED FOR A PURPOSE – PART 1

We were chosen from the beginning to be His.
Ephesians 1:11 LB

Do you realize that before you were born God's plan for you was already decided? Paul writes, "All things happen just as he decided long ago" (Eph 1:11 TLB). Notice, it says "all things." That includes the things you want to run from!

When Jonah tried to run from God's will, God said, "No way. My word is already established. If I let you escape, I wouldn't be God. If I have to send tornadoes, rock your boat, shake up your comfort zone or put your entire life on hold, I'll do it in order to accomplish my purpose."

When Jonah could go no lower, he cried from the depths and God delivered him – just in time to preach in Nineveh. You can go the easy way or the hard way, but you'll go! David said, "Thy way . . . is in the sanctuary" (Ps 77:13). He also said, "Your way is in the sea [storm]" (Ps 77:19). The choice is yours.

You've been picked for a purpose; God's got too much invested in you to let you get away with things. If you have to come on one leg, with one eye, or on a stretcher, when He calls you – you'll come. If you have to leave behind a bottle, a habit, or an addiction – you'll come. And you'll know it's God, because you'll be able to leave behind you those things which now mean *nothing* for those things which have suddenly come to mean *everything*. Aren't you glad He chose you?

PICKED FOR A PURPOSE – PART 2

Each one of you is a separate and necessary part.
1 Corinthians 12:27 TLB

The disciples came from very different backgrounds: a fisherman; a tax collector; a medical doctor. Seem like strange choices? No, the Lord knows each of our strengths and weaknesses. He *never* makes mistakes because He created the plan – including the part *you* are supposed to play in it.

And the great thing is when you know *He* picked you, you no longer need the approval of others to feel good about yourself. Whether you're outspoken like Peter or gentle like John, He accepts you and gives you space (and grace) to be who you are.

Everybody doesn't have to be like you in order for you to *work* with them or enjoy them. Paul says, "The body has many parts . . . [God] has put each . . . where He wants it . . . all of you together are the one body . . . each one of you is a separate and necessary part" (1Co 12:14, 18, 27 TLB). Did you get that? *You* have an important part to play, and so have all the *others* God sends into your life. There are no unnecessary parts!

Don't let anybody intimidate you into forfeiting your individuality. If two of us were identical, one of us would be unnecessary. It's okay to admire somebody else's talent so long as you don't try to become a carbon copy. God delights in you just the way you are! Listen, "We have become gifts to God that He delights in . . . we were chosen from the beginning to be His" (Eph1:11 TLB). Rejoice – you're hand-picked!

DO YOU NEED STRENGTH?

They that wait upon the Lord shall renew their strength.
Isaiah 40:31

God doesn't tell us *how* He'll answer our prayers, or even *when,* but He does promise one thing to those who wait on Him – strength. Tony Evans points out that the word *wait* comes from a Hebrew word used in the *making of rope.* Every rope starts as a thread, and every thread added just increases its strength. Getting the idea? Every time you wait on the Lord you add another thread to the rope; you get a little stronger, a little more able to cope. Feel like you're hanging on today by a thread? Wait in God's presence and let Him turn it into a rope.

But waiting isn't always passive, sometimes it's active; like waiting on a customer and seeing that his or her needs are met. Waiting is not so much a position, it's a *focus.* Isaiah says, "Thou wilt keep him in perfect peace whose mind is stayed [focused] on thee" (Isa 26:3). Whether it's sitting prayerfully in God's presence, or actively carrying out His will, you've got His assurance that your strength will be renewed. Listen to these promises:

(1) "Wait on the Lord; be of good courage, and He shall strengthen your heart; wait, I say, on the Lord" (Ps 27:14 NKJV). (2) "Wait silently for God alone, for my expectation is from Him" (Ps 62:5 NKJV). (3) "As the eyes of servants look to the hand of their masters . . . so our eyes look to the Lord our God" (Ps 123:2 NKJV). Need more strength? Wait on God more!

LIVING IN WAR MODE!

I want to serve God with all my heart . . .
but I'm pulled by the influence of sin.
Romans 7:23 TM

When does the battle begin? The moment your feet hit the floor! Paul writes, "The moment I decide to do good, sin is there to trip me up. I truly delight in God's commands, but . . . not all of me joins in that delight" (Ro 7:19 TM).

What's happening? Your *flesh* is at war with your *spirit,* seducing you into relaxing your defenses. The moment you do, it'll "nail you." It whispers, "Go ahead, it's no big deal; everybody does it. Who'll know anyway?" Learn to identify that voice *before* it becomes a thought entertained, a deed done, a habit formed, and a character ruined.

Your new birth doesn't do away with your old nature, it just brings it into sharp contrast. You may be redeemed, but you still live in a carnal body. If you try to fight the flesh in the power of the flesh, you'll just end up fighting yourself. What's the answer? "Walk in the Spirit, and you shall not fulfill the lust of the flesh" (Gal 5:16 NKJV). How do you do that? By obeying God's Word instead of doing what comes naturally.

If you "blow it" occasionally, don't get discouraged. You were programmed from birth to walk in the flesh. Now you're learning to walk in the Spirit, with a new set of values, new companions, new priorities, new resources, and new management. Your new birth began a new battle. If you're gonna win it, learn to live in "war mode!"

DON'T MISS WHAT GOD'S GOT FOR YOU!

Let him . . . on the housetop not come down
to take anything out of his house.
Matthew 24:17

The Bible uses words like *straightway, immediately* and *suddenly,* to remind us that when God moves, He does it *quickly.* He doesn't announce it with trumpets and fanfare, so you need to stay prepared; especially for something you've been waiting for a long time. God actually moves so quickly that one day you'll feel like you're going through hell, and the next like you're seated in heavenly places. And in both instances it's "God which worketh in you" (Php 2:13).

Stay alert! You may be just *a moment* away from the answer you've been seeking. That's all the time it takes for God to change things. Don't let procrastination steal your opportunity. Listen, "Let him which is on the housetop not come down to take anything out of his house" (Mt 24:17). You've got to decide if you're going to go with what God has for you now, or return to the house – because your *unfinished business* can cause you to miss it.

Others may also cause you to miss your opportunity. A sick man missed his healing for thirty-eight years because he waited for others to act. He said, "I have no one to help" (Jn 5:7 NLT). For years he sat beside the solution, but others caused him to miss it.

Nothing is more important than what God wants to *say* to you and *do* for you today; not what's going on in your house; not the opinions of others. *All* that matters is being *ready* to receive what He has for you!

"THE SHELTER!"

He who dwells in the shelter of the Most High will abide in the shadow of the Almighty.
Psalms 91:1 NAS

It's much easier to *visit* the secret place than it is to *dwell* in it! We make excuses, but the truth is we're as close to God as we really want to be. Listen: "He who dwells in *the shelter*" (Ps 91:1 NAS). "Sheltered from what?" you ask.

(1) *From mistakes!* If you don't learn to spend more time on your knees, get used to spending it flat on your face. Examine your mistakes; either you didn't pray about them, or you didn't stay in God's presence long enough to hear what He had to say (Jas 1:5-6).

(2) *From defeat!* You can't stop the enemy from attacking you, but you can keep him from defeating you. His attack just proves your value to God! When you're in the secret place you're not only beyond his reach, you're actually being strengthened to come out and win the next battle (Lk 4:13-14).

(3) *From broken focus!* We get so busy that we forget what's really important. E. Stanley Jones said, "If I throw out a boat hook, catch hold of the shore and pull, do I pull the shore to me or do I pull myself to the shore? Prayer is not pulling God to my will, but aligning myself with His."

David wrote, "When thou saidst, Seek ye my face; my heart said unto thee, Thy face, Lord, will I seek" (Ps 27:8). *Listen to your heart today and get back to "the shelter!"*

HOW ARE YOUR MANNERS?

Be courteous.
1 Peter 3:8 NKJV

Common courtesy is becoming less common every day. And that's too bad because God says, "Be courteous . . . that you might inherit a blessing" (1Pe 3:8-9 NKJV).

We wonder about pleasing God. Preachers have made it complicated; a series of long, drawn-out, deeply painful acts designed to appease a peeved deity who takes delight in making us squirm. But Micah simplifies it, "What does the Lord require of you? To love *kindness*" (Mic 6:8 NAS). Could language be clearer? Here are 10 "not-so-common" courtesies you might want to work on.

(1) Go out of your way to speak to people: "Pleasant words are . . . healing" (Pr 16:24 NIV). (2) Try to remember their names – it shows that you value them. (3) Smile; it increases your face value. (4) Be friendly and helpful. If you do people will reciprocate (Pr 18:24). (5) Show genuine interest. You can like almost anybody if you try. (6) Be generous with your praise and cautious with your criticism. (7) Be slow to judge. There are three sides to every story – your side, their side, and the right side. (8) Seek to be of service; "By love, serve one another" (Gal 5:13). (9) Learn to trust people; it builds lasting relationships. (10) Finally, add a sense of humor, a good dose of patience, and a dash of humility.

Courtesy says a *lot* about the parents who raised you and the family to which you belong. Jesus said, "Live so that [people] will . . . praise your father" (Mt 5:14-16 NCV). It also determines the level of your blessing!

MAKING IT WORK FOR YOU!

Our . . . affliction . . . is working for us.
2 Corinthians 4:17 NKJV

Stress comes from having too many hats but only one head. Feeling stressed out? Do these four things:

(1) *Find God's purpose in it.* Paul experienced levels of stress that would push most of us over the edge, yet he wrote, "Our . . . affliction . . . is working for us" (2Co 4:17 NKJV). Instead of letting it drive you crazy, let it drive you closer to God. Need to work on your patience? Or your character? Listen, "Troubles produce patience. And patience produces character" (Ro 5:3-4 NCV).

(2) *Guard your mind.* Listen, "Capture every thought . . . make it . . . obey Christ" (2Co 10:5 NCV). Don't let your negative surroundings infect your spirit. Listen again, "Though the fig tree may not blossom, nor fruit be on the vines . . . yet I will rejoice in the Lord" (Hab 3:17-18 NKJV). Instead of reacting, rise above it and focus on God – your solution!

(3) *Don't major in minors.* Don't reach the end of your life only to discover you've spent it on things that don't matter. Life's about choice. Be "intentional" about where you direct your energy. David prayed, "Teach us to number our days, that we may gain . . . wisdom" (Ps 90:12 NKJV).

(4) *Count your blessings.* Have you been complaining a lot lately? Resenting what others have? How much would you take for your *health?* Or your *family?* Or the home that's waiting for you in *heaven?* "Count your blessings, name them two by two; count your blessings name them four by four, count your blessings, name them by the score, and it will surprise you there are *millions* more."

LET IT GO!

Forgive . . . as quickly and thoroughly as . . .
Christ forgave you.
Ephesians 4:32 TM

Some scientists set out to capture a rare species of monkey and bring it back alive and unharmed. To do this they devised a trap; a small jar with a narrow neck into which they placed a handful of nuts. Smelling the nuts, the monkeys reached in to get them. But when they tried to withdraw their hands, they discovered that they couldn't get their clenched fists back out. They were trapped; *unable to escape but unwilling to let go!*

Sometimes we're just like those monkeys, aren't we? Unable to escape our past but unwilling to let it go! Has somebody mistreated you? Have you said to yourself, "I'll never forget this as long as I live?" Whether you know it or not, you're not holding on to resentment – it's holding on to you. You're trapped! The real victim of resentment is the one who carries it. Are you a carrier? If so remember, hate prolonged is just a slow form of suicide.

Do you think the other person is the one who needs forgiveness? Think again. Jesus said, "Forgive . . . as quickly and as thoroughly as . . . Christ forgave you" (Eph 4:32 TM). How did Christ forgive you? (a) When you were completely undeserving of it. (b) With no strings attached. (c) With full knowledge that you'd fail Him again.

"What's the answer?" you ask. Forgive and forget! More issues are forgotten than are ever resolved. To forgive is to set a prisoner free – and discover that the prisoner is you!

THERE'S POWER IN SACRIFICE

I remember you in my prayers at all times.
Romans 1:9-10 NIV

In The Old Testament tabernacle the altar of incense (prayer) was lit from the altar of sacrifice. It takes sacrifice to pray. A lady in her nineties, when asked how she was able to recall the names of people others had difficulty remembering, replied, "Because I *pray* for them each day." It's hard to forget somebody you're praying for, isn't it?

Paul sacrificed his will, his safety, and his comfort to serve the Lord and His people. His great success can be tied to the degree to which he gave his life for others.

There's power in sacrifice. The cross is the ultimate sacrifice – and the ultimate power. The degree to which *you* lay down your life for others, is the degree to which *you* will experience God's power in your daily living.

Peter says we are "a royal priesthood." Think about that. The priesthood is about intercession, and intercession is not about *you.* It's about *others!*

"But I'm trying to *find* myself," you say. Listen to Jesus, "Self-sacrifice is the way, my way, to finding yourself" (Mt 16:25 TM). Has God been speaking to you about the need to intercede for others? If so do it. That could be your *calling.* Listen, "I have posted watchmen on your walls . . . they will never be silent day or night. You who call on the Lord, give yourselves no rest, and give him no rest till he . . . makes [whoever you're praying for] . . . the redeemed of the Lord" (Isa 62:6-7&12 NIV). Keep praying. God will answer!

SOMETHING NEW

I'm about to do a brand new thing. See, I have already begun!
Isaiah 43:19 NLT

When God says He's going to bless you, ignore the obstacles and keep walking. You're too important to Him to be derailed by a situation that was only meant to give you character and direction.

It was *grace* that enabled you to make it this far, right? God has already proved that He can bring you through the fire without so much as the smell of smoke, and out of the lion's den without even a bite mark (well, maybe one or two!) If you're afraid of the future check with the past. Has He ever failed you? No, and He never will!

His word to you today is, "I'm about to do a brand new thing. See, I have already begun!" (Is 43:19 NLT). After feeling like you've waited forever God will suddenly move, and if you're not ready you'll miss it.

When God brought Paul and Silas out of prison we read, "*Suddenly* there was a great earthquake . . . and *immediately* all the doors were opened and everyone's chains were loosed" (Acts 16:26 NKJV).

God's getting ready to open some doors that have been closed to you; to break some chains that have held you back. He says, "I'm about to do a brand new thing." "Like what?" you ask. How about a new relationship? Or a new assignment? Or a new anointing? Or a new approach to an old problem? God may not change, but He moves. So get ready to move with Him!

RUTH'S PRAYER

Therefore shall a man leave his father and his mother, and shall cleave unto his wife.
Genesis 2:24

Next to following Jesus there's not a more important decision than your choice of a mate. When Ruth Bell was a teenager she was sent to school in Korea. Intending to become a missionary, she envisioned herself as a confirmed "old maid" ministering to the people of Tibet. She did, however, give some thought to the kind of husband she *might* consider. Here's what she prayed for:

"Lord, he must be so tall that when he's on his knees he reaches all the way to heaven. His shoulders must be broad enough to bear the burden of a family. His lips must be strong enough to smile, firm enough to say no, and tender enough to kiss. His love must be so deep that it takes its stand in Christ, and so wide that it takes in a whole lost world. He must be active enough to win souls, big enough to be gentle, great enough to be thoughtful, and his arms must be strong enough to carry a little child." That's a pretty tall order!

Well, Ruth *did* become a missionary to Tibet. And she *did* find a man worth marrying – Billy Graham. As his wife she became a missionary to the whole world!

If you don't have a partner, consider the qualities you'd like in one and begin *praying* for them. That's right, pray! God knows *who* they are, and *when* the time's right He'll send them your way – if you'll just be faithful to Him!

LEARNING FROM ELIJAH

Elijah was a man just like us. He prayed earnestly.
James 5:17 NIV

Elijah did something we keep forgetting to do. When things got tough he recalled what God had assigned him to do – announce the end of a drought and the beginning of rain. What has God called *you* to do? Pull it up on your screen and start doing it. What has He promised you? Begin speaking it over your life today. Learn from Elijah:

First, "He bent down to the ground, and put his face between his knees" (1Ki 18:42 NIV). He deliberately positioned himself *not* to see his surroundings. Smart move! Hang up the phone. Turn off the TV. Lock the door. Get alone with God. *He* has your answers.

Next, he refused to give up. Six times his servant came back to say, "There's no rain. Not even a cloud." But Elijah *persisted* in prayer and told his servant to go look again. This time he came back to say, "I see a cloud like a man's hand." Next we read, "There was a great rain" (1Ki 18:44-45 AMP).

Here are three important things you need to remember today. (1) The greatest moments in your life will always come through prayer. God does things through prayer that He'll do no other way. (2) Instead of obsessing over your situation, start factoring in the God who can change it. (3) If you don't sense The Holy Spirit's power in your life, it may be because you've left the place of prayer too soon. Commit yourself to "pray without ceasing," and God will come through for you.

JOY!

The joy of the Lord is your strength.
Nehemiah 8:10

C.S. Lewis said, "There's too much rigidity in dealing with sacred matters, too much speaking in 'holy tones.' And the tragic loss in all this pious gamesmanship is to the individual in the pew. He begins to feel that in the midst of all the religious razzle-dazzle he can't get through to God himself. Joy is more than earthly pleasure and more than what we call happiness. *Joy is the enjoyment of God and the good things that come from Him.* If the Bible provides us the wonderful words of life, joy supplies the music. If the way to heaven is an arduous climb, joy sets up the chair lift."

Joy is the fuel on which God intends us to run. So why do we feel so uneasy about seeking more of it? For the same reason we feel guilty about taking time off. We think, "We're Christians; we're not *supposed* to enjoy ourselves." Read your Bible! "May the God of hope fill you with all joy" (Ro 15:13 NIV).

Ever notice how some people go through incredible difficulties yet still have joy; while others who don't go through half as much struggle just to keep their heads above water? "What's the difference?" you ask. The first group have a *well* within them from which they draw daily; a well that can't be drained by what's going on around them.

Nehemiah said, "The joy of the Lord [the joy that comes from knowing He's with you] is your strength" (Neh 8:10). What's blocking you from experiencing God's joy? Find out as soon as possible – and refuse to live without it another day.

REBUKING THE DEVOURER

Bring . . . [the whole tenth of your income] . . .
and I will rebuke the devourer.
Malachi 3:8-11 AMP

Tithing isn't the church's way of raising its budget, it's God's way of raising His children. Giving God the first tenth of your income demonstrates that He's *first* in your life. Those who practice tithing are guaranteed two things:

(1) *Blessing.* God says He'll "Open the windows of heaven . . . and pour you out a blessing, that there will not be room enough to receive" (Mal 3:10 NKJV). One farmer, a faithful tither, prospered while others around him were barely making it. When somebody asked him, "What's your secret?" He replied, "No secret. I just shovel it into God's bin and He shovels it back into mine – but God's got a bigger shovel!" *Think* what God's blessing could mean to your business, your family, your ministry, your future.

(2) *Protection.* "I will rebuke the devourer . . . he shall not destroy" (Mal 8:11). "What's the devourer?" you ask. Anything that devours your blessings. The dishwasher breaks down for the third time in a month. The kids are chronically ill and continually have to be taken to the doctor. The day after the warranty runs out on your car, the transmission fails.

One of the Hebrew words for tithe is *charam,* which means "marked for destruction." Your tithe becomes a force in the hand of God to destroy the works of the enemy. It puts a hedge of protection around you.

"Is God after my money?" you ask. No, He's after your *lack.* He wants you to be blessed and protected in *every* area of your life.

THROW OFF YOUR COAT!

The blind man jumped up,
left his coat there, and went to Jesus.
Mark 10:50 NCV

In Jesus' day people were identified by the clothes they wore. The Pharisees' clothing said, "I'm religious." The Roman soldier's clothing said, "I'm powerful." The beggar's clothing said, "I'm down and out."

When blind Bartimaeus heard the voice of Jesus he jumped up, threw off his coat, moved in the direction of the Master, and received a new pair of eyes, a new identity, and a new future.

Others probably chose the garments Bartimaeus wore; they might even have dressed him. But that day he decided, "I don't have to wear these anymore." And neither do you. Christ can change your self-worth, your outlook, and even your connection to the past. Listen, "If any man be in Christ, he is a new creature: old things are passed away; behold, all things are become new" (2Co 5:17).

But you can't just sit there and do nothing. You've gotta move! The moment Bartimaeus heard the voice of Jesus, he "jumped up, left his coat there, and went." He didn't sit on the sidelines while the answer passed him by. He was too desperate to stay in the place of no vision and no provision. He wouldn't be silenced by his critics and miss his day of grace. No, he cried out for help, threw off his pride, jumped up and ran to Jesus. When he did everything changed for the better – *everything!* He'll change your life too, if you'll come to Him today.

GOD'S NOT THROUGH WITH YOU

He has made everything beautiful in its time.
Ecclesiastes 3:11 NIV

Do you feel like you've failed God, yourself, and everybody else? *Shame* sneers, "You're no good; a complete failure. Nobody in church will even want to be around you." *Disgrace* insinuates, "You'll be treated differently now that you're plagued with the leprosy of divorce." *Fear* jibes, "What makes you think God could still love you? And if *He* can't, His children sure won't." *Deceit* whispers, "Why don't you just pull away from everybody? That way you can't be hurt anymore." *Seduction* adds, "The church is full of hypocrites, why don't you just go party with your old unsaved friends?"

How do you silence the roar of these confusing, intimidating voices? You begin by returning to Jesus, the source of life, health, strength, sanity, peace, love, joy, and restoration. He said "I am the way, the truth, and the life" (Jn 14:6). Now if Jesus is the *way,* that means He won't allow you to be lost. If He's the *truth,* He won't allow you to be deceived. If He's the *life,* He won't allow the circumstances to destroy you.

But you've got to keep your mind *open* to hear His voice. Pour out your heart to Him in prayer. Read His Word daily. Allow yourself to be embraced by the loving medics in His hospital (the church), who're trained to rescue and restore people just like you. *Don't despise the process.* You may not see it now, but the Lord can make something beautiful out of the mess you're in.

LEARN TO BE MORE FLEXIBLE

I have become all things to all men so that by all possible means I might save some.
1 Corinthians 9:22 NIV

Your *principles* should be set in concrete, but not your *methods.* Never stop asking, "Is there a better way?" Knowledge in most fields is doubling every five years, so any program *that* old should be brought in for an examination, an overhaul, and possibly the last rites!

As great a businessman as Henry Ford was he had poor people skills. He believed that the Model T ended the need for any other car. When people started saying to him, "We'd like a different colored car," he answered, "You can have any color you want – as long as it's *black!"* And that's when his business began to decline.

If what you're doing isn't working, you can: (1) look for somebody or something to blame; (2) rationalize, so that you can live with it more comfortably; (3) find comfort in the fact that others are in the same boat; (4) be willing to change.

In the movie *Five Easy Pieces,* Jack Nicholson goes into a restaurant and asks for a side order of toast. When he's told it's not on the menu, he comes up with a creative solution. He orders chicken salad on toast, then instructs the waitress, "No mayonnaise, just butter, and hold the chicken salad."

If you're too rigid you'll break (or go broke). Paul's great success can be summed up in one verse, "I have become all things to all men, so that by all possible *means* I might save some" (1Co 9:22 NIV).

HEY, WISE UP!

Make no provision for the flesh, to fulfill its lusts.
Romans 13:14 NKJV

"I keep a close watch on this heart of mine, I keep my eyes wide open all the time." Good song; even better theology! The definition of insanity is doing the crazy things that others do, hoping for a better result. Wise up! David seduced another man's wife and ended up with a blighted conscience, a ruined reputation, and two shattered families. Run while you still can!

Sound old fashioned? Try talking to some of the folks you thought "got away with it." They paid in ways they don't like to talk about, like: (1) *fear:* "What the wicked dreads will overtake him" (Pr 10:24 NIV); (2) *lack of confidence:* "If our hearts do not condemn us, we have confidence before God" (1Jn 3:21 NIV); (3) *regret:* "I have played the fool, and I have erred exceedingly" (1Sa 26:21).

Solomon had it all – a home that took thirteen years to build, forty thousand stables for his horses, a fleet of ships, a thousand beautiful women, and more money than he could spend in ten lifetimes. Yet he ended up turning his back on God and on the very advice he gave others. Why? Because he lacked personal discipline. Here's how he sums up his life: (1) "I denied myself nothing" (Ecc 2:10 NIV). (2) "I hated all the things I had toiled for" (Ecc 2:18 NIV). (3) "Better a poor but wise youth, than an old but foolish king who no longer knows how to take warning" (Ecc 4:13 NIV). Hey, wise up!

"COMPARTMENTALIZED."

Love the Lord your God with all your heart.
Deuteronomy 6:5 NIV

Is your life like a chest of drawers with a separate one for each interest, value, and pastime? One for work, one for play, one for church; every one requiring a separate set of values and a different language? Every new situation you encounter demands yet another drawer to ensure complete appropriateness and safety. So rather than having oneness and integrity of character, your life is fragmented by many roles.

Modern living is custom-made for compartmentalized living. We hardly know the family next door. We commute to a church miles away, often walking in and out in near anonymity. We work with one crowd and play with another. The opportunities for undercover activity are almost limitless. Since no one knows us in any other context, we are free to reinvent ourselves in each aspect of our life.

But God doesn't see you as a row of compartments or a collection of separate performances. He sees you as a whole person. The person you are when no one's looking is just the same to Him as the person you are when you're standing in plain view.

God asks for integrity (wholeness) in our lives. Why? Because it doesn't work any other way! God made us with one will, one mind, one heart, and one spirit. It's Satan's lie that "we can have it both ways" which leaves us fractured and paralyzed. What's the answer? Listen, "Love the Lord your God with *all* your heart, and with *all* your soul, and with *all* your strength" (Dt 6:5 NIV). Refuse to live a "compartmentalized" life!

LOVING THE LORD – AND OTHERS!

For even the Son of Man did not come to be served, but to serve and to give His life.
Mark 10:45 NIV

No two ways about it, if you love the Lord you'll love people and lay down your life – your comforts, rights, schedule, etc. – for them. When you read The Gospels you can't escape the fact that the Lord's first love was always for *people.* People of all races, in all situations, whether powerful or not, acceptable or not, young and beautiful, or old and infirm. How many destinies were changed that day when He stopped to bless the children?

The early church understood this. They shared everything (see Acts 2:44). They were even willing to *sell* their possessions to take care of one another. Rather than thinking of their own needs, they thought of others first – and amazingly their own needs were taken care of in the process. Their willingness to humbly serve one another also brought them favor with outsiders, who were then introduced to God's love. That's how it works!

When you give yourself to God you become committed to what He's committed to – loving people. Bruce Wilkinson points out: "God didn't come to the Garden of Eden to tend His prize-winning grapes, He came to tend His children. Christ didn't come to erect public buildings, shore up retirement accounts, write a literary masterpiece, or win a spot on the school board." No, He came to minister to hurting people, to put their lives on track and to give them joy. Hey there goal-oriented, purpose-driven, time-conscious, go-getter, are you forgetting something? *Others!*

INTIMACY WITH CHRIST – WHY NOT?

Behold, I stand at the door, and knock.
Revelation 3:20

The picture is powerful – Christ aggressively pursuing us. So why don't we open the door to Him? Two reasons:

(1) *Fear.* Thomas Keating writes, "Because trust is so important, our spiritual journey may be blocked if we carry negative attitudes toward God from early childhood. If we're afraid of God, or see Him as an angry father-figure, a suspicious policeman, or a harsh judge, it will be hard to develop enthusiasm or an interest in building a relationship with Him!" What's the answer? Pray, "Lord, I believe; help thou mine unbelief" (Mk 9:24). Grasp this: God will never use or abuse you. No one who ever trusted Him has been disappointed!

(2) *Self-sufficiency.* Listen, "I am rich, and have become wealthy, and have need of nothing" (Rev 3:17 NAS). The church at Laodicea thought that because they had no material needs, they didn't need God. They relied on what they "consumed" to satisfy, sustain, and secure themselves. Sound familiar? Today many of us believe we don't need a purpose. The mechanism doesn't require it. Consumption keeps the workers working, the paychecks coming, the people spending, the inventors inventing, and the investors investing, which means there's even more to consume. The system operates independent of values, and needs no philosophy to prop it up. It's a perfect circle, complete in itself – but *empty* in the middle.

Don't go a step further without Jesus. Open the door of your heart and invite Him in. When you do, everything in your life will change for the better – *everything!*

NEVER STOP CHANGING

He takes us firmly by the hand
and leads us into a radical life-change.
Romans 2:4 TM

The greatest mistake you can make is to be afraid of making a mistake. It's tragic when success goes to your head, but even worse when failure does. Larry Anderson, former pitcher for the *San Diego Padres,* liked to say, "If at first you don't succeed, failure may be your thing!" You may smile, but too many of us, fearing that failure is "our thing," cling to whatever we feel comfortable with even when it doesn't work.

Although we don't say it in so many words, our attitude is, "Don't look, you might see. Don't listen, you might hear. Don't think, you might learn. Don't make a decision, you might be wrong. Don't walk, you might stumble. Don't run, you might fall. Don't live, you might die. Don't change, you might grow!"

In the 1940's eighty percent of all watches sold were made in Switzerland. In the late 1950's the digital watch was presented to them, but they rejected it because they already *had* the best watches and the best watchmakers. The man who developed it subsequently sold his idea to Seiko – and the rest's history!

In 1940 Swiss watch companies employed 80,000 people. Today they employ 18,000. In 1940 they made eighty percent of all watches sold. Today they make twenty percent – and they're all digital! This story demonstrates what happens when an *organization* or an *individual* chooses to die rather than change. Today pray, "Lord keep me open to change."

GROWING OLD – GRACIOUSLY

Teach the older men . . . teach the older women.
Titus 2:2-3 NIV

In *Time Out Ladies,* Dale Evans shares this prayer:

"Lord, you know better than anybody that I'm getting older and will someday be old. Keep me from being talkative; from the fatal habit of thinking I've got to say something on every subject and on every occasion. Release me from the need to straighten out everybody's affairs. Keep my mind free from the recital of endless details; give me wings to get to the point. I ask for grace to listen to the tales of others' pains, and to endure them with patience. But seal my lips when it comes to my own aches and pains, for they're increasing, and my love of rehearsing them is becoming sweeter as the years go by. I ask for improved memory, but even more for a growing humility and a lessening cocksureness when my memory seems to clash with the memory of others. Teach me that occasionally I may be mistaken. Keep me reasonably sweet. I don't want to be 'a saint' because some of them are so hard to live with – and a sour old person is one of the crowning works of the devil. Make me thoughtful, but not moody; helpful, but not bossy. With my vast store of wisdom, it seems a pity not to use it; but you know, Lord, I still want to have a few friends at the end. Give me the ability to see good things in unexpected places, and talents in unexpected people, and give me the grace to tell them so. Amen."

ONE SIZE FITS ALL!

My yoke is easy and My burden is light.
Matthew 11:30

Beware of the "one size fits all" mentality. We may all be saved by grace, but we each have a *different* journey – a personal one pre-planned by God.

You'll only have grace for the assignment *God's* given you; outside of that you're running on your own steam. When Jesus said, "*My* yoke is easy, and *My* burden is light" (Mt 11:30), His listeners understood Him clearly. You see they lived off the land and they knew that nothing was worse than an ill-fitting yoke that constantly irritated the ox and made the plough twice as hard to pull.

The plan of God for you will be a comfortable fit. You won't chafe under it, and you won't burn out. If you do, it's a good indication that you're laboring under the weight of somebody else's expectations – not God's!

Where God guides He provides. With His instructions come His wisdom and His strength. Paul writes, "It is God which worketh in you both to *will* and to *do* of his good pleasure" (Php 2:13). He'll give you: (a) the desire; (b) the ability; (c) the right conditions and connections. Need a little more assurance? "I will make you wise and show you where to go. I will guide you and watch over you" (Ps 32:8 NCV). "If you go the wrong way – to the right or to the left – you will hear a voice behind you saying, 'This is the way'" (Isa 30:21 NCV). What more do you need?

A DECLARATION OF GOD'S GREATNESS!

O magnify the Lord with me . . .
Psalm 34:3

The word *magnify* means "to enlarge." Your problem isn't too big; your concept of God is too small! The following words are a *declaration* of God's greatness. Begin repeating them over your circumstances each day and watch what happens.

He is the first, the last, the beginning and the end. Keeper of creation, Creator of the universe, Manager of all time. He always was, always is, and always will be. The world can't understand Him; its armies can't defeat Him; its schools can't explain Him; its leaders can't ignore Him. Herod couldn't kill Him; the Pharisees couldn't confuse Him. Nero couldn't crush Him. Hitler couldn't silence Him. He's the Power of the powerful, The Ancient of Days, the Ruler of rulers, the Leader of leaders. He is holy, mighty, and true. His ways are right, His word eternal, and His will unchanging. He is my Redeemer, Savior, Lord and Guide.

When I fail, He forgives. When I'm weak, He is strong. When I'm lost, He is the way. When I'm afraid, He is my courage. When I stumble, He steadies me. When I'm broken, He mends me. When I face persecution, He shields me. When I face loss, He provides for me. When I face death, He carries me home. He said it and that settles it. He is on my side. God is in control – it is well with my soul! Amen.

WHAT ARE YOU EXPECTING?

What I dreaded has happened to me.
Job 3:25 NIV

One autumn some Native American Indians asked their new Chief to predict whether the winter would be cold or mild. He hadn't a clue, so to be safe he told them to collect lots of wood. Meanwhile he called the National Weather Service. "It'll definitely be cold," they said. So the chief told them to collect *more* wood. A week later, having again called the Weather Service who confirmed their earlier forecast, he told his people to gather even more wood. Two weeks later he called the Weather Bureau again and asked, "Why are you so *sure* it'll be a cold winter?" The weatherman replied, "We know – because the Indians are collecting wood like crazy!"

Satan wants to influence your future by getting you to expect the worst. When you do, he'll provide you with the right circumstances, symptoms, and opinions. He'll even supply "experts" who'll confirm your worst fears. If you don't take hold of God's Word and rise above them, you'll end up like Job, lamenting, "What I dreaded has happened to me" (Job 3:25 NIV).

Each time you speak doubt over your future you're: (a) sowing negative seeds; (b) shaping your outlook; (c) influencing those around you; (d) contradicting the God who said, "The plans I have for you are good" (See Jer 29:11); (e) creating a self-fulfilling prophesy.

Put ice cream and milk in a blender and you get a milk shake. Put in dirt and water and you get mud! What goes in, comes out. Stop the negative projections! Start sowing seeds of faith and expect only God's best.

JUST WHAT GOD'S LOOKING FOR!

The Father seeketh such to worship Him.

John 4:23

Men thought she was a plaything. Women felt threatened by her so they despised her. But Jesus is in the "rehab" business. He looks for treasure in the trash – and this woman was just who He was looking for. This redeemed, re-commissioned woman was granted two privileges denied to everybody else:

(1) *She was the first person ever to introduce the Gospel to Samaria.* The disciples had traveled there a few days before and they returned with a sack of groceries. She went – and came back with a harvest of souls! She had impact. Why? *Because the greatest testimony of all is a life you can't explain without God!*

(2) *She was the first person to whom Jesus introduced Himself as The Messiah.* Why didn't He do that earlier when He called His disciples, was baptized by John, challenged the religious order of His day by cleansing the temple, performed His first miracle, or even when He conducted that famous interview with Nicodemus where He said, "You must be born again" (See Jn 3:3)?

The Bible doesn't say, but this much is clear – God loves to take the lost, the last, the least, and the lowest, and make something beautiful. He invites them to come and be made whole. Why don't you come too? You've nothing to lose except: (1) the baggage of your past; (2) the emptiness of your present; (3) the sad prospect of a future without God. Today He says, "Come, drink of the water of life that I give, and you'll never thirst again" (See Jn 4:14).

DO IT AGAIN, LORD!

Wilt Thou not revive us again:
that Thy people may rejoice in Thee?
Psalm 85:6

After the terrorist attack on America on September 11, Max Lucado wrote: "Dear Lord, as the innocent are buried, our innocence is buried as well. We thought we were safe; we should have known better but we didn't. We don't ask You for Your help, we *beg* You for it! We know what You can do. We've read the accounts, pondered the stories, and now we plead, *'Do it again, Lord.'*

"Remember the Hebrews in Egypt? You protected their children from the Angel of Death. We have children too Lord! You took Daniel the captive and made him a King's counselor. You took Peter the fisherman and made him Peter the Apostle. David went from leading sheep to leading armies. Do it again Lord, for today we need . . . counselors . . . apostles . . . leaders.

"At Calvary You saw . . . innocence slaughtered . . . goodness murdered . . . mothers weeping . . . evil dancing . . . heaven's sweetest song buried beneath a rock. But You turned the darkest Friday into the brightest Sunday . . . Grant us a September Easter.

"Thank you for these hours of unity. Christians praying with Jews. Republicans standing with Democrats. Skin colors covered by the ash of burning buildings. The enemy sought to bring us to our knees and succeeded. *He had no idea however, that we would kneel before You.*

"Grant those who lead us, wisdom. Have mercy on the souls who have departed and the wounded who remain. Give us grace that we might forgive, and faith that we might believe. Look kindly on Your church. For two thousand years You've used her to heal a hurting world. *Do it again, Lord. Do it again!"*

GET OVER IT!

Remember ye not the former things, neither consider the things of old. Behold, I will do a new thing.
Isaiah 43:18-19

When Eve awoke on planet earth she was already a wife! Imagine waking up beside a man when you had never seen one before! She found herself in the ultimate sink-or-swim situation. Eve was created without a childhood and she never got to grow up. She stepped right into being a wife and then a mother. Did that happen to *you?*

A lot of us found ourselves having to be parents before we had a chance to be children and know what it meant to be innocent, to trust, or to receive genuine love. If that's your story, God has a word for you, "Remember not the former things, neither consider the things of old. Behold, I will do a new thing."

Refuse to blame your past for your present, or let it ruin your future. You can't go back and make things different. You're not the person now you were then, and you're never going to be. You can't re-live your first marriage or your early childhood. Accept it, dismiss what used to be, and move on!

Often we hold on to the past because there's something we think we still need there. We cling to things because we fear we'll never be able to replace them!

Don't you know that God has more for you? If you're trusting Him for your future, then you haven't seen your best days yet. There's more ahead of you than behind you. So get up, get over it, and move on!

"DIS-APPOINTING" GOD

Until Christ is formed in you.
Galatians 4:19 NIV

In *The Life You've Always Wanted,* John Ortberg writes, "I'm disappointed that I still love God so little and sin so much. I'm capable of dismaying amounts of jealousy if somebody succeeds more visibly than I do. I'm disappointed at my capacity to be small and petty. I cannot pray for very long without my mind drifting into a fantasy of angry revenge over some past slight I thought I had long since forgiven, or some grandiose fantasy of achievement. I can convince people I'm busy and productive, yet waste large amounts of time watching television. Although I'm aware of how far I fall short, sometimes it doesn't even bother me. I'm disappointed at my lack of disappointment."

Where does this disappointment come from? It comes from *"dis-appointing"* or removing God from the central role He longs to play in our lives, and appointing ourselves in His place. It's what Paul had in mind when he said he was, "In the pains of childbirth until Christ is formed in you" (Gal 4:19 NIV).

One of Michelangelo's masterpieces, *Pieta,* is a marble statue of Mary holding the crucified Christ. Some years ago a fanatic took a sledgehammer and began smashing it. Although the damage was significant, Vatican artists were able to restore it to near-perfect condition.

Know what? God's determined to overcome the defacing of His image in us. His plan isn't to repair most of our brokenness; it's to make us "new creatures." Maybe that will help you to understand why He's been so hard at work in your life revealing, removing, and restoring.

WHEN THE STRUGGLE PRODUCES NOTHING

That night they caught nothing.
John 21:3

The disciples, including Peter a master fisherman, struggled all night and "caught nothing." Based on their experience alone you'd think they'd have caught *something* – but not this time. There's a lesson here.

Sometimes God lets us struggle to teach us that despite all our skill and experience, some problems can't be solved by planning, budgeting, or trying to figure them out. They're resolved, "Not by might, nor by power, but by my spirit, saith the Lord" (Zec 4:6).

Maybe you're ready to give up the fight because what worked for you in the past isn't working now. If so, here are two things about Jesus you need to remember:

(1) *He's closer than you think!* Listen: "When the morning was now come, Jesus stood on the shore" (Jn 21:4). In spite of your turmoil, your experiences with those who've disappointed and hurt you, the frustrations and futility of your own efforts, Jesus is closer – much closer – than you think! David says, "Weeping may endure for a night, but joy cometh in the morning" (Ps 30:5). Did you hear that? Joy is coming; don't lose hope!

(2) *He's there – even when you can't see Him!* When morning broke the disciples were able to see the Lord on the beach. It wasn't that He couldn't reach them, it was just that He didn't need to become embroiled in their struggle to speak into it and deliver them.

Hang in there, God's at work! When the morning comes you'll see Him as you've never seen Him before, and understand things in a way you've never understood them before.

"HAVE YE ANY MEAT?"

Jesus saith . . . Children, have ye any meat?
John 21:5

Why would an all-knowing God ask simple fishermen a question when He already knew the answer? Their response certainly couldn't enlighten Him. God's intention is always to make you think about *how* you answer His questions.

He asked Adam, "Where art thou?" (Ge 3:9). He asked Abraham, "Is anything too hard for the Lord?" (Ge 18:14). He asked Ezekiel, "Can these bones live?" (Ez 37:3). In this passage He was asking the disciples, "Have ye any meat?"

What God really wants you to consider is whether or not what you're doing is working. The long hours of overtime, the frenetic pace, the scrimping and saving, the unwillingness to trust Him. And how about all that baggage you've carried for years; the hard heart, the angry walls you've built to keep from being hurt again? Have you "any meat" to show for all your efforts?

God's not interested in the size of your boat or who's on board! In fact, some of us have bragged so much about the size of our church and the big name celebrities in the pulpit, that we can't admit we no longer catch fish! We're so competitive and worried about what people think, that we're afraid to confess the truth!

Deliverance always begins with confession. The disciples replied, "We have fished all night and caught nothing." They first had to acknowledge that their best wasn't good enough.

When you don't have any meat there's only one thing to do. Unplug the phone, turn off the TV, get into your prayer closet and let God show you where to cast your net.

DON'T THROW IN THE TOWEL – THROW OUT THE NET!

Throw out your net . . . and you'll get plenty.
John 21:6 TLB

Just when the disciples were ready to give up, Jesus showed up and said, "Throw out your net on the right-hand side . . . and you'll get plenty." They did, and "couldn't draw in the net because of the weight of the fish."

When you're at your lowest point, when everything you've tried has failed, don't throw in the towel – throw out the net! You're closer to winning than you think. There's nothing wrong with your boat or your crew. *You're exactly where you should be.*

The enemy knows that with a few more pulls on the oar you'll be right in the middle of your biggest catch. He's tried to delay your blessing while you struggle, grow frustrated, and get weary. But he can't win, because God says, "No weapon that is formed against thee shall prosper . . . This is the *heritage* of the servants of the Lord" (Isa 54:17). Are you serving God? If so, this is your heritage! God's holding your blessing under the boat. He's even put your name on it, so don't worry about somebody else taking it. What you can't accomplish by struggling all night God can accomplish in an instant by His spoken word.

The strange thing is the disciples didn't recognize that it was Jesus who spoke to them the next morning. That's how God works; He just speaks a word and enables you to do what you couldn't do before. *So be encouraged today, don't throw in the towel – throw out the net!*

"YOU KNOW JOHN . . ."

Then the disciple whom Jesus loved said . . . "It is the Lord!"
John 21:7 NIV

John 21:7 talks about, "the disciple whom Jesus loved" without actually mentioning his name. Why? Because it's your *relationship* with Jesus that gives you your *identity!*

You know John . . . he was the disciple who lay with his head on Jesus's breast . . . the one who was always worshipping while the others argued about who should sit on the right or left . . . the one who outran Peter to the empty tomb to see whether or not Jesus was there. *You know John* . . . he's the one who's always standing up praising God in church . . . the one you can't see around . . . the one who's always in your way.

But don't despise John because he doesn't act the way you think he should. The fact is, you need him on your boat . . . or on your board . . . or in your pulpit. "Why's that?" you ask. Because when nobody else around you recognizes it, John will always tell you when the Lord is speaking. Listen: "Then the disciple whom Jesus loved said . . . 'It is the Lord.'" When you're looking for a fresh word from God – spend time with somebody who really knows Him. When you need an answer to your prayers – come into agreement with someone who knows how to pray!

You'll know John . . . he'll be the guy saying, "I will praise the Lord no matter what" (Ps 34:1 TLB). The one who believes, "He must become greater and greater, and I must become less and less" (Jn 3:30 TLB). How'd you like to have *that* kind of relationship with God? You can if you're willing to pursue it with all your heart!

THE "SUCCESS" DILEMMA

Peter heard that it was the Lord . . .
jumped into the water [and swam ashore].
John 21:7 NRS & TLB

Once "Peter heard that it was the Lord," he had to decide whether to leave his fish and go to Him, or stay behind with the catch for which he'd worked so hard.

Real tests don't necessarily come during the hard times – *anybody* can seek God then. No, they come when you've *accomplished* your objectives, your nets are full, and you've finally "arrived." The challenge then is – do you stay and guard your blessings, or leap overboard and go for the One who gave them to you? Do you want the Giver more than the gift?

When Paul faced his "success dilemma," he said, "You know my pedigree . . . from the elite tribe of Benjamin, defender of my religion, meticulous observer of . . . God's law" (Php 3:3-6 TM). Career-wise he had it made! But listen to him now: "Things I . . . thought were so important are gone . . . dumped . . . in the trash so that I could embrace Christ" (Php 3:8 TM). Temporal blessings begin to fade once you've met the Blesser!

To reach Jesus you'll have to leave behind those who want to stay with the fish. It felt like Peter was forfeiting everything, yet when he reached the shore he found Jesus busy – cooking fish! Whatever you need, God already has it! Just obey Him and He'll give you "a blessing so great you won't have room . . . to take it in" (Mal 3:10 TLB). That's His promise!

But here are His terms: "Seek first his kingdom . . . and all these things will be given to you" (See Mt 6:33 NIV). *Whatever you're willing to walk away from ultimately determines what God can trust you with.*

"GONE FISHIN'"

Peter said . . . "I'm going fishing."
John 21:3 TLB

Peter was a fisherman by trade. In fact, he was fishing when he first met Jesus and was called to be a disciple. So when he decided to go fishing again, he may have been making a conscious decision to get away from everything and everybody, and go back to where he had first met the Lord.

That was a good move! Why? Because when you get discouraged, confused, or stressed-out, you'll either go back to the One who saves, keeps, and satisfies, or you'll return to whatever was going on in your life before you met Him.

God says in Revelation: "I have watched your hard work . . . You have patiently suffered . . . without quitting. Yet there is one thing wrong; you don't love me as at first! *Think* about . . . your first love . . . and turn back to me" (Rev 2:2-5 TLB).

When your love for God grows cold, it's time to hang out your "Gone Fishin'" sign and get back to where you first met Him. It's time to seek Him again, like you did before you'd heard so much and seen so much; before life had worn you down.

"But I'm busy doing the work of the Lord," you say. That's the easiest place in the world to crash and burn. Oswald Chambers said, "Beware of anything that competes with your loyalty to Jesus Christ. The greatest competitor of devotion to Jesus is service for Him." Is it time for you to "Go Fishin'?"

WORDS! WORDS! WORDS!

God, has given me a well-taught tongue.
Isaiah 50:4 TM

Your words are like nitroglycerine: they can either blow up bridges or heal hearts. You can tell more about somebody by what *they* say about others, than by what *others* say about them. Never judge a person's horsepower by their exhaust; ignorance is always eager to speak. Wisdom dictates that the best time to hold your tongue is when you feel like you "just have to say something."

Some people speak from experience; others from experience don't speak. That's because they've learned better. Jesus said that your words actually determine your destiny. Listen, "Your words now reflect your fate then: either you will be justified by them or you will be condemned" (Mt 12:37 TLB). Solomon said, "Words kill, words give life; they're either poison or fruit – you choose" (Pr 18:21 TM).

Try to remember that your words have the capacity for good or evil; they either hurt or heal. If there's one place where we all need more discipline, it's in "the words' department." Isaiah says, "God, has given me a well-taught tongue, so I know how to *encourage* . . . people. He wakes me up . . . opens my ears to listen as one ready to take orders . . . God, stays right there and helps me, so I'm not disgraced" (Is 50:4-7 TM).

When you don't know what to say, say nothing! Just listen, observe, and let God lead you. After all, you're usually not learning while you're talking.

Just for today, try to refrain from all hurtful remarks and focus only on speaking words that encourage and bless others. You'll be amazed at the results!

DON'T LOSE YOUR PEACE

Do not give the devil a foothold.
Ephesians 4:27 NIV

There's power in peace! If the devil can't get you upset he has no power over you! He only gains control when you "lose it." He'll actually set you up to get you upset; that way he can steal your peace, confuse you, and make you run in circles.

Ever get into an argument just before church, then feel "hypocritical" while you were there? And all the while the devil is smiling and saying, "Gotcha!" That's because he knows God's Word can only be "sown in peace" (Jas 3:18). If he can keep you from receiving the seed of God's Word, he can rob you of the harvest of blessing that comes from it. That's why you must stay in peace.

Listen, "The wisdom that comes from heaven is first of all pure and full of quiet gentleness. Then it is peace-loving and courteous. It allows discussion and is willing to yield to others; it is full of mercy and good deeds. It is wholehearted and straightforward and sincere. And those who are peacemakers will plant seeds of peace and reap a harvest of goodness" (Jas 3:17-18 TLB).

Next time you get all worked up, ask yourself, "What's the enemy trying to do here? If I give in to these negative emotions what will the result be?" When you're upset you lose your joy, and when you lose your joy you lose your strength, because "the joy of the Lord is your strength" (Neh 8:10). *So today do your utmost to exercise self-control, and remain in peace!*

JESUS AT THE SCENE OF DEATH

Our friend Lazarus has fallen asleep;
but I am going . . . to wake him up.
John 11:11 NIV

What do you say to those who are heartbroken, angry, and questioning because of death? Tell them about Lazarus whom Jesus raised from the dead:

(1) *Jesus allows us to question!* Martha asked, in effect, "Where were you when we needed you, Lord?" Was Jesus upset with her? No. In moments like these we learn things about ourselves we never knew before. In times of heartache we discover, "His compassions fail not. They are new every morning: great is thy faithfulness" (Lam 3:22-23).

(2) *Jesus shows us how to grieve!* "Jesus wept," not because He was powerless, but because He was our example. If you bury your emotions, you bury them alive and they'll rise again to hurt you. The process of becoming whole involves: (1) feeling deeply; (2) dealing honestly; (3) making way for healing. Are you running from pain? Are you trading it in prematurely for some other feeling? That's not God's way. He says, "You will weep and mourn . . . but [eventually] your grief will turn to joy" (Jn 16:20 NIV).

(3) *Jesus gives us hope!* Listen, "Lazarus has fallen asleep; but I am going . . . to wake him up." Remember how great you feel after a good night's sleep? Well multiply that feeling by infinity and you still haven't come close! Goodnight here means good morning there. Jesus said, "In that life they are like angels and cannot die" (Lk 20:36 NCV). Wow! The "Uppertaker" puts every undertaker out of business! Don't you love it!

THE "CAN-DO-SPIRIT!"

Because . . . Caleb has a different spirit . . .
I will bring him into the land.
Numbers 14:24 NIV

Dr. James Dobson says that for years he was afraid to tackle the computer. As an author and broadcaster he recognized its potential value to him, but he kept putting it off until "someday." Finally, in his fifties, he faced down his fears and took lessons. Today he wonders how he ever coped without a computer.

What are the messages in *your* head saying each time you've an opportunity to add a new skill or take on a fresh challenge? "You can't teach an old dog new tricks?" "You never were any good at this?" "You'll only embarrass yourself?"

The ten spies Joshua sent into Canaan weren't defeated by the size of the giants but by their *perception* of them, and by what they *told themselves.* Listen, "They are stronger . . . we seemed like grasshoppers" (Nu 13:31-33 NIV). Such talk is terminal!

Because Caleb had the "Can-do-spirit," he saw his enemy and himself differently. Listen, "We can certainly do it" (Nu 13:30 NIV). Before achievement comes attitude. Always!

If having to do everything right the *first* time is your prerequisite to trying – you'll accomplish nothing. Actually, you'll end up wondering what you could've done had you been willing to: (1) take a risk; (2) learn from your experiences; (3) allow God to show you what He can do through you.

Every time you face down another fear, it loses its hold on you and you take one step closer to success. *Go ahead! You'll never know what God can accomplish through you until you step out in faith and make yourself totally available to Him!*

PARENTS – WAKE UP!

We will tell the next generation.
Psalm 78:4 NIV

Parents, wake up! You wouldn't permit a pornographic theater in your neighborhood, yet the enemy has taken *The Information Highway* and used it to transport his filth right into your child's bedroom – legally.

If we're to save our children we've got to make sure that what we say matches what we're *doing* to make it happen.

You can't just close your eyes and hope for the best. You can't delegate this responsibility to the childcare center, the schoolteacher, the scoutmaster, or even the church youth leader. You can't solve the problem by buying your kids more "stuff." You can't sacrifice them for your career, assuming that if there's no crisis underfoot at home everything must be fine. No, the best defense is a good offense. Listen to these sobering Scriptures:

The first one addresses the pedophile and pornographer: "If anyone causes one of these little ones who believe in me to sin, it would be better for him to have a large millstone hung around his neck and to be drowned in the depths of the sea. Woe to the world because of the things that cause people to sin! Such things must come, but woe to the man through whom they come!" (Mt 18:6-7 NIV).

The second is for parents: "What . . . we have heard and known, what our fathers have told us. We will not hide them from [our] children; we will tell the next generation the praiseworthy deeds of the Lord, his power, and the wonders he has done" (Ps 78:3-4 NIV). *Noah "saved his family" (Heb 11:7 TLB). Make sure you do too!*

THE ROGER CRAWFORD STORY

Be strong and courageous.

Deuteronomy 31:6 NIV

Roger Crawford is a successful author who speaks to *Fortune 500* companies, travels worldwide as a consultant, and is a professional tennis player. Not impressed? *Would* you be if you knew he has no hands and only one foot?

When he was born doctors said Roger Crawford would never be able to walk or take care of himself. But his parents disagreed. They sent him to regular schools, involved him in sports, and taught him to think positively. "They never allowed me to feel sorry for myself, or take advantage of my handicap," he says.

One day he got a call from a man who'd read about him. When the two met they discovered they had identical handicaps. Roger got excited thinking perhaps he'd found someone older who might act as his mentor. He was wrong! "Instead," he says, "I found someone bitter, who blamed all his disappointments on his body. He couldn't hold a job. He blamed that on discrimination, and not (as he admitted) on his constantly being late, absent, and failing to take responsibility. His attitude was, 'The world owes me.' The problem was the world disagreed! He was actually angry with me because I didn't share his despair. We kept in touch until I finally realized that even if some miracle were suddenly to give him a perfect body, his life wouldn't change much because – he was more the prisoner of his attitude, than of his circumstances."

Roger Crawford's philosophy is worth living by. *Handicaps can only disable us if we let them. The real limitations are in our minds, not our bodies.*

GETTING IT RIGHT

I have not shunned to declare unto you all the counsel of God.
Acts 20:27

Believe it or not one-hundred-and-fifty years ago some of our best preachers, including those who founded great denominations, used the Bible to defend *slavery.* There's a lesson there for us. The danger lies in deciding what we want and then using the Bible to justify it, instead of reading the whole counsel of God on the matter and bringing our thinking and lifestyle into agreement with it.

David prayed, "Oh Lord . . . Make *Your* way straight before me," because he didn't dare trust his own way. (See Ps 5:8 NAS). God's voice isn't all that difficult to hear. In fact, you almost have to be closing your eyes and stopping your ears to miss it. He shouts through our pain, whispers to us while we're relaxing on vacation, occasionally speaks to us in a song, and instructs us through the sixty-six books of His written Word. It's right there, ink-on-paper! Count on it – God's Word will never lead you astray. Never!

In addition to His own unfailing wisdom, God gives us wise counselors, friends, acquaintances, parents, teachers, and mentors who've earned our love and respect through long years. If you're wise, you'll filter what you believe to be the will of God through *their* thoughts and perspectives.

Does your conviction about the direction you're headed deepen daily? Or are you seeing lots of red flags and caution signs? Before you undertake a major life-change be sure it's *God's voice* you're hearing, and *God's Word* you're following. In other words – make sure you get it right!

"LORD, I SAID I WOULDN'T – BUT I DID!"

I decide one way, but then I act another.
Romans 7:18 TM

Are you feeling discouraged, or even disgusted with yourself? You said you wouldn't, but then the enemy put the pressure on and you folded like a house of cards. You're not alone. Paul writes, "I decide not to do bad, but then I do it anyway . . . Is there no one who can do anything for me? Isn't that the real question? The answer, thank God, is that Jesus Christ can and does" (Ro 7:18-25 TM).

Why do we keep failing? *Because flesh will always act like flesh!* After a season of doing everything right, you can fall flat on your face because you "give place to the devil," (Eph 4:27), or "[give] occasion to the flesh" (Gal 5:13).

The story is told of an old Native American who a few months after his conversion came back to his pastor and said, "It's like I have two big dogs constantly fighting inside me." "Which one of them wins?" the pastor asked. After thinking about it, the old Indian replied, *"I guess the one I feed the most."*

The power to live victoriously comes from feeding your spirit and disciplining your flesh. Listen, "His divine power has given us everything we need for life and godliness . . . He has given us His very great and precious promises, so that through them you may participate in the divine nature and escape the corruption in the world caused by evil desires" (2Pe 1:3-4 NIV). *Spiritual growth doesn't just happen; you have to work at it daily.*

"SUCKER-SHOOTS!"

He cuts off every branch . . . that bears no fruit.
John 15:2 NIV

Atlanta pastor Dr. Michael Youssef, who was born in The Middle East, says the branches which Jesus talked about cutting off, are "sucker-shoots." These tiny offshoots literally drain and disable the vine so that it produces leaves – but no fruit!

What are the "sucker-shoots" in your life? What's keeping you from being fruitful? You can be sure they didn't spring up overnight. Nobody makes a single leap from the pinnacle of commitment to the swamp of carnality. No, it's a slow downward spiral based on wrong choices. Unless you stop it, this week's wrong choice won't seem quite so bad next week. In fact, a month from now it might not seem like a bad choice at all.

A famous sculptor was once asked how he carved a lion's head out of a big chunk of marble. "I just chipped away everything that didn't look like a lion's head," he replied. That's how God works; He chips away at everything in us that doesn't look like Christ. (1) Our insensitivity to the needs of others. (2) Our drive for success at the expense of our family, or spiritual well being. (3) Our laziness and lack of personal discipline. (4) _________ (you fill in the blank.)

Sucker-shoots drain and disable us; that's why God is determined to remove them. Paul says, "We . . . are being transformed" (2Co 3:18 NIV). God is committed to it, and nothing we can do will dissuade Him! He stays at it; He's relentless. And He never runs out of creative ideas for bringing it about. Aren't you glad?

TRY AGAIN

Though I have fallen, I will rise.
Micah 7:8 NIV

Dan Rhodes met Dave Thomas long before Thomas opened his first *Wendy's.* Rhodes admitted he always knew young Thomas would, "Someday be something big." But still, given an opportunity to invest in *Wendy's* – he didn't. Later he met Colonel Sanders and had a chance to buy his stock before it went public. But he turned down that opportunity too, because he didn't agree with some of the Colonel's ideas.

When he was in the restaurant business, Rhodes often had a salesman named Ray Kroc in his office trying to sell him equipment. Rhodes admits that Kroc was a nice guy; however, he chose not to invest in his little hamburger joint – *McDonalds!* A few years later on an Alaskan cruise he met an attorney from Seattle who suggested that Rhodes invest in his son's new computer company. It had a funny name – *Microsoft!* Again Rhodes declined.

Now most of us would be pulling our hair out if we missed even *one* of those opportunities, but not Rhodes. He *learned* from his mistakes, kept *pursuing* his dream, and eventually saw his name on *Forbes Magazine's* list of the 400 most successful business owners in America.

Start seeing your failures as an investment in further knowledge. You paid too much to get where you are and understand what you know to quit now. Each time you plan, risk, fail, re-evaluate, and adjust, you get another opportunity to begin again – only *better* than the last time!

YOU'RE NOT HOME YET

Oh Lord, revive Thy work in the midst of the years.
Habakkuk 3:2

Beginnings are wonderful. So are endings. It's in the *middle* that we need help. It's in the *middle* of the race that we need our second wind. It's in the *middle* of the battle that we need reinforcements. If that's where you are today, listen: "Say to those with anxious heart, Take courage, fear not. Behold, your God will come" (Isa 35:4 NAS).

On their way home from a lifetime of missionary service in Africa, an elderly couple found themselves on the same ocean liner as President Roosevelt, who was returning from a big-game hunting expedition. They watched in awe at the fanfare surrounding the president and his entourage. When the ship docked in New York a band was waiting to greet him, the Mayor was there to welcome him, and the newspapers heralded his return.

Meanwhile the old missionary couple slipped quietly off the ship and found a cheap apartment. They had no pension, they were in poor health, and they were discouraged and fearful. The husband especially couldn't seem to get over how President Roosevelt had received such acclaim while their decades of service seemed to have gone unnoticed. "God isn't treating us fairly," he complained to his wife. "Why don't you pray about it?" she said. A short time later she noticed a big change in his attitude. "What happened?" she asked. He replied, "The Lord put His hand on my shoulder and said to me, *'Son, you're not home yet!'"* Hey, hang in there! The world's best days are now. Yours are still ahead!

DON'T JUST OPERATE – COOPERATE!

We have shared together the blessings of God.
Philippians 1:7 TLB

Andrew Carnegie said, "It marks a big step in your development when you realize that other people can help you do a better job than you can do by yourself." (After all, you can't whistle a symphony; it takes an orchestra!)

Your future is connected to certain people. Without them your destiny will be incomplete. If you're humble enough to accept that, your possibilities are unlimited.

A key player in the Billy Graham Association was his childhood friend, Grady Wilson. In 1948 Billy asked Grady to come and work with him. At first he said no. But Billy persisted: "God's told me you're to come and work with me. I need an evangelist; somebody who knows me and my ministry, somebody I can trust."

"I didn't want to come," Wilson later recalled. "After all, I already had a successful ministry of my own holding citywide crusades." But after praying he made the decision to follow Billy Graham (and God). He set aside his own dreams to be part of another man's. That decision made a *huge* difference, not only in his life but also in the lives of the multitudes they reached together until Grady Wilson's death.

Sometimes you have to sacrifice a smaller dream in order to fulfill a bigger one. It takes both courage and humility to do that. But look at the results. Heaven alone knows the impact that Grady Wilson and Billy Graham had together. And what was Wilson's take on his decision? *"I never regretted it!"*

BITTERNESS IS MORE DEVASTATING THAN BETRAYAL.

See to it that . . . no bitter root grows up to cause trouble.
Hebrews 12:15 NIV

Betrayal is something *others* do to you; bitterness is something *you* do to yourself! Look past the hurt and you'll see that your resentment is just a roadblock to your own success.

Eliminate words of bitterness from your conversation. *Don't* remind others of your experience, unless it's to teach and encourage them to rise above their own.

Lloyd Ogilvie says, "The hardest time to be gentle is when we know we're right and somebody else is wrong. It's when someone has failed us, admitted it, and their destiny or happiness is in our hands. Recently a friend hurt me in both word and action. Each time we met I enjoyed the leverage of being the offended one. At first I rejected all his attempts at reconciliation because I'd already pronounced judgment on him. My most difficult challenge now was to surrender my anger and work through the hurt.

"Finally, the Lord said, 'Lloyd, why is it so important to you who gets the credit just so long as My work gets done?' Right then I gave up my right to be what only God could be – this man's Judge and Savior. Immediately my heart tenderized and my attitude toward him changed."

When you withhold forgiveness you not only hurt the other person, but you hurt yourself more – much more! You lose the joy of living. It hangs over you like a cloud, affecting everything you do. But when you forgive, you release *peace* and *restoration* to the forgiven – and also to yourself. So today, forgive!

HOW DID I EVER GET HERE?

Keep the charge of the Lord your God . . .
that you may . . . prosper in all that you do.
1 Kings 2:3 AMP

First came a king's dying words to his son Solomon: "I go the way of all the earth . . . Keep the charge of the Lord your God . . . that you may . . . prosper." Then came a funeral and the son's coronation. Next came Solomon's prayer for "an understanding heart," and God was so pleased that He said, "I have also given you what you have not asked, both riches and honor" (1Ki 3:13 AMP). What could possibly go wrong? Everything! Here's why:

(1) *Solomon put a priority on possessions.* He made almost four billion dollars a year – most of it from forced labor – and kept it all for himself. (2) *He put a priority on pleasure.* He "loved many foreign women" (See 1Ki 11:1). Inexorably, they enticed him into worshipping their gods and building temples to honor them. What started as a king's right to pursue pleasure, turned into an outright act of rebellion against God. (3) *He put a priority on power.* Listen, "Solomon had forty thousand stalls of horses for his chariots, and twelve thousand horsemen" (1Ki 4:26 AMP). It's not that God doesn't like horses, it's that He doesn't want us depending on our own strength.

Read Solomon's writings – especially the Book of Ecclesiastes. Much of what he says can be distilled into one question – *"How did I ever get here?"* Tragically he went so far that he was never able to find his way back. How can *you* avoid that? By keeping "the charge of the Lord your God . . . that you may . . . prosper in all you do."

BREAKING HABITS

I made a covenant with my eyes not to look lustfully.
Job 31:1 NIV

To win the battle against lust you must decide once and for all to be fully committed to God. Steve Arterburn says that means establishing three perimeters of defense:

(1) *Your eyes.* Job said, "I made a covenant with my eyes not to look lustfully." It's the lingering look that opens the door to trouble. Before David messed up with Bath Sheba we read that he: (a) saw; (b) inquired; (c) took. Train yourself to pull your eyes away immediately. What you're looking at isn't yours. God says, "Leave it alone."

(2) *Your mind.* Paul writes, "Take captive every thought . . . make it obedient to Christ" (2Co 10:5 NIV). Does your mind traffic in double-entendres, daydreams, the Internet, magazines, movies, and anything else that can alter your mood at a glance? Replace these things with memorized scriptures, and mental images of your best moments with your mate. It'll work! With your transformed mind actively policing itself and capturing rogue thoughts before they capture you, your defenses will begin to grow strong.

(3) *Your heart.* Listen, "Above all . . . guard your heart" (Pr 4:23 NIV). Work on strengthening the bond with your mate. Begin to repay the debt you owe from the times you neither honored nor cherished them. Decide to love, even though you don't *"feel"* like it, and watch yourself become your mate's biggest fan. No matter how badly you've failed, victory can be yours if you're willing to humble yourself, ask for God's help, and make a covenant with your eyes, your mind, and your heart, to live in purity!

QUALIFIED BY WILLINGNESS

For who hath despised the day of small things?
Zechariah 4:10

Although raised in church he was spiritually ignorant. When he moved to Boston to make his fortune he began attending a Bible-preaching church. In April of 1855 a Sunday school teacher came to the store where he worked and led him to Christ. A month later when he applied to become a church member, one fact was obvious to everybody – he knew *nothing* about the Bible.

One of his Sunday school teachers later wrote, "I've never met an applicant for membership who seemed less likely to become a Christian of clear and decided views, much less fill any place of public usefulness." So they asked him to undertake a year of study, which he did. During his interview with the membership committee a year later, his answers were only *slightly* improved. He was barely literate and used atrocious grammar. Few thought God would ever use a person like him. But they were wrong!

God saw in the heart of D. L. Moody the raw material necessary to make a spokesman for His Word, and a changer of nations.

Every oak tree started as an acorn. Jesus began in a stable, but He didn't stay there. David had a slingshot, but he became King. Joseph was sold as a slave, but he became prime minister. Why? Because "God was with him . . . gave him favor and wisdom . . . made him governor over Egypt" (Acts 7:9-10 NKJV).

Whatever you have today is *enough* to create anything you'll ever need in your future. Just put it into God's hands and be willing to start small.

YOU MUSTN'T QUIT!

Every child of God can defeat the world, and our faith is what gives us this victory.
John 5:4 CEV

An unknown poet wrote: *Many a failure turns about when he might have won if he'd stuck it out; so stick to your task though the pace seems slow – you may succeed with one more blow.*

That was Irwin Rosenberg's philosophy. As a junior officer he was discharged from the Navy when he was diagnosed with cancer – standard military procedure at the time. But he was determined to get back both his health and his job. At one point he was given only two weeks to live. But with faith in God and dogged determination, his cancer was eventually brought under control.

Irwin then focused his attention on becoming a naval officer again. But he discovered that regulations forbade reinstatement of a person discharged with cancer. Everybody told him, "Give up. It can't be done. It would take an Act of Congress to get you reinstated." Their advice gave him an idea – he'd *pursue* an Act of Congress!

After years of waiting, petitioning, cutting through red tape and battling bureaucracy, President Truman eventually signed into law a special bill that allowed Irwin Rosenberg to re-enlist in the Navy – and go on to become a Rear Admiral in the United States 7th Fleet!

The poet concludes: *You can never tell how close you are, it may be near when it seems afar; So stick to the fight when you're hardest hit – it's when things seem worst that you mustn't quit!*

BE HONEST

Provide things honest in the sight of all men.
Romans 12:17

If you always tell the truth you'll never have to worry about remembering what you said. Nothing's more important than credibility. Lose that, and you've lost everything!

George Jones started out as a clerk at a grocery store. He quickly gained a reputation as a bright, ambitious employee – a man known for his work ethic, good manners, and easy-going personality. But the foremost trait people referred to when praising George was his *honesty.* That's what later got the attention of Henry J. Raymond, the renowned journalist. Together they started *The New York Times.*

Years later when *The Times* waged a crusade against "Boss Tweed" and his corrupt dynasty, Jones received an under-the-table offer of $500,000 – a vast sum at that time. All he had to do was retire to Europe. "You can live like a prince the rest of your days," said the con man making the offer. "Yes," replied Jones, "And know myself every day to be a rascal."

The poet wrote:

I have to live with myself and so, I want to be fit for myself to know. I want to be able as days go by, always to look myself in the eye. I don't want to stand in the setting sun, and hate myself for the things I've done. I don't want to keep on a closet shelf, a lot of secrets about myself; and fool myself as I come and go, into thinking nobody else will know – the kind of man I really am.

Today, be honest!

GOD ENCOUNTERS

A certain Samaritan, as he journeyed, came where he was.
Luke 10:33

One night a man walking to church saw four boys hanging out on a street corner, so he invited them to go with him. They did, and they returned with him the following Sunday. Actually they became the nucleus of a Sunday school class he began to teach. Years later his friends decided to contact the boys to see what had happened to them, and to invite each one to write a special birthday letter to be read at a surprise party for their old teacher.

Their letters were real eye-openers. One boy had become a missionary to China, one was president of the Federal Reserve Bank, one was private secretary to President Herbert Hoover, and the fourth was – President Hoover himself!

Be alert! God-encounters usually take place on your way to *somewhere else.* If you're not sensitive to God's Spirit you'll miss: (1) a real blessing; (2) a chance to grow; (3) an opportunity to put God's interests ahead of your own.

Jesus left the comfort of heaven to walk the road of human need. He didn't set up a throne in each town and say, "This is My place; if you want to see Me, come here." No, He went to the market place. He went to the boats of fishermen. He went to the homes of people. He "went through the towns, preaching the gospel and healing everywhere" (Lk 9:6 NKJV).

The moment your compassion is activated, stop! You may be on the verge of a God-encounter!

ANGELS WATCHING OVER YOU!

He will command His angels concerning you
to guard you in all your ways.
Psalm 91:11 NIV

Remember that "close call" you had? That wasn't "luck," that was your angel guarding you in "all your ways."

Chuck Swindoll tells of a group of church kids who got lost on a mountain-climbing expedition. A snowstorm suddenly covered the trail and their leader hadn't a clue where they were or how to get back to camp. The sun was setting. The temperatures were plunging. The danger was real.

Trudging through the snow and getting more panicky by the moment, they heard someone on the slopes above yell, "Hey, the trail's up here!" They glanced up, and to their relief saw another climber about one hundred feet above them. Quickly they made their way up to the big boulder where the man had been sitting. But when they arrived they found *nobody there,* not even a *footprint* in the snow. When they looked, however, the trail stretched out before them leading safely back to camp.

The Bible says, "Some people have entertained angels without knowing it" (Heb 13:2 NIV). "Are you serious?" you ask. Absolutely! Even your children have guardian angels watching over them. Jesus said, "Despise not one of these little ones; for . . . their angels do always behold the face of my Father" (Mt 18:10). Paul discovered that when you go through storms, God assigns an angel to protect you. Listen, "There stood by me this night the angel of God, whose I am . . . Saying, 'Fear not'" (Acts 27:23-24). *Hey, relax, God's got you covered!*

JOSEPH'S COATS

Israel loved Joseph . . .
and he made him a coat of many colors.
Genesis 37:3

Joseph's life story is told by two coats that he wore. One was the coat of *favor,* the other was the coat of *temptation.* Let's look at them:

"Jacob loved Joseph more than all his children . . . and he made him a coat of many colors" (Ge 37:3). That coat symbolized the special favor that would rest on Joseph all his life. Even in prison, "The Lord . . . granted him favor . . . So the warden put Joseph in charge of all" (Ge 39:21-22 NIV). And later we read, "Pharaoh said to Joseph, 'I hereby put you in charge of the whole land of Egypt' " (Ge 41:41 NIV). Five times in one chapter we read, "The Lord was with Joseph." That's favor!

But the favor of God doesn't exempt us from attack. Listen, "Joseph was . . . handsome . . . and . . . his master's wife . . . said, 'Come to bed with me!' But he left his coat in her hand and ran" (See Ge 39:6-12 NIV). When God begins to bless you, the enemy will use whatever he can to pull you down and keep you from fulfilling your destiny. God's plan was to save a *nation* through Joseph. What if he'd given in to temptation? Wise up! The battle isn't just about you – it's about those God plans to bless *through* you, like your children, your grandchildren, and your circle of influence.

Satan will offer you the pleasures of a moment in exchange for the high privilege of fulfilling God's will. Don't go for it! Pull your priorities back up on the screen. Get back into focus. Walk with God and live with the future in view.

"TAKE OFF YOUR SHOES!"

Put off thy shoes from off thy feet.
Exodus 3:5

Why would God tell Moses to take off his shoes? Because *men* made shoes – God made feet! Perhaps that's why God told His people, "Every place whereon the soles of your feet shall tread shall be yours" (Dt 11:24).

What's the point? It's this: *you can only stand on what God has given you. You can only walk in what He's ordained for you.* Anytime you launch out without consulting Him or allowing Him to lead, you get into trouble. If God doesn't order it He doesn't pay for it!

Listen, "Trust in the Lord with all thine heart; and lean not unto thine own understanding. In all thy ways acknowledge him, and he shall direct thy paths. Be not wise in thine own eyes" (Pr 3:5-7). God wants to bring you to the place of total dependence on Him – not your talent, or your intellect, or your connections, just *Him!* He'll allow you to *use* those things, but never to *lean* on them.

When you awoke this morning you faced these questions. Whose kingdom will be first today, His or mine? Will His will be done in my life on earth, even as it is in heaven? Will His right to rule be honored in *every* area, including my business, my finances, my family, and my private life?

Take off your shoes means: (1) stand only on the Word God has given you; (2) walk only in the plan He's ordained for you; (3) do nothing in your own strength; (4) do all things for His glory alone!

DEALING WITH CHANGE

Be diligent . . . so that everyone may see your progress.
1 Timothy 4:15 NIV

If you think *accepting* change is difficult – try *introducing* it to others! You'll have for enemies all those who've done well under the old system, and only lukewarm defenders among those who aren't sure how well they'll do under the new one. Resistance to progress is universal; it seizes every generation by the throat and attempts to stop all forward movement.

In 1553 Admiral Richard Hawkins recorded that during his career on the high seas, 10,000 men under his command had died of scurvy. He also noted that oranges and lemons (Vitamin C) completely cured it. But his observations went unheeded for *two hundred years,* during which time thousands more sailors died needlessly. In 1753 James Lind, a British Naval surgeon, published a book saying that scurvy could be eliminated with lemon juice. He even cited case histories to prove it. But instead of being honored, he was ridiculed by the Lords of the Admiralty and by the leading physicians of that day. In fact, his advice was ignored for another *forty years.* Not until the year after his death in 1794 was a Naval Squadron supplied with orange juice before a voyage. On that voyage which lasted *twenty-three weeks,* there wasn't one case of scurvy. Even so, another *ten years* passed and thousands more died before regulations were enacted requiring sailors to drink a daily ration of lemon juice. With that enactment, scurvy finally disappeared from the British Navy.

What a lesson! Don't let complacency, prejudice, or the fear of change, rob *you* of the joy of becoming all God intends you to be.

ENCOURAGE SOMEBODY TODAY!

If a man's gift is . . . encouraging, let him encourage.
Romans 12:6&8 NIV

There's no better exercise for strengthening your heart than stooping to lift somebody else. Think about it: your best friends are the ones who encourage you. Who wants to hang around somebody who always puts them down?

Dr. Maxwell Maltz interviewed the son of a successful businessman. The boy had refused to take over the family business after his dad's death, even though it would've made him wealthy. He explained, "You don't understand the relationship I had with my father. He was a driven man who came up the hard way. His objective was to teach me self-reliance, and he thought the best way to do it was *never* to encourage or praise me. Every day we played catch in the yard. The idea was for me to catch the ball ten straight times. I'd catch it eight or nine times, but always on that tenth throw he'd do everything possible to make me miss it. He'd throw it on the ground, or over my head so I'd no chance of catching it."

He then paused tearfully and said, "That's why I have to get away; I want to catch that tenth ball!" This young man grew up feeling he could never measure up, never be perfect enough to please his father. Sound familiar?

William James said, "The deepest principle in human nature is the craving to be appreciated." Most of us *think* wonderful things about people, but we never tell them. Praise only becomes valuable if you impart it. Today go out of your way to encourage somebody.

CONFIDENCE – PART 1

Do not throw away your confidence.
Hebrews 10:35 NIV

You can spot them in any group. They have that special "something" that sets them apart. What is it? A sense of direction – an assurance that they know where they're going! An awareness of their own abilities! Sincerity! Past successes! The ability to make eye contact and use body language! In a word – confidence!

Paul had it. Listen, "I have learned [during a lifetime of walking with God] the secret of being happy at any time in everything that happens, when I have enough to eat and when I go hungry, when I have more than I need and when I do not have enough. I can do all things through Christ, because he gives me strength" (Php 4:12-13 NCV). These verses cannot be separated because there's a definite correlation between experiencing life's lows and enjoying its highs. Paul rests in the assurance that his strength comes from *Christ alone.* Knowing *that* gave him the ability to handle every circumstance he encountered!

Confidence is taking your present situation – whatever obstacle you're facing, whatever limitation you're living with, whatever chronic condition wears you down, whatever has smashed your dreams, whatever factors in life tend to push you under – admitting you don't like it, but *never* saying "I can't cope." As soon as you say that you: (1) contradict the promises of God; (2) fail to draw on the resources that He's already given you.

Confidence means having the ability to stand up to any test, because Christ has made His strength available – through you!

CONFIDENCE – PART 2

Do not throw away your confidence.
Hebrews 10:35 NIV

Want to become more confident? Do these three things:

(1) *Establish your worth according to God's value system, not the world's!* God demonstrated your importance to Him in two great acts. First, He created you in His own image, which means you have "creative abilities." Next, had you been the only person who ever lived, He'd still have sent His Son to redeem you. That makes you priceless! Those two unchanging truths should be the enduring basis of your self-worth.

(2) *Surround yourself with confidence-builders, not confidence-busters.* Confidence-busters give you "The Charlie Brown Complex." One day Lucy put her hands on her hips and said, "You, Charlie Brown, are a foul-ball on the line-drive of life! You're a fifth putt on the eighteenth green! You're a dropped rod and reel in the lake of life! You're a missed free throw, a shanked nine-iron, and a called third strike! Have I made myself clear?" No wonder Charlie struggled! If you want to be confident, surround yourself with people who bring out the best in you.

(3) *Quit comparing yourself with others.* Comparisons only leave you feeling like the two cows reading the ad on the side of a passing milk truck: *Pasteurized, Homogenized, Standardized – Vitamin A Added.* One looked at the other and said, "Makes you feel kind of inadequate – doesn't it?"

You're more than equal to the task. God has fully equipped you for your assignment. Discover your gift, develop it, then go out and use it for His glory.

CONFIDENCE – PART 3

Do not throw away your confidence.
Hebrews 10:35 NIV

Confidence is contagious! It spreads throughout your sphere of influence. How many giant-killers were in Saul's army? None! When Goliath challenged the armies of God they quaked with fear. Yet David, who came to bring food to his brothers, sized up the situation, went out in faith and killed the giant.

After David became king how many other giant-killers arose in Israel? Lots! Listen, "Then Sibbechai . . . killed Siphai, one of the descendants of the giants, and they were subdued. And there was war with the Philistines again, and Elhanan . . . killed Lahmi the brother of Goliath the Gittite, the shaft of whose spear was like a weaver's beam. Again there was war at Gath, where there was a man of great stature who had twenty-four fingers and toes, six fingers on each hand and six toes on each foot; and he also was descended from the giants. When he taunted Israel, Jonathan the son of Shimea, David's brother, killed him. These were descended from the giants in Gath, and they fell by the hand of David and by the hand of his servants" (1Ch 20:4-8 NAS).

Now why do you suppose there were no giant-killers in Saul's army? Because Saul himself wasn't one! However, under David's leadership they became numerous, because David was a giant-killer! This illustrates the "it takes one to make one" principle that runs throughout the Bible!

When *you* develop confidence, those around you – friends, family, associates – will increase their confidence levels too. Why? Because confidence breeds confidence!

PUSH!

I press on toward the goal.
Philippians 3:14 NIV

When you commit to bringing forth all that God has placed within you – you may have to push against everything people ever *did* to you or *said* about you. You may have to battle years of suppression, oppression, and depression. You may have to push in order to release the treasure God has placed inside you. He'll help you bring it out, but it's up to you to push. In fact, it may not happen if you don't.

But what do we push against? Against Satanic attacks in all their debilitating forms, such as bad memories, low self-esteem, and feelings of unworthiness. The devil may have spent years pushing you aside, pulling you back and putting you down, but today God's saying to you, "I want to open you up, I want to empower you to give birth to that which I've placed within you."

The time has come for you to rise up and say, "It's my turn to conceive, for the treasure within me to come forth, for me to be loosed to do what God created me to do."

When a baby is born *everything* in the family changes. The same is true for you. When you give birth to what God's placed within you, everything around you will be affected. God's blessing is an overflowing blessing and it'll touch *every* area of your life.

Every woman knows when she's pregnant. The same is true in the spiritual realm. Don't fail to give birth to what God has put in you. Now is the time for the treasure to come forth. So push!

LOOK TO GOD

My God shall supply all your need.
Philippians 4:19

There's a big difference between your *wants* and your *needs.* Your desires come from many different sources. Some come from your peers and friends, others from your age and stage in life. And believe it or not, something as commonplace as a television ad or a catalog can actually influence what you think you need.

Amidst all these influences, God will not grant you everything you request. A good father doesn't give in to his child's every whim. No, he carefully considers what they need, and then decides: (a) what's best for them, (b) when they're ready for it.

This means growing up! It means understanding and accepting that if God doesn't grant it, you don't need it – at least not yet! If it were a genuine need He'd have supplied it already. Anytime there's a discrepancy between what you *think* you need and what's actually being supplied, trust God and thank Him for knowing what's best.

Remember, you are to prosper and be in health – *as your soul prospers* (See 3Jn:2). If you're not growing spiritually, *that* should be your primary concern! Every other supply will flow "as your soul prospers."

That's why it's so important to maintain a healthy heart towards God; for what would it profit if you gained the whole world and lost your soul? (See Mk 8:36). Don't stress out, burn out, become jealous, or strive for *things.* Keep your head in the right place. Seek His kingdom first, and all these *things,* whatever they are, will be added to you (See Mt 6:33). God guarantees it!

STAND

Having done all . . . stand.

Ephesians 6:13

Since we're born with all sorts of human weaknesses, what are we to do when the enemy comes along? Listen, "Having done all . . . stand." In Romans 14:4 Paul says that, "God is able to make [you] stand." Not in your own strength, but in the strength of Jesus Christ. By yourself you're an easy target for the enemy, but in the strength of the Lord you can stand and not give in.

So today when Satan shows up with his temptations, announce that you're going to stand in Christ. Let him know that you're going to stand until the shaking stops, until you feel peace again, until the wave of loneliness passes, until your marriage is restored, until you come out of debt, until the struggle is over, and until the tempter loses his power to either trap you or topple you!

When you do the standing – God does the strengthening! Paul said, "I can do all things through Christ who strengthens me" (Php 4:13 NKJV). God doesn't just strengthen you once, He'll strengthen you again and again. He'll strengthen you every time you face a difficult challenge, every time a memory comes back to haunt you, every time you're reminded of your imperfect past, every time you face a difficult decision.

Drawing from God the strength you need to stand up to the enemy may take *effort.* It may take your praise, your prayer, and your getting into His Word with an intensity you've never had before. *But the fact is – you can stand if you really want to!*

YOU'RE NO ACCIDENT!

He chose us in Him before the foundation of the world.
Ephesians 1:4 NAS

You were in God's mind before you were in your mother's womb. Your parents didn't create you – God did. It doesn't matter if you were conceived during an act of date rape, or born to a welfare mother who had children by several different fathers. *God* created you! He didn't allow you to be aborted, miscarried, stillborn, or die of crib death. Those events didn't take you. Why? Because God has a purpose for your life. Never forget that!

Even when you were abused as a child, He never took His hand off you. He brought you through and kept you from losing your mind. He's the One who brought you to an understanding of Jesus Christ as your Lord and Savior. He's the One who raised you up in spite of every attempt of the enemy to destroy you, diminish you, defame you, or discourage you.

The fact is, if you hadn't gone through everything you've been through, you wouldn't be the person you are today – and God knows that! He has been in the process of creating you, molding you, refining you, and perfecting you since the moment He first thought of you.

He gave you your own personality, your own abilities, your own spiritual gifts, and your own identity in Christ. Why? So that you, and you alone, might *praise* Him the way you do, *give* the way you do, *serve* the way you do, and *love* the way you do. Rejoice, you're His unique creation and He loves you!

VOICES – PART 1

Your ears will hear a voice . . . saying . . .
this is the way; walk in it.
Isaiah 30:21 NIV

Have you ever decided to launch into a new venture when suddenly a voice within you whispered, "You must be out of your mind. You're not capable of this. Those little accomplishments you had before were pure luck; you just happened to be in the right place at the right time. Now you're in over your head." That voice will wake you in the middle of the night with the bitter taste of bile in your mouth and shudders of fear up your spine. It can be heard in every boardroom, bedroom, closet, and sidewalk. It's an evil voice – it doesn't play fair. It preys on your deepest anxieties, basest frailties, past failures, insecurities, and inhibitions.

But there's another voice – God's! Attuning your ears to His voice doesn't mean all your problems are automatically solved, or that the other voice just fades away. No, it's more like having an intimate conversation with an old friend in a noisy, crowded place. There may be other voices around you, but you don't hear them because you're so focused on what your friend is saying.

It's the same with the voice of God. Whether He speaks to you through the Scriptures, through a friend, or through your life circumstances, He's *always* communicating with the heart that seeks Him. His promise to you is, "Your ears will hear a voice . . . saying 'This is the way; walk in it.'"

One word from God, just one, can change everything for you. So today take the time to listen for His voice!

VOICES – PART 2

Your ears will hear a voice . . . saying . . .
this is the way; walk in it.
Isaiah 30:21 NIV

To be successful at anything God calls you to, you must: (a) constantly be in touch with the Holy Spirit within you; (b) learn to recognize when He speaks to you through His Word.

When the pressure is on and you're tempted to move too quickly, you'll hear His voice saying: "You will not leave in haste or go in flight; for the Lord will go before you . . . God . . . will be your rear guard [He'll come behind you and back you up]" (Isa 52:12 NIV).

When you're about to make a wrong turn or a bad decision, His voice will reassure you, "In his heart a man plans his course, but the Lord determines his steps" (Pr 16:9 NIV).

When you don't have the wherewithal to get the job done, His voice will whisper, "The Lord will guide you always; he will satisfy your needs in a sun-scorched land and will strengthen your frame. You will be like a . . . spring whose waters never fail" (Isa 58:11 NIV).

When you run out of answers and don't know what to do, His voice will whisper, "I will instruct you and teach you in the way you should go; I will counsel you and watch over you" (Ps 32:8 NIV).

When the load becomes too heavy to carry, you'll hear His voice saying, "Cast your cares on the Lord and he will sustain you; he will never let the righteous fall" (Ps 55:22 NIV). Today take time to listen for God's voice.

GOD'S GOT YOU COVERED!

He allowed no man to do them wrong . . .
saying, touch not My anointed.
1 Chronicles 16:21-22 AMP

Nebuchadnezzar took God's sacred vessels from the temple at Jerusalem and placed them in a pagan temple at Shinar (Dan 1:1-2). After his son Belshazzar became king, one night during a drunken feast, "They brought in the . . . goblets . . . from the temple of God . . . and the king . . . and his concubines drank from them" (Dan 5:3 NIV). That was a bad move!

If they'd defiled some worthless old cups it mightn't have mattered, but God had too much invested in these sacred vessels to allow them to be mishandled. That night Belshazzar and his entire kingdom were destroyed. Why? Because of this Bible principle: "He allowed no man to do them wrong; yes, He reproved kings for their sakes, Saying, Touch not My anointed, and do My prophets no harm." Even in hostile surroundings, God's chosen vessels still belong to Him, and the enemy disturbs them at his peril.

You may have to live and work in a difficult situation. You may have to endure great hardship for your faith. But understand – God's got too much invested in you to let you be destroyed! Anytime Satan tries that, God will disrupt his party and say, "This vessel's off limits; it took Me too long to teach this woman how to pray . . . I've devoted too many hours training this man how to overcome. They've just learned how to stand amidst trials . . . they've suffered too much for My sake for Me to let you harm them. The party's over – they're Mine!" *Rejoice – if you belong to God, you're fully protected!*

RUNNING TO WIN

In a race all the runners run, but only one gets the prize.
So run to win!
1 Corinthians 9:24 NCV

In life you only get to run once, so run to win! To avoid stumbling and losing your place, don't look back. You can't change the past, but thank God you can learn from it and leave it behind. Don't be anxious about the next *lap;* focus only on the next *step.* If you miss *that* you may fall and not get up again.

Before you know it you'll soon have more laps behind you than ahead of you. So make every lap count. Listen, "Let us run the race that is before us and never give up. We should remove from our lives anything that would get in the way and the sin that so easily holds us back" (Heb 12:1 NCV).

Many of us carry the weight and worry of burdens which older and wiser people understand are of no real importance. We spend our energies extinguishing fires that, if left alone, would burn out on their own. Time is your most valuable resource; save it and you've increased your assets and decreased your liabilities.

Get rid of the baggage of old relationships, pointless fears, and false indebtedness to those who seek to manipulate you. There are enough painful trials in life; why endure the ones you can lay aside? When blind Bartimaeus heard that Jesus was within reach, he threw off his coat (lest it trip him up) and ran toward Him. Today you need to do the same.

THE CHURCH'S ALL-TIME BIGGEST BLUNDERS

I will build My church.

Matthew 16:18

It's never too late for the church to learn from its blunders. Here are seven:

(1) *We've made unbelief a doctrine.* While third-world nations believe God for New Testament results, we teach our seminary students that God doesn't do miracles anymore.

(2) *We've tolerated division.* Who needs Satan when we're so adept at hating one another in the name of denominational loyalty?

(3) *We've cultivated a religious spirit.* We've taught that Christianity is about avoiding things like smoking and drinking. As a result we've lost our joy, because intimacy with God cannot be achieved through performance.

(4) *We've encouraged "super stars."* Consequently, some of our preachers have stopped modeling servanthood, and forgotten that Jesus washed feet and rode on a donkey.

(5) *We've equated money with success.* We've found a way to "theologize" greed, instead of using our God-given prosperity to feed the poor and reach the world with the Gospel.

(6) *We've stayed in the pews and become irrelevant.* We freak out when somebody uses rap or rock music to reach the younger generation. Instead of engaging the culture, we're hiding from it.

(7) *We've taught people to be escape-artists.* Instead of "occupying till He comes," we'd rather be astronauts and fly away. We read rapture novels when we should be praying for those living on the verge of martyrdom. Why don't we have their kind of faith? We can – if we're willing to pay the price and commit ourselves fully to God!

TRY TO GET MORE SLEEP

He giveth His beloved sleep.
Psalms 127:2

John Ortberg writes, "I discovered when trying to live in a loving fashion for one whole day, that love requires an enormous amount of energy – and I was just too tired to give it. I realized that as unspiritual as it sounds, if I was serious about becoming a more loving person, I was going to have to get more sleep. I also discovered that I have a very hard time thinking, feeling, and acting like Jesus, when I lack sleep."

Sleep is an act of trust: when you go to sleep the world's in God's hands, not yours. It'll get along very well even though you're not awake to control things! At the appropriate time your eyes will open and you'll receive the gift of another new day. David said, "I lie down and sleep; I wake again, because the Lord sustains me" (Ps 3:5 NIV).

Have you ever tried to *pray* when you were lacking sleep? It's hard. Before Elijah was able to spend any prolonged time in prayer, the Angel of the Lord made him take not one, but *two* long naps. Contrast that with the disciples in Gethsemane who couldn't pray because they kept falling asleep.

Sleep is a gift from God; listen, "It is vain for you to rise up early, to sit up late . . . for so he giveth his beloved sleep" (Ps 127:2). *Maybe the single most spiritual thing you could do right now is to put this book down and take a nap!*

ALL IN THE FAMILY – PART 1

Obey His laws . . . so that things will go well for you and your children.
Deuteronomy 4:40 NCV

Periodically we all need a jolt to wake us up to the less-than-ideal way we treat our family members.

John Maxwell tells of a man he met through *Promise Keepers.* One day the man's daughter, who was in second grade, was asked by her teacher to draw a picture of her family. She loved to draw so she willingly tackled the assignment. That evening she proudly brought her artwork home and showed it to her parents. When her dad looked at the picture he said, "What's this picture of?" His daughter replied, "That's us and our house. The teacher asked me to draw a picture of our family." He looked at the picture more carefully and saw that every one was there – except him. "Sweetheart," he asked, "Am I in the picture?" "No," she replied. "Why not?" he asked. *"Because this is a picture of us at home, and you're never here!"*

It was as if she'd dropped the piano on him! She'd stated a simple fact without malice or any desire to inflict guilt. That was the day he decided he was going to turn his bus around and head back to his family.

If *you've* been traveling down the road to success, but neglected to bring your family along, it's time to make a U-turn. Go back and pick up the people who matter most! Commit yourself to traveling only on a journey that includes *them!*

ALL IN THE FAMILY – PART 2

Enjoy life with your wife [and your husband], whom you love.
Ecclesiastes 9:9 NIV

Benjamin Franklin said, "Those things that hurt, instruct." If we're to grow as families, to be as successful there as we are in other areas, we must learn how to cope with difficulties at home. Marriages *start* because of love, but they continue because of commitment. Here are some suggestions for troubleshooting at home:

(1) *Attack the problem, not the person!* You're all on the same team, so don't take your frustrations out on your loved ones.

(2) *Get all the facts.* Before you offer (or impose) solutions, make sure you really understand the problem. Think before you speak. Nothing's more damaging than jumping to conclusions.

(3) *List all your options.* When you do you'll be less emotional and more objective. If you had a problem at work that's how you'd handle it, so why not do the same for your family?

(4) *Look for the positives.* Scott Peck writes, "It's only because of problems that we grow mentally and spiritually. It's through the pain of confronting and resolving them that we learn." No matter how bad things seem at the time, every situation holds something positive – so look for it.

(5) *Never withhold your love.* No matter how rough the going gets, never withhold your love. It's okay to tell your family how you feel, so long as you do it graciously. But make sure they know that you love them unconditionally despite the problems. Why? Because when people feel loved and supported they can weather just about any crisis!

ALL IN THE FAMILY – PART 3

Be kind to one another, tender-hearted.
Ephesians 4:32 NAS

The average couple spends about thirty-seven minutes a week in meaningful communication. They spend five times more each day watching television! No wonder we're in trouble! Like anything else, good communication doesn't just happen; it must be developed, and that takes time and effort. Wanna communicate better? Here's how:

(1) *Build platforms for communication.* Be creative. Take walks together as a family. Call your partner during the day. Try to meet for lunch once a week. Offer to drive the kids to soccer practice so you can talk to them. Communication can happen anywhere.

(2) *Control communication killers.* TV's and phones are the chief culprits. Restrict the time you give them and you'll be amazed how much more time you'll have together.

(3) *Encourage honesty and transparency.* Differences of opinion are healthy and normal in any family. Encourage every member to speak his or her mind, and when they do, don't criticize or retaliate.

(4) *Adopt a positive communication style.* Be conscious of the way you interact with your family. You may unwittingly have adopted a style that stifles communication. The fastest way to do this is to: (a) *retaliate* – that has a degrading effect; (b) *dominate* – that has an intimidating effect; (c) *isolate* – go off in a huff; that has a frustrating effect. Instead, *cooperate* – that has an encouraging effect. If you're in the habit of using any communication style other than a cooperative one, start working immediately to change it. You'll have to if you want to build a good relationship with your family.

THE NEED TO TURN ASIDE

I must turn aside and look.
Exodus 3:3 NRSV

One day Moses walked past a shrub he'd probably seen a hundred times before, only this time it was on fire with God's presence. Moses said, "I must turn aside and look at this great sight." Everything depended on his willingness to "turn aside" – to interrupt his daily routine and pay attention to God. He didn't have to. He could've looked the other way and said, "I'm busy," and kept right on going. But then he'd have missed his calling and the reason for his existence. He'd also have missed knowing God. What a loss! But he didn't – he "turned aside."

God wanted to begin a new nation and He wanted Moses to lead it. God's timing seemed strange. Forty years ago Moses was young; the product of the finest education system in the world. Then he had powerful connections and high hopes. But now he was a nobody, an anonymous shepherd in a forgotten desert, rejected by his own people and a fugitive from the Egyptians.

"Who am I that I should go to Pharaoh?" Moses asked. "Nobody knows me. I'm slow of speech. I'm disappointed in myself." What God said to Moses, He's saying to you as you read this: "I've seen your track record and it doesn't matter – for I will be with you. Your guilt and your inadequacies are no longer the ultimate truth about you. You are what you are, but you're not yet what you will be – because I'm with you!" *Need direction today? Slow down, turn aside, and listen to God!*

POSITIVE PEOPLE

As he thinketh in his heart, so is he.
Proverbs 23:7

Are you a positive person? Before you answer check out the following attributes of positive people:

(1) *They believe in themselves.* Dr. Joyce Brothers said, "Many people succeed even when others don't believe in them, but rarely does a person succeed when he doesn't believe in himself."

(2) *They look for the best in others, and usually find it.* People will generally rise to meet your expectations. Your words of encouragement become the wind beneath their wings.

(3) *They see opportunity everywhere.* Opportunities are all around us just waiting to be seized. Always try to say yes, because nothing good happens for people who always say no.

(4) *They focus on solutions.* Anybody can see problems, faith-filled people focus on solutions. Ever notice how things turn out best for those who make the best of how things turn out?

(5) *They look for ways to give back.* Psychiatrist Carl Menninger says, "Generous people are rarely mentally ill, because giving to others is the highest level of living."

(6) *They are persistent.* Many people fail because they subscribe to the adage, "If at first you don't succeed – try something else!" Dreams come true for those who refuse to let discouragement get the upper hand.

(7) *They take responsibility for themselves.* Positive people understand that nothing good happens until you're willing to step forward and take responsibility for your thoughts and actions. Only then can you look yourself in the eye, discover your strengths and weaknesses, and begin to change.

STRUGGLING WITH LOW SELF-ESTEEM?

It's in Christ that we find out who we are and what we are living for.
Ephesians 1:9 TM

Until God tells you who you are, you'll know neither your *worth* nor your *purpose.* And worse, others will be able to label and control you. That's why Paul writes, "It's in Christ that we find out who we are and what we're living for." Until you really know who you are you'll: (1) always worry about how you look; (2) always worry about what others think of you; (3) always worry about whether or not you're going to fail. But when you believe in yourself, you're free to focus on improving and reaching your God-given potential.

If you're struggling with low self-worth, here's a prayer to help you: "Father, sometimes I think I'm of no use, that I can't do anything right, that nothing I do is ever good enough. Then I remember that when You look at who I am, and who I can be – You see Jesus! And He is good enough!

"It's good enough that He shed His precious blood to cover my unworthiness. Good enough that He paid the price for every sin I'll ever commit. Good enough that He's perfecting me each day. Good enough that I am the righteousness of God in Christ. Good enough that He's interceding for me right now. Good enough that He's washed me clean and made me whole. Good enough that His love for me is everlasting and guaranteed.

"Thank you Father that everything Jesus does is good enough, and that in Him, I'm good enough too!"

"FIGHT ONE MORE ROUND"

Be strong and let your heart take courage,
all you who hope in the Lord.
Psalm 31:24 NAS

When prizefighter James Corbett was asked what it takes to become a champion, he replied, "Fight one more round!" Did you know that: (1) Somerset Maugham earned only five hundred dollars during his first ten years as a writer? (2) Enrico Caruso was a factory worker who studied voice for twelve years before getting his first small break? (3) Gershwin composed one hundred melodies before he sold one – for five dollars? (4) Zane Grey didn't sell a single story during his first five years as a writer?

Study the lives of those you most admire and you'll discover that they spent years surmounting obstacles, facing their deepest fears, learning from repeated failures, rising above the predictions of those who said, "You'll never make it."

If you're looking for a neat, clean, respectable, no-loose-ends formula for success, forget it! Success is sweat, perspective, and dirt under your fingernails. It's discipline, commitment, and a long distance view. It's the tenacious bulldog quality of a Churchill rising in the darkest hours of World War II to tell the nation, "What is our aim? I can answer in one word: victory . . . at all costs, victory, in spite of all terror, victory, however long and hard the road may be; for without victory there is no survival."

Don't be discouraged if your dream hasn't come true yet. Keep pursuing it. Pray over it daily. Study and learn. Grow by experience. *Keep working. Victory always goes to the man or woman who's willing to "fight one more round!"*

UNFORGIVENESS

Confess your faults one to another,
and pray one for another, that ye may be healed.
James 5:16

Jesus said, "When you offer your gift to God at the altar, and you remember that your brother or sister has something against you, leave your gift . . . Go and make peace . . . then come and offer your gift" (Mt 5:23-24 NCV). It's pointless to pray for other things until you've first made things right with those you need to forgive, or ask forgiveness from.

But what if it's impossible to be reconciled because the person has died? You can't get a hearing, yet you're still troubled about it. Here's a suggestion: share your feelings with somebody you trust – a spouse, a counselor, a pastor. Be specific and completely honest. Pray with them, openly confessing your wrongs and the guilt you feel. You'll be surprised at how prayer and the presence of an understanding, affirming friend, can provide the relief you so desperately seek.

After David had indirectly murdered Uriah, Bathsheba's husband, his guilt was enormous. Adultery and hypocrisy just about wiped him out. When he could take it no more, he broke his silence and sought God's forgiveness. But Uriah wasn't around to hear his confession; he'd been dead almost a year. So the broken king called on the prophet Nathan and poured out his soul saying, "I have sinned." Nathan listened patiently, then said, "The Lord has taken away your sin" (2Sa 12:13 NIV).

When you've hurt somebody, have the heart of a servant. Stop, go make things right, and then move forward with confidence.

YOU CAN'T DO IT BY YOURSELF

You . . . became my partners.
Philippians 4:15 TLB

At midnight November 20, 1988, a nineteen-year-old woman who'd fallen asleep behind the wheel, plunged her car through a guardrail. It dangled sixty feet in the air. Some motorists stopped, grabbed ropes, tied them to the back of the woman's car and hung on until emergency units arrived. A ladder was extended from below to help stabilize the car while fire fighters chained the vehicle to two trucks. Every time her car moved she screamed. It took over two hours for passers-by, the Highway Patrol, tow-truck drivers and fire fighters – about twenty-five people in all – to pull her to safety. "It was kinda funny," L.A. Fire Captain Ross Marshall recalled later. "She kept shouting, 'I'll do it myself!'"

Are you like that? Trying to do it all on your own? On his office wall, Alex Haley, the author of *Roots,* has a picture of a turtle sitting on top of a six-foot fence post. The caption reads, "You can be sure he had help getting up there!" Haley says, "Anytime I feel too proud to ask for help, I look at that picture."

Somebody within your reach knows something you need to know; something you'll never learn on your own. They're your mentor. Get close to them. Drop your bucket into their well and begin to draw water.

Paul recognized his limitations so he connected his life to others. Listen, "You Philippians became my partners in giving and receiving" (Php 4:15). Some of us know how to give but not receive. Others know how to receive but not give. Winners know how to do both!

LEADERSHIP – PART 1

I heard the Lord saying, "Whom shall I send?" and I said, "Here am I, send me."
Isaiah 6:8 NIV

The need for good leadership has never been clearer, the price has never been higher, the temptations have never been greater. If you've been called to lead in any area of life, you'll need these three qualities:

(1) *Compassion.* Anthony DeMello saw a starving child shivering in the cold. Angrily he lifted his eyes to heaven and said, "God, why don't you do something?" God answered, "I did – I made you!" Leadership isn't using others to build your kingdom, it's loving and serving them in order to build God's!

(2) *Creativity.* Homer wrote, "Adversity has the effect of eliciting talents which in prosperous circumstances would have lain dormant." The story is told of a chicken farmer whose land flooded each spring, killing all his chickens. In despair he told his wife, "I've had it; I can't afford to buy another place, and I can't sell this one. What can I do?" Calmly she replied, "Buy ducks!" The true leader looks for a creative solution in every problem, then acts on it.

(3) *Commitment.* Real leaders don't quit – they couldn't even if they wanted to. One young man said to his pastor, "It must be really hard living for others, leading an exemplary life, handling all the pressures, and having to set a good example with people waiting for one sign of human frailty so that they can jump on you. How do you handle it?" Sheepishly he replied, "I stay at home a lot!" *Before you say, "Lord, send me," ask yourself, "Do I have what it takes?"*

LEADERSHIP – PART 2

We who teach will be judged more strictly.
James 3:1 NIV

Years ago some wag scrawled on the walls of Canterbury Cathedral, "The Archbishop cheats at Scrabble." Apparently even archbishops can have chinks in their armor! But then again, don't we all? The important thing is to discover your flaws and deal with them. You can avoid mistakes by listening for "alarm bells." Maybe these questions will ring some for you:

(1) *Is my personal walk with God up to date?* If that question doesn't prompt a quick yes, you're getting too close to the edge. A disciplined daily walk is your best protection. David says, "Your word have I treasured in my heart that I may not sin against you" (Ps 119:11 NAS). What we think about is what we become! Look out! If you're not spending time with God, you're spending it on whatever has become more important to you than Him.

(2) *Are my priorities in order?* Priorities have a way of sneaking out of position when we're not paying attention. Too many of us only become "successful" at the cost of broken homes or lost health, because at some point along the road to success our priorities shifted.

(3) *Am I accountable to anybody?* You should be scared of following anybody who isn't! Only God can handle ultimate, unquestioned authority. Paul writes, "Appreciate those who . . . have charge over you in the Lord" (See 1Th 5:12-13 NAS). We all need people in our lives with 20/20 vision to cover our blind spots and keep us balanced. Authority without accountability equals disaster. *Still think you're called to lead?*

LEADERSHIP – PART 3

To whom they entrusted much,
of him they will ask all the more.
Luke 12:48 NAS

Let's pick up where we left off yesterday.

(1) *Am I asking myself the difficult questions?* What questions are they? (a) Why am I doing this? You may be doing a great job, but if you're doing it with the wrong motives, don't count on God to bless your efforts. Remember, "By Him actions are weighed" (1Sa 2:3 NKJV). (b) How should it be done? The danger of presumption is ever present, especially to those called to a ministry of faith. (c) When should I do it? Aggressive leaders, like Abraham, have a tendency to run ahead of God and produce an "Ishmael."

(2) *Am I overly concerned with image building?* When pretense replaces passion we're in trouble. Check yourself in these areas: (a) *Character;* do I make decisions based on what's right or what's popular? (b) *Change;* do I behave differently according to whom I'm with? (c) *Credit;* do people see more of God than of me? Is my goal that He should receive all the glory? (d) *Channel;* is God working through my life to change others? If not, it's a good indication that I'm building my kingdom, not His.

(3) *Am I sensitive to what God says through others in the Body of Christ?* If not, you've no checks and balances! God not only uses others to speak, He uses them to correct and challenge us; in other words – to be better than we are. Have you been called to lead? If so, talk to God about these issues.

LEADERSHIP – PART 4

Simon . . . do you love Me more than these?
John 21:15 NAS

The question the Chief Shepherd most wants His under-shepherd to answer isn't, "How much do you *know* about Me?" Or even, "How much are you telling *others* about Me?" No, it's, "How much do you love Me?" If you really love Him and want to do His will, answer these questions:

(1) *Am I a loner in my service to my Lord?* When Dr. David Yonggi Cho, Pastor of the world's largest church (800,000 members), spoke to 1,000 ministers in Buffalo, New York, he introduced one of his staff members. "I always bring this man with me," he said, "Because I am susceptible to sexual temptation and he's my safe-guard." The auditorium was silent, but everybody knew what he meant.

(2) *Am I honest about my weaknesses?* Most of us have a tendency to try to cover them up. What are your areas of weakness? Do you smile publicly, but secretly resent it when others disagree with you? Do you get into things simply because they're ego gratifying? Do you set a standard for others that you don't live up to yourself? The first step to overcoming is admitting you have a problem.

(3) *Is my commitment to God constantly before me?* Paul writes, "Stay the way you were when God called you" (1Co 7:20 NCV). There's nothing more tragic than losing your focus and getting side-tracked. When Paul stood before King Agrippa he said, "I was not disobedient unto the heavenly vision" (Acts 26:19). If you've been truly called of God to lead, you'll be able to say that too!

OFF LIMITS!

We have this treasure in earthen vessels, that the . . . power may be of God, and not of us.
2 Corinthians 4:7

Do you know there are people who are literally "off limits" to Satan? It's not that they're spiritual giants; it's that they're vital to God's plans. They're ordinary clay pots filled with extraordinary ointment. The glory doesn't come from them, but from what God has placed inside them. As a result Satan can't touch them.

We run into problems when we think that these people aren't made from the same "stuff" as we are – because they are! We must always be careful to make the distinction between the treasure and the vessel. Never allow anyone to expect you to be the treasure. Paul says, "We *have* this treasure," he didn't say we *are* the treasure.

God uses people we'd never use; like Rahab, working the red light district in Jericho. She was well known in the neighborhood. She was a walking commercial. Her bracelets jingled when she walked down the street so the guys could check her out! But when she placed her faith in God, He used her to help win the Battle of Jericho, and then included her in the lineage of Christ. Isn't grace amazing?

God specializes in restoring broken vessels. He takes things that aren't productive, like marriages that don't work, people who've failed, and teaches them how to be victorious and fruitful in His service.

Knowing this can give you the tenacity and strength to face whatever comes. Because you know that when God places His treasure inside you, unless *He* takes you down, nothing else can!

LESSONS FROM A TAVERN

Men will know that you are My disciples,
if you love one another.
John 13:35 NIV

Chuck Swindoll writes: "One day a Marine Corps buddy who came to Christ told me, 'Chuck, the thing I still miss most is the fellowship I had with the guys at the tavern. I can't find it amongst the Christians I've met. I no longer have a place to admit my faults and talk about my struggles, where somebody won't preach, frown, quote a verse, or blab it all over the place.'

"The neighborhood tavern's an attractive counterfeit for the church. Ever watch *Cheers?* It's an imitation, dispensing liquor instead of grace, and escape instead of reality. But it's an accepting and inclusive fellowship; unshockable and democratic. You can tell them your secrets and they usually won't tell others. It flourishes not because its patrons are all alcoholics, but because each of us has a God-given desire to know and be known, love and be loved, and we seek these things for the price of a few beers.

"Christ wants His church to be unshockable; a fellowship where people can come and say, 'I'm beat . . . I've had it,' and find real answers! Now before you shoot me for comparing your church to a tavern, ask yourself, (a) If you discovered your spouse had been unfaithful, who could you confide in? (b) If your biopsy confirmed cancer, who would you turn to? (c) If you were lonely, where would you go?"

Jesus said, "Men will know you are my disciples, *if you love one another.*" And love ain't what you say, it's what you *do!*

TRAINING – NOT TRYING!

For it is God who works in you to will and to act according to His good purpose.
Philippians 2:13 NIV

You don't *try* to run a marathon, you *train* to run it, otherwise you end up exhausted and defeated. The kind of training we're talking about isn't a teeth-gritting, white-knuckle, do-or-die attitude toward things like prayer and Bible reading. No, it's training yourself to be more sensitive to God. It's learning to do the right thing, at the right time, in the right way, with the right spirit.

Your goal may be to read several chapters of the Bible each day, but what if God tells you to linger at a certain Scripture because He wants to make that particular truth a *reality* in your daily life?

The difference between trying and training is like the difference between a motorboat and a sailboat. You can turn one on and drive it away, but with the other you have to wait for the wind. Jesus said, "The wind blows wherever it pleases. You hear its sound, but you cannot tell where it comes from or where it is going. So it is with everyone born of the Spirit" (Jn 3:8 NIV). It's the wind that does the work. We can't turn it on or off. We can't engineer it or take credit for it. But like good sailors we can train ourselves to "read" it and respond to it.

Once we learn to do that, we're walking in the Spirit instead of straining in the flesh. Today ask God to help *you* live that way.

DON'T BE AFRAID!

When I am afraid . . . I will trust the promises of God.
Psalms 56:3-4 TLB

Have you any idea how much it's costing you to fear things that *never* happen? Meteorologists say that a fog capable of covering seven city blocks is made up of only *one glass* of water divided into sixty million particles. But when it settles it can obscure your entire vision! A little fear can do the same thing!

Why do almost *half* of us suffer from stress-related disorders? Because instead of walking by faith, we think we're supposed to fly like jets on supercharged adrenaline – and we pay for it in terms of fear and anxiety.

It's so easy for fear to replace faith because they've got something in common – *both challenge you to believe that what you can't see is about to happen.* Fear will convince you to run from something that's not after you at all. Billy Sunday said, "Fear knocked at my door. Faith answered. There was no one there."

How do you overcome this fear? By faith – and faith comes by hearing the Word of God (See Ro 10:17). Begin to feed your faith on the Scriptures, and watch your fears starve to death!

Howard Chandler says, "I spend the first fifteen minutes of every morning filling my mind with God's Word, that way there's no room left for worry." Good formula! David says, "When I am afraid, I will . . . trust the promises of God" (Ps 56:3-4 TLB). And you've got to do the same! Today, get into His Word and you'll discover that God's got everything under control.

A MEMO FROM GOD

How precious . . . to realize that
You are thinking about me constantly!
Psalms 139:17 TLB

"I knew you before time began. I even know how many hairs are on your head! Like parent, like child; you're created in My image. Not only have I got plans for you, I've also given you the talents needed to fulfill them. And what I give, nobody else can take away. But don't neglect them; remember to exercise them and stir them up daily.

"Rest assured that I've started a good work in you and I'm going to finish it. I always complete what I begin. My Word concerning you is forever settled in heaven. My commitment to you is unending.

"In this life you'll have challenges, but cheer up; I've robbed Satan of his power to hurt you, and the world of its power to destroy you! When you're in trouble, remember I'm a very present help. Give Me your burdens and I'll sustain you. When you're stressed-out or weighed down by the pressures of life, lean on Me. I'll be your Rock, your Fortress, your Deliverer and your Strength. Even though you fall from time to time, you won't be destroyed because I'm holding you.

"But a word of caution: don't take advice from those who are spiritually blind, and don't hang out with skeptics. Delight yourself in My Word, and like a big oak tree growing by a river, you'll be fruitful and prosper in all that you do." PS: "I'd love to hear back from you. See you at My place on Sunday!"

PERSUADED BEYOND DOUBT

I am persuaded beyond doubt . . . that [nothing] will be able to separate us from the love of God.

Romans 8:38-39 AMP

Doesn't it blow your mind to think that nothing – absolutely nothing – can ever cause God to turn His back on us? Most of us are just religious enough to believe that there are certain sins God can't get over – you know, like the ones *we* never commit!

But how about the destructive power of gossip, or stubbornness, or pride? Remember the Pharisee who prayed, "I thank you that I am not like other people" (Lk 18:11 TM)? Ever feel that way? Come on, be honest! God's standard is "perfection" and you couldn't reach it in *a thousand* lifetimes. Grace, God's unmerited favor, is the only hope any of us have!

Your level of love will always correlate to the level of forgiveness you've received. Jesus taught that those who've been forgiven much, love much! (See Lk 7:47 NIV). Paul writes, "Where sin abounded, grace did much more abound" (Ro 5:20). That means though you're a big sinner, Jesus is a bigger Savior. It means God doesn't always approve of your *behavior,* but He always loves and accepts *you.*

Ever try to reconcile your checking account, and no matter what you do it won't balance? Spiritually speaking, that's why you need the cross. Listen, "God was in Christ, *reconciling* the world unto himself" (2Co 5:19). At Calvary God balanced your account. Your slate's been wiped clean. Now He says, "Come and be reconciled to me. Let's have a relationship. You've nothing to fear, for nothing can separate you from My love."

YOU'RE FREE!

The Lord has anointed me . . .
to proclaim liberty to the captives.
Isaiah 61:1 NKJV

During WWII an American professor and a British Army chaplain were imprisoned in a German POW camp – the professor on the American side, the chaplain on the British side. Since the Americans had secretly built a homemade radio, the two friends would meet at the fence each day to discuss the latest news. (To communicate they used an ancient Gaelic language that their captors didn't understand.)

When the professor heard over the radio that the Germans had surrendered three days earlier, he told his friend on the other side of the fence. Moments later a roar of celebration went up from the British barracks. When the news reached the German guards several days later, they fled leaving the gates unlocked, and the British and Americans walked out together as free men.

Jesus said He came, "to proclaim liberty to the captives" (Is 61:1 NKJV). Good news – Satan is now a defeated foe. Your prison door is open; your freedom has been won at Calvary – *accept* it, act on it, and stop living like a prisoner!

Did you know that the African impala can jump ten feet high and cover a distance of ten yards? Yet this magnificent animal can be confined within walls only three feet high. Why? Because unless it first sees where it's going to land it's afraid to jump.

Faith is the ability to jump and trust God, even when you can't see. It opens doors and frees you from every prison of fear. Today, "The Son has made you free" – start acting like it!

"HEART PRINTS"

Love suffers long and is kind . . . is not provoked . . . endures all things.
1 Corinthians 13:4-7 NKJV

When William McKinley campaigned for president he was hounded by an impoverished young reporter who continually attacked him. One bitterly cold night the reporter, who didn't have a winter coat, sat shivering outside the coach in which the future president was traveling. When McKinley saw him he stopped and said, "Here, put on my overcoat and ride inside with me." "But you don't know who I am," the reporter stammered, "I've been ripping you to pieces." "I *know* who you are, it makes no difference," McKinley replied. "Put on my coat and come inside where it's warm."

That's love in action! When Jesus was teaching His disciples about going the extra mile He said, "If any man . . . take away thy coat, let him have thy cloak also" (Mt 5:40). Margaret Mead said, "Never believe that a few caring people can't change the world, indeed that's all who ever have." That night William McKinley touched a young man's life, because "Love suffers long, and is kind."

We leave fingerprints on whatever we touch – walls, furniture, doorknobs, dishes, and books. There's no escape; when we touch anything we leave our identity on it. So today pray, "Lord, wherever I go let me leave *heart prints!* Heart prints of understanding, love, kindness, and genuine concern. May my heart touch a lonely neighbor, a runaway son or daughter, an anxious mother, or an aging grandfather. And if somebody should say, 'I felt your touch,' may it be because they sensed *Your love through me.*"

ARE YOU RESPONDING TO PRESSURES OR PRIORITIES?

He shall . . . wear out the saints.

Daniel 7:25

One day a caterpillar met a friend at the psychiatrist's office and asked, "Are you coming or going?" His friend replied, "If I knew that I wouldn't be here!" Satan's goal is to wear you out until you don't know whether you're coming or going! He does it by weighing you down with things that aren't necessarily *sinful,* but drain you physically and emotionally. Daniel says that in the last days the enemy will "wear out the saints." If you doubt it, look at the pressures you face every day – work, finances, church commitments, and family. No wonder you're frazzled!

Paul says, "Let us lay aside every weight . . . and . . . run . . . the race . . . set before us" (He 12:1). Knowing what to pick up and what to set down is *your* job – not God's.

Establish priorities, then discipline yourself to live by them. Nobody was more dedicated to God's work than Jesus, but even He needed time alone with His Father. One of the first priorities set by the New Testament church leaders was to dedicate themselves to God's Word and prayer. How? By assigning others to handle the administrative load. (See Acts 6).

Learn: (a) what to offload, (b) what to delegate, (c) what not to pick up in the first place. And saying, "I don't have time," doesn't cut it. Everybody gets the same twenty-four hours to respond to either pressures or priorities. Decide what to set aside for now, and what to unload for good. *Don't get so involved with the work of God that you neglect the God of the work!*

WHERE'S THE BREAD?

The bread of [Thy] Presence.
Numbers 4:7 NRSV

Bread in The Old Testament symbolized God's presence. That's why Numbers 4:7 refers to "the bread of [thy] Presence." When famine drove Naomi and her family out of Bethlehem *(House of Bread),* they left for the same reason people leave churches today – no bread!

Tommy Tenney writes: "Why do so many people flock to clubs and bars looking for crumbs? Because they tried the church and found only old recipes and cold ovens; there was no presence of God in the pantry.

"For some churches it's a pride thing; through tradition, they try to preserve the image of where God's been, at the expense of where He is *now!* They talk about what He *used* to do – but what about *now?* It's time we set aside our personal agendas and man-made games; it's time to say, 'He must increase, but I must decrease' (Jn 3:30).

"When people experience the presence of God it overrides human theologies and changes hearts. Why? Because someone with an experience is never at the mercy of someone with an argument. On the other hand, when people experience only a *hint* of God mixed with other things, it immunizes them to the real thing.

"The problem isn't that God's not *in* the church, it's that sometimes there's not *enough* of Him to make the needed difference! Ezekiel said, 'I saw water coming out from under the threshold of the temple' (Ez 47:1 NIV). If living water is to reach this generation, it must first flow down through the church aisles and out through *us!*"

SPEAKING GOD'S LANGUAGE – PART 1

Say unto this mountain, be thou removed.
Mark 11:23

Stop talking *about* your mountain and start talking *to* it! Listen: "Whoever says to this mountain, Be . . . thrown into the sea and does not doubt . . . it will be done" (Mk 11:23 AMP). How do you talk to a mountain?

(1) *By using God's Word.* When Satan tempted Him in the wilderness, Jesus responded three times, "It is written," and Satan couldn't stand up to Him. The enemy doesn't respect what you say, but he trembles every time God speaks. Because *His* Word is power-packed and Satan hopes you never discover that!

(2) *By being persistent.* Ever wonder how you can hammer a rock ninety-nine times and nothing happens, yet on the one hundredth blow it shatters? That's because all the previous blows have weakened it. Keep speaking God's Word in faith over your situation and "It will be done."

(3) *By forgiving.* One pastor asked his congregation, "How many of you are willing to forgive your enemies?" Everybody was, except one elderly man. "Why won't you forgive your enemies?" the pastor asked. "Because I have none, I've outlived them all!" Listen: "Whenever you stand praying, if you have anything against anyone, forgive" (Mk 11:25 AMP). Before you can speak to a mountain of trouble – and get results – you must first speak forgiveness to others. God's promises depend on your obedience. Remember, "If you will *listen* diligently . . . watchful to do all His commandments . . . *these blessings shall come*" (Dt 28:1-2 AMP). That's how you talk to a mountain!

SPEAKING GOD'S LANGUAGE – PART 2

Do all things without . . . complaining.
Philippians 2:14 AMP

If somebody gave you a dollar every time you complained and collected one every time you showed gratitude, would you be rich or poor? Maybe you're thinking, "If you had *my* problems you'd complain too!" Listen, "Do all things without . . . complaining" (Php 2:14 AMP). That's not a suggestion it's an order! Why? Because the more you complain, the worse things get. Consider this:

(1) *Complaining is addictive.* The cycle goes like this: (a) You've got a problem. (b) You complain and remain stuck in the problem. (c) Satan pours on the "poor me's" and you complain even more. (d) You end up living in constant crisis.

(2) *It's also destructive.* Would it surprise you to know that God sees your complaining as criticism of His provision? In fact, when the Israelites did it He destroyed them. Listen, "Do not grumble, as some of them did – and were killed . . . These things . . . were written down as warnings for us" (1Co 10:10-11 NIV). Think maybe it's time for an "attitude check?"

(3) *It can make you sick.* Solomon said, "A calm and undisturbed mind and heart are the life and health of the body" (Pr 14:30 AMP). How many "calm and undisturbed" complainers do you know?

(4) *It can ruin your future.* People who build their lives around past problems never move forward. Paul writes, "Forgetting those things which are behind, and reaching forth unto those things which are before" (Php 3:13). You'll never connect with your future till you disconnect from your past. So starting today, make up your mind to "Do all things without . . . complaining!"

SPEAKING GOD'S LANGUAGE – PART 3

I will not tolerate anyone who . . . slanders.
Psalms 101:5 TLB

It bothers God when your tongue praises Him on Sunday and tears somebody apart on Monday. James says, "These things ought not so to be" (Jas 3:10). Slander stems from pride, from an attitude that says in effect, "I'm right and everybody else is wrong." Remember, "All a man's ways seem innocent to him, but motives are weighed by the Lord" (Pr 16:2 NIV). Too many people flock to church altars for healing from the wounds inflicted on them by Christians. Gossip has broken their spirits.

A leading Bible teacher writes: "I went through a period of trying to overcome my tendency to gossip. But I'd still tell it to my husband. Although I knew he wouldn't repeat it, I soon realized that by exposing him to it I was poisoning his spirit. That's when I decided to change what was coming out of my mouth." Wow!

What you say about somebody in a careless *moment* can color how others see them for a *lifetime.* One pastor tells all his new members, "If you hear another member slandering somebody, stop them right away and say, 'Excuse me – who hurt you, ignored you, or slighted you? We'll pray together so that God can restore peace to this body, but we *won't* let you talk about people who aren't around to defend themselves.'" Ninety-nine times out of a hundred the issue dies right there, or the offender leaves!

Paul writes, "Be . . . gentle, and patient, accepting each other in love" (Eph 4:2 NCV). Today, refuse to let the enemy use *your* words to hurt others.

DOING IT GOD'S WAY

He gave them their request, but sent leanness into their soul.
Psalms 106:15 NKJV

O*ld Blue Eyes* used to sing, *"The record shows, I took the blows and did it my way."* Sometimes God will let you do things your way, then let you deal with the consequences! When you insist on having something that He in His wisdom has withheld, He steps back and says, "Okay, have it your way."

The Bible says that because the Children of Israel: (a) "forgot His works, (b) did not wait for His counsel, (c) lusted exceedingly, (d) tested God . . . He gave them their request, but sent leanness into their soul" (Ps 106:13-15 NKJV). That's the formula for spiritual barrenness!

When God called Moses to deliver the Children of Israel, Moses decided to do it his way. He saw an Egyptian beating a Hebrew slave, but instead of consulting God he took matters into his own hands by killing the abuser. Before he did, the Bible says he "looked this way and that" (Ex 2:12 NKJV) – but he never looked up! He was more concerned about "audience response" than "God response."

God had to teach Moses that his orders came from *Him!* After Moses dug a hole and tried to hide the work of his flesh, God allowed it to be exposed. Why? To show Moses that by doing things his own way he couldn't keep a single soldier buried in sand, whereas by doing things God's way he was able to bury a whole army in the depths of The Red Sea! *So today make up your mind to do it God's way!*

WHAT WILL YOUR LEGACY BE?

The just man walketh in his integrity:
his children are blessed after him.
Proverbs 20:7

In 1927 a Georgia real estate and insurance company folded, short-changing 500 stockholders. The owner, a man called Mercer, was a person of integrity who vowed if possible to repay every single penny. But despite his best efforts his company never did make a comeback. After he died his son remembered his father's vow, and *twenty-eight years later* deposited a check in a Savannah bank to reimburse every last stockholder.

That young man was the successful singer/songwriter Johnny Mercer. One of the songs he wrote from which he earned the royalties to pay the stockholders was, *"Accentuate the Positive."* You've probably heard it.

When you go, leave your children something more than money to remember you by; leave them a legacy of integrity! Listen, "The just man walketh in his integrity: his children are blessed after him."

If you can't be trusted on *all* counts, you can't truly be trusted on *any.* Ethical principles are not flexible. A little white lie is still a lie; theft is theft whether it's one dollar or one million. Philips Brookes said, "Character is made in the small moments of our lives."

Sociologists suggest that people of poor character might have been different if they'd grown up in a better environment. Character is a choice. Your circumstances are no more responsible for your character than the mirror is for your looks. What you see only reflects what you are – and what you are is what you've spent your life building!

"AN ATTITUDE OF ENTITLEMENT"

Correct your young ones . . . save them from something worse.
Proverbs 23:12 TM

An "attitude of entitlement" is deadly. It destroys a child's motivation and self-esteem. Our kids develop this attitude when we allow them to think that they don't have to work for anything because it's "owed" to them.

Parents, love your children and provide a secure home environment – but hold them accountable for their actions! Here are three reasons we fail to do this:

(1) *Misguided love.* "My kids shouldn't have to struggle like I did" or "I want them to have a good time growing up." Kids interpret that kind of indulgence as: (a) lack of interest, (b) taking the easy way out. Their demands then increase because what they're really saying is, "I don't want more stuff, I want you!"

(2) *Low expectations.* Self worth comes from achievement, and that can't be inherited, it must be earned. Raise the bar. Give them something to reach for. Don't rob them of the sense of fulfillment that comes from working hard to improve their grades, clean their rooms, and earn their way.

(3) *Guilt.* Life's busy; we all feel bad at times about not spending enough time with our kids. Other pressures produce guilt, too. One sixteen-year-old told her dad he "owed" her a car. And she got it! Know why? Because her parents were divorced, and dad felt guilty about "letting her down." Don't try to "buy" your kids' affection or you'll only end up paying later.

Want some advice? Don't encourage an attitude of entitlement, "Correct your young ones . . . save them from something worse" (Pr 23:12 TM).

COLOR-BLIND

You are all one in Christ Jesus.
Galatians 3:28 NIV

Spiritual advantage has nothing to do with the color of your skin – and everything to do with the contents of your heart! "But," you say, "My ancestors came over on *The Mayflower* with the Pilgrims." So what? "There is neither slave nor free . . . you are all one in Christ" (Gal 13:28 NIV). Being born with a silver spoon in your mouth doesn't mean a thing to God. In His kingdom social status doesn't count.

And He doesn't consider gender either, because "There is neither male nor female . . . you are all one in Christ."

God won't even discount you because of your moral background. Rahab was a harlot until she exercised faith in God's Word. Once that happened she never returned to her old profession. In fact, she's even mentioned alongside Sarah, Abraham's wife, because she believed and was blessed.

Faith is the only thing that creates true equality. When you have it you can walk with your head held high in spite of your past failures. It doesn't matter what *people* say about you, it's what *God* says about you, and consequently what *you* say about yourself, that matters!

Jesus healed a woman who'd been stooped over for eighteen years with severe spinal curvature. When He saw her Jesus said, "Woman you are free . . . and immediately she was able to stand up straight" (Lk 13:12-13 NCV). The moment you place your complete faith and trust in Christ, you too will find the power to stand up straight. Once that happens – your potential's unlimited!

BOUND WITHIN

If I were still trying to please men,
I would not be a servant of Christ.
Galatians 1:10 NIV

Until you quit agreeing with those who've mistreated you, or the events that have crippled you emotionally, you'll remain locked in a prison of your own making. Too many of us have made it our life's work to change somebody else's opinion of us. We're determined to prove to them that we're valuable.

Never allow someone else's approval to become your goal. The truth is some folks may *never* like you. They may *never* see your good qualities.

Any time you agree with somebody who rejects or abuses you, you put yourself into bondage to them. By saying either in word or deed, "You were right to hit me, or leave me, or hurt me," you're tying yourself up with *their* opinion, rather than God's. Furthermore, when their opinion of you becomes *your* opinion, you've built a prison inside your soul with only one prisoner – you!

Are you prepared to accept that the person you've spent your life trying to impress may never be impressed? And are you prepared to accept that from God's perspective it doesn't matter? *To deal effectively with others, you must be able to work alongside them without allowing yourself to be controlled by their moods, or governed by their opinion of you.*

In all probability you don't need to be delivered from Satan or anybody else; you just need to change the wrong beliefs you have about yourself. When you can acknowledge that, you've taken the first step toward freedom.

SERVING

I have set you an example that you should do as I have done for you.
John 13:15 NIV

Is your ambition to serve or be served? Ponder that before you answer! Jesus didn't wait for His disciples to make the first move, He taught them by going first. He "rose from supper and laid aside His garments, took a towel . . . poured water . . . and began to wash the disciples' feet" (Jn 13:4-5 NKJV). Incredible! The Master steps down to become one of them – and serve!

He laid aside His garments – not only for them, but for us too. He came to earth stripped of the glory He'd enjoyed in heaven with His Father. Jesus had no time for form or fashion. Real ministry is done with a complete loss of distinction. To make a lasting impact on these men He had to cover Himself in humility.

As He kneeled to wash their feet, Peter was embarrassed to think that his Lord would allow Himself to be seen in such a demeaning light. Then Jesus spoke, "I have set you an example that you should do as I have done . . . no servant is greater than his master . . . Now that you know these things, you will be blessed if you do them" (Jn 13:15-17 NIV). Want to be blessed? Serve!

If you believe that God wants to use you, don't join the "spiritual elitists," who're impressed by their own speeches and accomplishments. Lay aside everything in which you privately glory, and pick up the towel of servanthood. Don't wait for others. Somebody at your table needs to start the trend. *Today let it be you!*

LET HIM COMFORT YOU

The God of all comfort, who comforts us.
2 Corinthians 1:3-4 NIV

God can make you comfortable in the most uncomfortable places. He can pull you out of situations you thought you'd be stuck in forever. He can give you peace, even in the midst of trauma.

Before your life is over, you'll live, love, and experience loss. Losing some things will actually help you to appreciate the things you still have. It's the taste of failure that makes success so sweet. How can you celebrate victory unless you've known defeat?

You'll live each day not knowing what tomorrow holds, but knowing that God holds all your tomorrows. They're not in the hands of your boss, your broker, your mate, or anybody else. Nor are they in *your* hands to manipulate and control. No, all your tomorrows are in God's hands!

So whatever you do, get to know Him, because you'll need Him. And He'll be there for you. He'll be there when everybody and everything else has gone. He'll be there for you in the dark places. His promise to you is, "Weeping may endure for a night, but joy comes in the morning" (Ps 30:5 AMP). However long the night, morning always comes, and with it His joy.

Just think, no matter how dark the night, you've always lived to see the morning, right? Somehow His grace has protected you, provided for you, secured you, calmed and comforted you, and brought you through. Times and seasons change, but not God. *He's always "the God of all comfort," and He's watching over you today!*

CARING FOR EACH OTHER

Marriage involves . . . wanting to please your spouse.
1 Corinthians 7:34 TM

Marriage is about giving not taking. When you marry somebody you marry everything they *are* and everything they've *been.* You inherit their strengths, their fears, and their weaknesses. It's impossible to choose the parts you want and leave the ones you don't. It's a package deal!

If you ask God, He'll give you *grace* to minister to your spouse (and to the child within them). Be patient! You may not see immediate change. It takes time for even a small cut to heal. It's a process. If you ask Him, God will give you the oil of compassion and the wine of love to pour into their wounds.

The Bible teaches that we're not to be so spiritual that we become *unavailable.* God says, "I want those who are married to be concerned about pleasing their mates." Your first ministry is to your *own home* . . . your first calling is to your own *spouse.* Your priorities need to start there, then they can spread to your career, your vocation, and other pursuits.

God builds the house but we've got to do our own decorating! In effect, He says, "I release those who are married from the level of consecration I expect from those who are single, so they'll be able to spend time working on their relationship."

"But I need to spend time with the Lord," you say. True. The Bible doesn't release you from your relationship with the Lord, it just sets some priorities. You are called to be committed to God – *and* to your partner!

SEEING HIM

The Lord . . . revealed Himself to Samuel through His Word.
1 Samuel 3:21 NIV

God revealed Himself to Moses through a *burning bush,* but He revealed Himself to Joshua as a *military captain.* Why the difference? Because Joshua was facing Jericho – the biggest battle of his life – and he needed somebody with a strategy for conquering it.

After the resurrection Jesus appeared as a *traveler* to Cleopas and his companions: one who answered their questions about the cross and removed their doubts about the resurrection. Looking back they said, "Did not our heart burn within us while He talked with us on the road, and . . . opened the Scriptures to us" (Lk 24:32 NKJV). He can do that for you too!

How wonderful! God doesn't just show up at the right *time,* He reveals Himself in the right *way.* Whether it's as a burning bush, a military captain, a traveling companion, or through His Word as He did to Samuel, when God reveals Himself to you – you'll never be the same again!

The question is, are your eyes open to see Him? Are your ears tuned to hear Him? In Revelation 3:20 Jesus stands knocking, but nobody hears Him. Inside it's "business as usual." Nobody's even missed Him. What a fearful place to be!

At the final judgment some will say, "Lord, When did we see you sick, or hungry, or naked?" Then He will reply, "Whatever you did not do for one of the least of these, you did not do for me" (See Mt 25:37-45). Be sensitive today, Jesus may come to you in the form of somebody else's pain or unmet need. If you miss the opportunity, you'll miss *Him.* Make sure that doesn't happen!

GIVE THANKS

In every thing give thanks.
1 Thessalonians 5:18

Gratitude works like a vaccine. It stops you from becoming infected with a "spirit of grumpiness." It's the antitoxin that counteracts the poisonous effects of ingratitude.

Have you noticed that we live in a thankless society? Paul said, "In the last days . . . people will be . . . *ungrateful"* (2Ti 3:1-2 AMP). This generation lacks godly principles; they've neither learned to pray at home nor in school. Because they've witnessed the fall of high-profile church leaders, they've concluded that "religion" doesn't work.

But thanklessness is a problem among Christians, too. We ask God for things, then when we get them, we complain about having to take care of them! Ever do that?

If you want to know God's will, listen: "In everything give thanks; *for this is the will of God . . . for you"* (1Th 5:18 NKJV). We're supposed to demonstrate thankfulness!

Paul says, "With thanksgiving let your requests be made known" (Php 4:6). Why? Because thanksgiving moves them through God's approval process. It also demonstrates that you're mature enough to handle whatever He sends. After all, why would He send more if you don't appreciate what you already have?

Sometimes thanksgiving is a *sacrifice.* It's easy to give thanks when you feel well. It's when you don't feel well and give thanks anyway that it becomes a sacrifice. David said, "I will offer . . . the sacrifice of thanksgiving and . . . call on the . . . Lord" (Ps 116:17 AMP). Notice: he only called on God *after* he'd offered the sacrifice of thanksgiving.

Your flesh will always find reasons to be dissatisfied. Your spirit will always search for reasons to be thankful. So today – *be thankful!*

STILL PRAYING THE PRAYER OF JABEZ?

Jabez was more honorable than his brothers . . .
and [he] cried out to the God of Israel.
1 Chronicles 4:9-10 NIV

Jabez prayed a short prayer and his life changed forever. He prayed for: (1) *Greater success:* "Oh, that You would bless me indeed." (2) *Greater influence:* "And enlarge my territory." (3) *Greater power:* "That Your hand would be with me." (4) *Greater protection:* "That You would keep me from evil, [and] God granted him what he requested" (1Ch 4:10 NKJV).

Why does this prayer work? Because when you pray it, you're asking God for exactly what He wants you to have. Why does it work for some and not others? Because all God's promises come with *conditions.* Listen, "Jabez was . . . *honorable.*" If you want what he had, you've got to do what he did.

Now you don't have to do anything to earn God's love, but you do have to do certain things to experience His blessing. "We . . . receive whatever we request because we obey him" (1Jn 3:22 NLT).

Are your motives right? James writes, "You do not receive, because you ask with wrong motives" (Jas 4:3 NIV). Is your heart right? David said, "If I regard iniquity in my heart, the Lord will not hear me" (Ps 66:18). Sin will clog the pipeline of all future blessings.

Once you have the "all-clear" from God, you can start praying the Prayer of Jabez and expect breakthroughs and blessings because God knows *what* you need, *when* you need it, and *how* to get it to you!

STAND IN YOUR PLACE

Having done all [the crisis demands] . . .
stand [firmly in your place].
Ephesians 6:13 AMP

Paul Harvey says, "In times like these it's helpful to remember that there have always been times like these." The question isn't, "Will trouble come?" but, "How will I handle it when it does?"

Here's how: "Having done all [the crisis demands] . . . stand [firmly in your place]." What place? *In Christ.* (See Eph 2:6). Can you think of a safer place to stand?

Listen, "We which have believed do enter into rest" (Heb 4:3). In times of trouble do what God leads you to do, then relax, stand still, and watch God work on your behalf. (See Ex 14:13). *Go ahead and enjoy your life while God works on your problems!*

Too many of us have the idea that it's wrong to enjoy ourselves when we have problems. We think that if we can't do anything else, the least we can do is look solemn and miserable.

Paul addresses this: "Do not [for a moment] be frightened . . . for such [constancy and fearlessness] will be a clear sign . . . from God" (Php 1:28 AMP). This Scripture plainly lays it out – when you're attacked, stay in peace! That tells Satan he's defeated. *He doesn't know what to do with you when he can't get you upset.* You've taken one of his greatest weapons out of his hands! Your peace also assures you of being delivered by God, because an attitude of rest shows that you're trusting Him *completely.*

ARE YOU IN A RUT?

Restore unto me the joy of Thy salvation.
Psalm 51:12

Henri Nouwen is a distinguished professor of theology with an impressive resume from Harvard and Yale. In his book *In the Name of Jesus* he writes "As I entered my fifties, I came face to face with this simple question: did becoming older bring me closer to Jesus? After twenty-five years of ministry, I found myself praying poorly, isolated from other people, and very much preoccupied with burning issues. *Something inside was telling me that my success was putting my own soul in danger.* I woke up one day with the realization that I was living in a very dark place and that the term 'burn out' was a convenient psychological translation for spiritual death."

When Nouwen asked the Lord what he wanted him to do, he was told to go join the L'Arche Communities for mentally handicapped people. God said "Go and live among the poor in spirit, and they will heal you." The lessons he learned there were painful . . . humbling . . . and necessary.

First he experienced a deep spiritual change within his own being. Second, the master teacher learned to become a humble servant. Third, the self-confident individualist became a compassionate, caring friend. What a transformation!

God probably won't tell you to go live in a monastery, but he *will* challenge you about your coldness of heart, your callous attitudes, and your critical words. He'll let you know that you're stale and that you need something fresh in your life. *Are you willing to listen to what he has to say and obey him?*

A CALL FOR FATHERS

He will turn the hearts of the fathers to their children, and the hearts of the children to their fathers.
Malachi 4:6 NIV

After trying to get through to a rebellious fifteen-year-old whose father had left four years earlier, a noted psychologist wrote these sobering words in *Newsweek:*

"Most adolescent boys can't make use of professional counseling . . . what they need, and all too often don't have, is the fellowship of men – at least one man who pays *attention* to him, who spends *time* with him, who *admires* him. A boy needs a man he can *look up to.*

"The great majority of youthful offenders are male, most without fathers involved in their lives: many have never even met their fathers.

"Where are the fathers of these boys? Well, I can tell you where they're not. They're not at PTA meetings or piano recitals. They're not teaching Sunday school. You won't find them in the pediatrician's office holding a sick child. Where are they? They're in diners and taverns, drinking, conversing and playing pool with other men. They're on golf courses, tennis courts, fishing on lakes and rivers. They're working from early morning till late at night. Some are home watching television, out mowing the lawn, or tuning up the car. *In short, they're everywhere, except in the company of their children!"*

Sobering words – huh? Dad, do you have a free day or a few available hours? Are you tempted to fill them with projects, or a trip to the links? Before you do, stop and ask yourself, "Why not spend some time with one of my children?" *Go ahead, circle a few dates on your day-timer. Before it's too late – take time!*

YOU CAN'T GIVE AWAY WHAT YOU DON'T HAVE

There is no fear in love; but perfect love casteth out fear.

1 John 4:18

God loves you unconditionally – at all times. But you must *believe* that and *receive* His love. Only when you do that can you begin to give that love back to God – and then bestow it on others. *But you can't give away what you don't have!*

Listen, "God's love has been poured out in our hearts through the holy spirit who has been given to us" (Ro 5:5 AMP). When you commit your life to Christ, God's spirit comes to live in your heart, and He brings with Him – love! The question is, what are you doing with that love? Are you rejecting it because you don't think you're good enough to be loved? *Has it occurred to you that you have a relationship with yourself? That until you learn to love yourself, you'll never be able to love God or anybody else?*

John says, "There is no fear in love. But perfect love drives out fear" (1Jn 4:18 NIV). I tried for years to walk in "perfect love," and I failed daily. I thought perfect love referred to my loving others perfectly. Then God showed me that the only perfect love was His love for me – He's the only One who can love perfectly!

Once that became clear I started confessing, "I can love what God can love. I don't love everything I do, but I love myself as I am because God loves me that way. I know I need to change and I want to change. In fact, I believe God is changing me daily. But in the meanwhile, I will not reject what God accepts. I will accept and love myself as I am right now, knowing that I will not always remain this way." Make that your confession today!

DIVINE PROVIDENCE

The Most High ruleth in the kingdom of men.
Daniel 4:25

There are three words you need to *drop* from your vocabulary right away; *luck, chance,* and *fate.* Instead, use the word *providence.* It means, *"to see in advance and to provide for."*

You can't improve on the Westminster Confession written in the 17th century. Listen, "God the great creator, doth uphold, direct, dispose, and govern all creatures, actions, and things from the greatest event to the least, by his most wise and holy providence." Aren't you glad He's still in charge?

But you ask, "What about our human will? Can't we act independently?"

R.C. Sproul writes, "God's sovereign providence stands over and above our actions. He works out his will through the actions of human wills, without ever violating the freedom of those wills."

Look at Joseph; his brothers tried to destroy him, but their efforts only put him on the throne and fulfilled the will of God. Later Joseph said, "You meant evil against me; but God meant it for good, in order to bring about this present result" (Ge 50:20 NAS). It was Judas' worst act of wickedness that helped bring about the best thing that ever happened: the atonement.

Are you confused because of what's going on around you? That's because we only use about ten percent of our mental capacity, therefore, we only "know in part" (1Co 13:9). Some day God will explain it all to us. *Until then trust Him and rejoice, because "He's got the whole world in His hands." That includes you!*

KNOWING THE FUTURE

Do not turn to mediums or seek out spiritists,
for you will be defiled by them.
Leviticus 19:31 NIV

Guess who was nominated for *The Most Admired Woman in the World* for three consecutive years? Need a hint? She's syndicated in 450 newspapers, and is a personal confidant to presidents and kings. She's the world's leading astrologer – Jeanne Dixon! Her logo reads, "Behold the revelation of your destiny." *Can you believe it? What was once practiced behind closed doors is now big business.*

Look out! The enemy of your soul has a field day when you take the restraints off your curiosity, and dabble in the so-called mystical world. Just substitute the word *demonic* for the word *mystical* and you won't be so tempted!

Two thousand years ago Paul met a girl who made a fortune for her owners by forecasting the future. He cast the evil spirit out of her, ended her career, and caused a riot in that town (Acts 16:18 NIV). He'd probably get the same response in your town too!

If God had wanted us to gaze into the future His Word wouldn't say, "Come now, you who say, 'Today or tomorrow we shall go to such and such a city', you do not know what your life will be like tomorrow . . . instead you *ought* to say . . . 'If the Lord wills we will live and also do this or that'" (Jas 4:13-15 NAS). *Everything you need to know can be found in God's Word or in His presence. Don't mess with anything else!*

SUCCESS – AS GOD DEFINES IT!

Accept the authority of the elders . . . humble yourselves . . . give all your worries and cares to God.

1 Peter 5:5-7 NLT

Listen, "Accept the authority of the elders . . . humble yourselves . . . give all your worries and cares to God for he cares what happens to you" (1Pe 5:5-7 NLT). Let's look at these three things:

(1) *Submit yourself to those who are wise.* Listen to their counsel, be accountable, accept reproof, take suggestions, respect experience, and follow a worthy example.

(2) *Humble yourself "under the mighty hand of God"* (1Pe 5:6). God's hand symbolizes two things: His discipline and His deliverance. When you humble yourself before Him, you accept His discipline as being for your good, and you acknowledge His deliverance, by whatever means He chooses. In other words, you let God be God in your life.

(3) *Throw yourself on the mercy and care of God.* Trouble and disappointment will come, but when they do, throw them back on the Lord. The situation may be too big for you but it's not too big for Him!

Does this mean there's no place for planning, goal-setting, and hard work in your life? No! It just means doing it God's way!

LIVING IN THE AMBER ZONE

Christ has really set us free . . . make sure that you stay free.
Galatians 5:1 NLT

Isn't it strange how some of us find it hard (or impossible) to give ourselves permission to think, say, or enjoy certain things just because others disapprove of them? So often we live by their convictions instead of ours! There's no bondage like religious bondage!

The church I grew up in said we shouldn't attend a soccer match (that would involve "mixing with the world"); or wear makeup (heaven knows some of us needed it!) Our standard answer to most of these issues was, "We were taught differently!" Such was the reasoning of an over-sensitive conscience nurtured in the school of tradition!

Paul jumped all over the Galatians for trying to "police" others and force them to live by *their* standards instead of *God's*. Listen, "Make sure that you stay free, and don't get tied up again in slavery to the law."

Train yourself to *care much less* about what people think and much *more* about what God thinks! Some people are always going to be upset because you do certain things they don't feel they can do – because they won't give themselves permission to enjoy their freedom in Christ.

If you fail to press on while the light's green, you'll spend your life in the amber zone waiting for "just the right moment" or, "a time when most people will understand." Finally you'll find yourself on your deathbed filled with regrets. Don't let that happen to you! Listen again, "Christ has really set us free . . . make sure that you stay free." Selah!

LOVE IN ACTION

If anyone . . . sees his brother in need but has no pity on him, how can the love of God be in him?

1 John 3:17 NIV

Tim Hansel tells of a seminary professor who set up his preaching class in an unusual way. He scheduled his students to preach on *The Good Samaritan.* One by one they were to go from classroom to classroom, preaching love and compassion for others. Some students had ten minutes between classes, but others had less time, which forced them to rush in order to meet the schedule. Each student had to walk down a certain corridor and pass by a "beggar" who'd been deliberately "planted" there by the professor.

What happened next is a powerful lesson! The number of aspiring preachers who stopped to help this man was extremely low; especially among those who were under time pressure. *Rushing to preach their sermon on The Good Samaritan they all walked right past the beggar at the heart of the parable!*

Today I read again these words: "I was hungry and you formed a humanities club to discuss it. I was imprisoned and you stayed home to pray for my release. I was naked and you debated the morality of my appearance. I was sick and you thanked God for your health. I was homeless and you preached to me about the shelter of God's love. *You seem so holy and so close to God; but I'm still hungry, lonely, cold, and in pain. Does it matter?" (Read Mt 25:35).*

IS CHRIST LIVING IN YOU?

Christ liveth in me.
Galatians 2:20

If you could change through self-effort you wouldn't need the Lord. Furthermore, any attempt on your part to earn or deserve His acceptance disqualifies you right away. Why? Because you're trying to be the source of your own salvation, you own significance, and your own strength. Talk about making God angry – that'll do it every time! So what's the answer? Die to "self" and allow Christ to live through you!

Listen to these challenging words, "Those who think they can do it on their own end up obsessed with measuring their own moral muscle, but never get around to exercising it in real life . . . If God Himself has taken up residence in your life, you can hardly be thinking more of yourself than of Him.

"Anyone, of course, who has not welcomed God won't know what we're talking about. But for you . . . in whom He dwells – *even though you still experience all the limitations of sin* – you yourself experience life on God's terms.

"It stands to reason, doesn't it, that if the alive-and-present God who raised Jesus from the dead, moves into your life, He'll do the same thing in you that He did in Jesus, bringing you alive to Himself" (Ro 8:5-11TM).

How can you tell when Christ is alive in you? That's simple; when others look at you they'll see Him. When they listen to you they'll hear Him. When they walk with you they'll discover they're following Him. *Is Christ living in you?*

BROUGHT DOWN TO SIZE

Acquaint now thyself with Him, and be at peace: thereby good shall come unto thee.

Job 22:21

In an age when preachers prance like peacocks, athletes strut like deity, and "one-upmanship" has become an art form, we *all* need to be reminded who's calling the shots. There's only one Alpha and Omega – and pardon my grammar – it ain't you or me!

There are two benefits to realizing the greatness of God. (1) You're no longer tempted to try to reduce Him down to manageable terms. (2) You're no longer tempted to try to manipulate His will or defend His ways. Think carefully about that!

How many times does God need to tell us, "My ways are higher than your ways" (Isa 55:9), before we believe Him? How often must He prove to us that He's the Shepherd and we're the sheep, or that He's the vine and we're the branches, before we bow and pray, "Have thine own way Lord?"

If the Son of God found it necessary to pray, "Not what I desire – but what You will and desire" (Mt 26:39 AMP), wouldn't it be wise for us to pray those words often as well – like every day?

How long has it been anyway since you've taken time out to just sit silently in His presence, and catch a fresh glimpse of the One who's awesome and incomprehensible? Job said, "Acquaint now thyself with Him and be at peace; thereby good shall come unto thee" (Job 22:21). *Do you know Him? If so, how well?*

THANK GOD FOR A BETTER WAY!

This is the fresh, new, life-giving way which Christ has opened up for us.
Hebrews 10:20 TLB

In the Old Testament you'll find more laws than anybody could ever keep. Every time somebody failed they had to offer an animal sacrifice to atone for it. The result was people were always trying and failing; feeling guilty and trying harder; failing again and making more sacrifices. It was a never-ending cycle! Then Jesus came and offered "a new way." His way included mercy for failure, forgiveness for sin, and replacement of sacrifices with faith in Him. For many it was just too good to be true, so they kept right on working trying to impress God with their goodness. Do *you* ever do that?

I lived that way for years. It meant having to do everything perfectly, otherwise I was in trouble with God. Since this was an impossible standard to keep, it stole all my peace and joy. While I was trying to walk in love, I wasn't a very loving or merciful person. *I couldn't give others what I didn't know how to receive myself!* I didn't accept God's mercy for my failures, therefore I couldn't give it to anybody else. I tried to follow all the rules; many that weren't even scriptural – just more things to feel guilty about!

But thank God I don't have to live that way anymore (you either!) Now I'm not working to be saved, I'm working because I am saved! My salvation isn't based on what I do, it's based solely on what Jesus has already done. *When you understand that, your relationship with God is no longer a job – but a joy! Do you have that joy?*

JUST LEAVE IT TO GOD

Cast your cares on the Lord and He will sustain you.
Psalm 55:22 NIV

There are days when the best thing you can do is just – leave it to God. "But there's so much to be done," you say. "What about all those go-getters who get up before the sun, skip breakfast, and set new records while I'm busy 'leaving it to God?'"

Look at Jesus; He didn't really get started until he was thirty. All those wasted years! He just left them to God; He never hurried anywhere. He never worried about anything. And what did He do about those who heard the Gospel, shrugged, and walked away? He just left them to God. And what about those nit-picking Pharisees who gave Him so much grief? He left them to God, too!

In his book *The Finishing Touch,* Charles Swindoll tells of a time when he felt "driven and drained" by the never-ending demands of ministry. He says, "If folks weren't changing, I felt responsible. If some drifted, somehow I was at fault. If there wasn't continual growth, I acted as if I needed to make it happen. If a sermon failed to ring with clarity and power, I struggled all of Monday and half of Tuesday. Talk about wasted energy! Time has helped, so has age. Virtually all of the things that once stole my joy and assaulted my motivation – I now just leave it to God.

"Don't I care? Of course I care! *But those cares are now placed in the hands of One who can handle them. What once bothered me, I have now learned to give over to Him who doesn't mind being bothered.* Whereas criticism used to cripple me for days, I now do my best to sift, shift, and sail; I learn what I can – then turn the rest over to God." *Is God saying something to you through this?*

DEAL WITH YOUR DOUBT

May the God of hope fill you with all joy and peace . . . as you trust in Him.
Romans 15:13 NIV

How's your relationship with God? Do you doubt His love? His call on your life? Your ability to hear from Him? That He's pleased with you? For years I felt like I could never do enough, or be good enough to please Him. Then I discovered this verse: "May the God of hope fill you with . . . joy and peace . . . as you trust in Him" (Ro 15:13 NIV). Note: when you stop trusting God and start trusting in your own efforts, the first things to go are your joy and peace. Have you lost yours today? *If you want them back, get out of doubt and get back into faith!*

How's your relationship with yourself? For a long time the only relationship I had with myself was one of doubt. I doubted my decisions, my appearance, whether I was saying or doing the right thing, whether I was in any way pleasing God – or anybody else. *I knew I wasn't pleased with myself – so how could anybody else be pleased with me?*

Those years of misery are now behind me, because I know that God's grace covers me like a blanket. Now I know it's through Jesus alone that I'm made righteous and acceptable before God (See Col 2:10). What a confidence!

I was once so bound by legalistic religion that I'll probably always have to be on guard against it. But now I know how to recognize its symptoms. Paul says, "Stand fast then, and do not . . . submit again to a yoke of slavery [which you have once put off]" (Gal 5:1 AMP). *The word for you today is – evict your doubts, believe God, and get moving!*

BLIND GUIDES

Leave them, they are blind guides.
Matthew 15:14 NIV

There are plenty of good leaders around; don't be afraid to follow them. But what about these "blind guides" who lead you into a ditch? Here are some signs to help you identify them.

(1) *Inflexibility!* A true leader has a teachable spirit and a servant's heart. He rejoices in your growth and isn't threatened by your development. He won't try to keep you "in the nest" when it's clear that you're ready to fly.

(2) *Elitism!* Look out for the "We-alone-are-right" club. When you can't acknowledge and fellowship with the members of God's larger family, there's something wrong. The word *exclusive* is often just another word for *paranoid.*

(3) *Money-grubbing!* Here's God's standard for leadership: "Not greedy for money, but eager to serve" (1Pe 5:2 NIV). Paul says good leaders are "Worthy of double honor" (1Ti 5:17). But look out for the man who teaches you to sow all your seed into His field and nowhere else.

(4) *Accountability!* Beware of the untouchable, "I'm God's anointed" types. No matter how gifted we are we all have blind spots, and we all need to be counseled and confronted. Solomon said, "Pity the man who falls and has no man to help him up" (Ecc 4:10 NIV).

When choosing a pastor you don't need a blind prima donna, you just need a shepherd. Think about it!

ACCEPTING YOURSELF – AS YOU ARE!

God saw everything that He had make, and,
behold, it was very good . . . and He approved it completely.
Genesis 1:31 AMP

You can't deal with anything until you first accept it as it is – and that includes yourself! The dictionary defines *acceptance* in three ways: (1) to accept willingly; (2) to view as right; (3) to agree with.

First, acceptance involves your will. You can choose or not choose to accept yourself! It's up to you! Next, when something's acceptable it's viewed as being right. We reject ourselves because we see only what's wrong with us and never what's right! This outlook was probably instilled in us by those who majored on our weaknesses instead of our strengths. Sadly, we still carry their opinions with us even today!

The word *acceptance* also means, "to agree with." If you're having a problem accepting yourself, then you need to get into agreement with God. Whatever *He* says about you, believe, and begin to say the same about yourself! Listen, "Can any two walk together except they be agreed?" (Amos 3:3). To walk with God you must agree with Him. God says He loves you and accepts you as you are, so when you agree with Him you can no longer hate and reject yourself.

When God made you He said, "It was very good" (Gen 1:31) – and He hasn't changed his mind! *He's not through with His creative work in your life yet, but He wants you also to see yourself as "good," and learn to love yourself while you're "under construction."*

REAL INTIMACY!

Marry a believer, and have the blessing of the Master.
1 Corinthians 7:39TM

The Bible teaches that the basis for a good marriage isn't simply sharing the same bed. It's having the same values and goals! Without that you'll be talking to each other in a foreign language. Furthermore, you'll never be able to agree because you'll each be governed by a different set of rules. To reach the same destination you must follow the same road map!

Sex alone isn't enough. That might get you through the night, but it takes genuine friendship and a shared faith to get you through the years. I'm talking here about partners who often communicate without a word, because the same thing is in each of their hearts. When problems arise – and they will – they both seek solutions from the same source!

When life fell apart for Adam and Eve, they both came before the same God, because they each shared the same convictions. *How can you correct a problem if one of you doesn't even believe there is one?*

Real intimacy occurs when the sex is over but the commitment is stronger than ever. It allows you to be with someone without always needing to impress them. When we know we're loved because of who we *are,* we become healthier in mind and more intimate in expression. Why? Because we are freed from the fear of rejection, and loosed from the anxiety of having to perform. Now there's something to think about!

BECAUSE YOU HAVE A LAWYER!

We have an advocate . . .

1 John 2:1

On those days when you wonder how God can *stand* you, much less *love* you, remember these words, "We have an advocate." When your thoughts aren't fit to print, and your actions aren't much better, listen: "He ever liveth to make intercession for [us]" (Heb 7:25). It works like this: when righteousness declares you "guilty," grace steps in and says, "I've got him covered, because he's trusting in the shed blood of Jesus; no less will avail, no more is needed!"

In the Old Testament the blood of the Lamb was poured daily on top of the mercy seat. The Ark of the Covenant which contained the broken law – the record of our guilt – was placed underneath it. *Hence the only way God could see the record of our failures was through the blood – and it's still the same today!*

If you're wondering why God continues to love and accept you, it's because you have a lawyer. Here are some of His credentials: (1) *He's fully qualified to represent you.* "This is my beloved son in whom I am well pleased" (Mt 3:17). (2) *He's never lost a case.* "He is able also to save them to the uttermost, that come unto God by him" (Heb 7:25). (3) *He offers His services to you freely;* "Without money and without price" (Isa 55:1). That's why the Bible says, "Let us then approach the throne of grace with confidence, so that we may receive mercy and find grace to help us in our time of need" (Heb 4:16 NIV). You can come to Him confidently today!

DR. MAYO ON WORRY!

Do not worry about anything.
Philippians 4:6 NCV

Worry's like a rocking chair; it uses up all your energy but gets you nowhere. Leo Buscaglia writes, "Worry never robs tomorrow of its sorrow, it only saps today of its joy." He's right!

Dr. Charles Mayo of the famous Mayo Clinic says, "There's a growing mountain of evidence to suggest that worry is the chief contributor to depression, nervous breakdowns, high blood pressure, heart attacks, and early death. Stress kills. I've never known a man to die from hard work, but I've known a lot who died from worry."

Mathematically speaking, it doesn't make sense to worry. Psychologists tell us that roughly thirty percent of what we worry about *never* happens; another thirty percent has *already* happened; twelve percent is about unfounded health concerns, and an additional twenty percent involves "sweating the small stuff."

That leaves only eight percent. Think about that! We worry ninety-two percent of the time for no good reason at all, and if Dr. Mayo is right, it's killing us.

You ask, "What's the answer?" Listen, "Do not worry about anything, but pray and ask God for everything you need, always giving thanks. And God's peace, which is so great we cannot understand it, will keep your hearts and minds in Christ Jesus. Brothers and sisters, think about the things that are good and worthy of praise. Think about the things that are true and honorable and right and pure and beautiful and respected . . . and the God who gives peace will be with you" (Php 4:6-9 NCV). *That's* God's answer to worry!

HOW COULD "THEY" DO IT?

Christ died for us.
Romans 5:8

When I saw the movie *Schindler's List* I walked away thinking, *"How could they do it?"* The gas chambers . . . the ovens . . . the smokestacks belching out human ashes . . . the trains arriving with mothers, fathers, and little children – herded like cattle on their way to a slaughterhouse. And worst of all, the soldiers who did it without even a twinge of conscience. *How could they do it?* The answer is *sin!* And if you think Hitler and his henchmen had a monopoly on it, think again! David says, "I was brought forth in iniquity, and in sin my mother conceived me" (Ps 51:5 NAS).

Listen to this resume: "They've all taken the wrong turn; they've all wandered down blind alleys . . . their throats are gaping graves, their tongues slick as mud-slides . . . They open their mouths and pollute the air. They race for the honor of sinner-of-the-year" (Ro 3:9-17 TM). If God did an autopsy on any one of us, that would describe it! But in order to *really* appreciate this you have to understand this scripture: "God demonstrates His love toward us, in that while we were yet sinners, Christ died for us" (Ro 5:8 NAS).

When you read those words the question then becomes, *"How could He do it?"* We didn't get what we *deserved,* we got what we *needed!* The songwriter wrote, "O the love that drew salvation's plan; O the grace that brought it down to man. O the mighty gulf that God did span – at Calvary!" Take a moment today to thank Him for the grace that redeemed you. *Where would you be without it?*

THE FINAL BID

Whoever accepts and trusts the Son gets in on everything, life complete and forever!
John 3:36 TM

The wealthy English Baron Fitzgerald had only one child, a son. Early in his teens the boy's mother died. Tragically, in his late teens the boy died also. In the meantime Fitzgerald's financial holdings greatly increased due to acquiring the artwork of the "Masters."

Before his death, Fitzgerald left explicit instructions that an auction be held at which his entire art collection would be sold. A big crowd of prospective buyers gathered. Among them were many well-known museum curators and private collectors eager to bid.

The artwork was displayed for viewing before the auction began. Among the paintings was one that received little attention. It was of poor quality, and by an unknown local artist. It happened to be a portrait of Fitzgerald's only son.

As the auction began the auctioneer read from Fitzgerald's will, which clearly instructed that the first painting to be sold was of "my beloved son." Because of its poor quality, the painting didn't receive any bids – except one. That bidder was the old servant who'd helped raise the boy, and had dearly loved him. For less than an English pound he bought the painting.

At that point the auctioneer stopped the bidding and asked the attorney to read again from the will. The crowd was hushed as he read, "Whoever buys this painting of my son, gets all my art collection – the auction is over!"

Christ: without Him you have *nothing* – with Him you have *everything!*

BECAUSE MARY BELIEVED

I'm . . . ready . . . Let it be with me just as you say.
Luke 1:38 TM

When the angel appeared to Mary he asked her to believe the impossible. Virgin birth? How would *you* have reacted? Mary had no way of knowing that heaven had already prepared for the Messiah she would deliver, or how much depended on her obedience. What she *did* know, however, was that when God spoke it was her job to believe Him and say, "I'm . . . ready . . . Let it be with me just as you say" (Lk 1:38 TM).

You *say* you believe God can do the impossible (Lk 1:37). Yes, but doesn't it blow your mind to think He can do it through somebody like *you?*

This teenage girl not only believed what she heard, she staked her reputation and her future on it! First faith, then fulfillment. That's how it works! Listen, "Blessed is she who believed, for there will be a fulfillment of those things which were told her from the Lord" (Lk 1:45 NKJV).

When God speaks to us, everything needed to fulfill His plan for our lives is *already* in place. His challenge is getting *us* to where we need to be.

Just as Mary couldn't imagine the results of her obedience, neither can you. God's already got a plan to save your loved ones, to meet your financial needs, to salvage your marriage, and to put things together for you. The question is – will you *believe* Him and do what He says?

CHRISTMAS GIFTS

May God give peace *to you . . . and* love, *with* faith . . .
May God's grace . . . *be upon all*
who sincerely love our Lord Jesus Christ.
Ephesians 6:23-24 TLB

It's easy to get caught up in the "craziness" of Christmas; in fact, it's exhausting just thinking about it! Imagine, however, that when you awoke this morning you found four gifts you'd overlooked, tucked away under the tree.

You open the first and find yourself filled with an awesome sense of *peace;* a peace you've never known before. You open the second and experience an overpowering *love* for others – even those who've wronged you. You open the third and you're energized with a *faith* that enables you to believe God for anything – even things you once thought impossible. Finally, you open the fourth and receive such *grace* that you're able to handle criticism and hurt without retaliation.

Sound far-fetched? Not at all! Listen: "May God give peace to you . . . and love, with faith . . . May God's grace . . . be upon all who sincerely love our Lord Jesus Christ" (Eph 6:23-24 TLB).

And think, you won't have to return any of these gifts, because they're just what you need. And the best part is God's *already* given them to you – all you have to do is receive them by faith, and start using them.

It's Christmas Day, the day that changed the calendar – and everything else! Why don't you take a moment and thank God for His wonderful gifts to you – including the gift of His Son. After all, without *Him* we'd have nothing to celebrate.

THE DANGER OF PAST VICTORIES!

If you think you're standing firm, be careful that you don't fall.
1 Corinthians 10:12 NIV

The time to be most careful is when you've *reached* a goal! There are three distinct phases in every battle. The *easiest* one is usually the battle itself. The most *difficult* phase is the period of indecision just before it begins – deciding whether to fight or run away. But by far the most *dangerous* phase is the aftermath. It's then, when all your resources are spent and your guard's down, that you have to watch out for discouragement, overconfidence, dulled reactions, and faulty judgments.

Remember David? He chose to "sleep in" rather than go to battle. Maybe his impressive record of successes made him soft, or careless, or arrogant – who knows. But while his affair with Bathsheba was brief, it changed everything. His peace vanished, his character was blasted, and his family life was destroyed.

Don't fall prey to the peril of past victories! Remember your "H.A.L.T." sign. When you're **H**ungry, **A**ngry, **L**onely or **T**ired you become vulnerable, so do something about it!

Resting on your laurels can be just another way of flirting with disaster. Danger awaits the man or woman who stays too long in the comfortable land of accomplished dreams, so stay on guard today.

TAKE YOUR TIME

Let the foundations thereof be strongly laid.
Ezra 6:3

God is a builder of people, and when He builds He emphasizes foundations. He knows the weight-load you'll be called to carry and the kinds of storms you'll have to face, so He lays your foundation accordingly. The Bible says Jesus, "Increased in favor with God and with man" (Lk 2:52), so allow yourself time to grow too!

Look at Moses, the messiah of the Old Testament. Who'd have thought looking at his church of "goat-deacons" and "gnats-for-choir-members" that he'd one-day lead the greatest movement in the history of the Old Testament? And what about Abraham? One moment he's sitting on the edge of the bed with an embarrassed look and the next he's fathering nations! *You can't tell just by looking at somebody what's inside them!*

God establishes patience, character, and focus while we're in the school of "nothing-seems-to-be-happening." Take the class. Get the credits. Let it work for your good! (See Ro 8:28).

No matter what you're trying to build – a business, a ministry, a relationship – give it time to grow! Some of the best friendships start out small. Some of the strongest Christians were once desperately in need of prayer themselves.

The word for you today is this – take the time to let God work in you!

SHIFT GEARS AND SHARE THE LOAD!

The thing . . . you are doing is not good.
You will surely wear out.
Exodus18:17-18 NAS

Ever feel like there just isn't enough of you to go around? If so you're probably taking on things God never asked you to take on! You see when He shows you His *purpose* for your life, He also gives you His *power* to carry it out. Usually it's simple and remarkably sane. In fact, one sure way to know you're walking with God is that you'll feel "led" and not "driven."

Are you resting less and working more? Are you praying and reading your Bible less and worrying more? Or are you like Moses, dashing from one appointment to another, eating on the run, meeting deadlines and solving everybody's problems? When Jethro his father-in-law asked, "What is this thing that you are doing?" Moses became defensive. (People who are too busy often do.) When Moses attempted to justify his schedule, Jethro wasn't impressed, he wasn't buying it! Instead he told Moses, "The thing . . . you are doing is not good. You will surely wear out."

So what's the answer? *Shift gears and start sharing the load!* (Ex 18:17-18 NAS). When you do, the Bible says, "It will be easier for you . . . you will be able to endure" (Ex 18:22-23 NIV). Since when did a bleeding ulcer become a sign of spirituality? Or a seventy-hour work week the mark of efficiency? The truth may be that you're just too stubborn to slow down, too insecure to say no, and too proud to ask for help. Think about it prayerfully!

THE WINNING LIFE

We should go up and take possession . . .
for we can certainly do it.
Numbers 13:30 NIV

The 12 spies Joshua sent into The Promised Land all saw the same thing. But 10 came back saying, "The people who live there are powerful, and the cities are . . . very large, we were as grasshoppers in our own eyes" (Nu 13:28-33 NIV). They caused such panic that the people wanted to stone Moses, pick a new leader, and go back into Egyptian slavery. Incredible!

But not Caleb! He had "a different spirit" (Nu 14:24). Listen, "We should go up and take possession . . . for we can certainly do it" (Nu 13:30). Years later, when Joshua was dividing the Promised Land amongst the tribes, Caleb steps forward and says, "Here I am today, 85 years old . . . just as vigorous as I was then. Now give me this hill country that the Lord promised me . . . Then Joshua blessed Caleb . . . and gave him Hebron as his inheritance" (Jos 14:6-14 NIV).

Caleb lived the winning life because: (a) he recalled the promises of God and acted on them; (b) he dared to take an unpopular stand; (c) he refused to quit when the pressure was on; (d) he saw possibilities when others saw only problems; (e) he kept his mind young, even when his body was old. Does that describe you?

Listen, "The eyes of the Lord run to and fro throughout the whole earth, to show himself strong on behalf of those whose heart is loyal to him" (2Ch 16:9 NKJV). As you face another year, God wants to show you what He can do *in* you, *for* you, *with* you, and *through* you! Will you let Him?

"TEAM HOYT!"

Two are better than one.
Ecclesiastes 4:9

Rick Hoyt is a quadriplegic who can't speak. When he was born doctors told his parents he'd be a vegetable, but they determined to raise him like any other child. When he was 10, Rick's life changed dramatically. Engineers at Tufts University created a device that enabled him to communicate via computer. His first words painstakingly typed out were, "Go Bruins!" That's when everyone realized he was a sports fan.

After a long battle, Rick got into public school where he excelled. Two years later he found out that there was a 5-kilometer fund-raising race to help a young athlete paralyzed in an accident. Rick told his father that he wanted to participate. His dad agreed to run and push his son in a modified wheel chair. They crossed the finish line – second to the last. But that day "Team Hoyt" was born! They got a more sophisticated chair and the quadriplegic teenager and his out-of-shape dad began running together. In 1981 they ran their first Boston Marathon. Since then they haven't missed one in 20 years.

Rick has since earned his degree and works at Boston University helping design computer systems for people with disabilities. As of March 2001, "Team Hoyt" had completed a total of 731 races, including 53 marathons and 135 triathlons. What do we learn from "Team Hoyt?"

(1)You don't have to live as a victim. (2) It's okay to acknowledge your limitations as long as you build your life around your dreams. (3) Focus on what you have, not what you don't. (4) Factor God in – for with Him "all things are possible."

WHAT'S YOUR CONCEPT OF GOD?

Come boldly to . . . our gracious God.
Hebrews 4:16 NLT

Nothing is more important than your concept of God – the picture you have of Him in your mind. That, and that alone, will determine how you approach Him, not only in times of need, but every time.

As long as you see God as an auditor before whom your books never balance, or a teacher whose class you dread and whose tests you can never pass, or a parent who abuses you but never affirms you, you won't "come boldly." You probably won't come at all!

If you need a new concept of God, listen: "We have a great High Priest who is gone to heaven, Jesus the Son of God. Let us cling to him and never stop trusting him. This High Priest of ours understands our weaknesses, for he faced all the same temptations we do, yet he did not sin. So let us come boldly to the throne of our gracious God. There we will receive his mercy, and we will find grace to help us when we need it" (Heb 4:14-16 NLT).

In *A Gentle Thunder,* Max Lucado writes, "If God had a refrigerator, your picture would be on it. If He'd a wallet, your photo would be in it. He sends you flowers every spring and a sunrise every morning. Whenever you want to talk, He'll listen. He can live anywhere in the universe, but He chose your heart. And what about the Christmas gift He sent you at Bethlehem? Not to mention that Friday at Calvary. Face it, He's crazy about you!"